"*The Color of Rain* is a testament to God's restoration and grace. Even in our suffering, there is beauty. It rarely makes sense, but it's always true: 'He makes all things beautiful, in His time.'"

— *Katie Davis, author of* Kisses from Katie

"Michael and Gina Spehn's *The Color of Rain* is not only an instant bestseller but also an instant classic, certain to be pressed into the hands of hundreds of thousands of grieving men and women by their closest friends, for it is a book that is painfully honest about the depths of sorrow but also full of the joy of the hard path back from near despair. There is no sugarcoating here, but simply a profoundly moving guidebook to the Valley of the Shadow, not only for the suffering but for those who suffer with them. *The Color of Rain* is another reminder that God is there, however dark the day, and that he will comfort those who call on him."

— *Hugh Hewitt*

"Michael and Gina personify the beauty that God can bring out of the ashes of sorrow."

— *Kathie Lee Gifford*

NEW YORK TIMES BESTSELLER

A **TRUE** STORY

THE COLOR OF rain

HOW TWO FAMILIES FOUND

FAITH, HOPE & LOVE

IN THE MIDST OF TRAGEDY

MICHAEL & GINA SPEHN

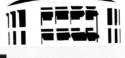
ZONDERVAN®

ZONDERVAN.com/
AUTHORTRACKER
follow your favorite authors

We want to hear from you. Please send your comments about this book to us in care of zreview@zondervan.com. Thank you.

ZONDERVAN

The Color of Rain
Copyright © 2011 by Michael Spehn and Gina Spehn

This title is also available as a Zondervan ebook.
Visit www.zondervan.com/ebooks.

This title is also available in a Zondervan audio edition.
Visit www.zondervan.fm.

Requests for information should be addressed to:

Zondervan, *Grand Rapids, Michigan 49530*

This Edition: ISBN 978-0-310-31889-7 (softcover)

Library of Congress Cataloging-in-Publication Data

Spehn, Michael.
    The color of rain : how two families found faith, hope, and love in the midst of tragedy /
Michael & Gina Spehn.
        p.   cm.
    ISBN 978-0-310-33197-1 (hardcover)
        1. Spehn, Michael. 2. Spehn, Gina. 3. Christian biography—United States. I. Spehn, Gina.
II. Title.
BR1725.S717A3   2011
277.3'0830922—dc22
    [B]   2011010568

All Scripture quotations, unless otherwise indicated, are taken from the Holy Bible, *New International Version*®, *NIV*®. Copyright © 1973, 1978, 1984, 2011 by Biblica, Inc.™ Used by permission. All rights reserved worldwide.

Any Internet addresses (websites, blogs, etc.) and telephone numbers in this book are offered as a resource. They are not intended in any way to be or imply an endorsement by Zondervan, nor does Zondervan vouch for the content of these sites and numbers for the life of this book.

Published in association with Yates & Yates, www.yates2.com.

Cover design: Rule29 Creative, Inc.
Cover photography: iStockphoto®, Julie Ferreri Photography
Interior design: Beth Shagene
Interior part image: iStockphoto®

Printed in the United States of America

---

12 13 14 15 16 17 18 19 /DCI/ 23 22 21 20 19 18 17 16 15 14 13 12 11 10 9 8 7 6 5 4 3 2 1

For our children
Charlotte • Jack • Drew • Sam • Dan

contents

PART THREE

the new day

This is a true story.

prologue

A tall man in a white coat walks into the room without speaking. He has dark skin, dark wavy hair, and, as it would turn out, a slight Middle Eastern accent. Seven adults are gathered in the room now, but no one makes a sound and the man chooses not to make eye contact with anyone. He moves quickly and quietly to the bedside. He unfolds a stethoscope from his hands and inserts the earpieces. Although this is a routine task that he has performed a thousand times before, he is keenly aware that all eyes in the room are focused on his every move. He never looks right or left, nor acknowledges anyone seated around the room. He simply goes straight to work.

The man places the listening piece on the patient's chest. He moves the stethoscope very slowly once, then pauses. He moves it again, gently, and listens. Finally, a third time. No one speaks. Not one sound can be heard. The nurse standing at the side of the bed looks away quietly.

Then the tall man in the white coat folds his stethoscope, glances nervously up at me, and speaks the only two words that I would ever hear him say.

"My condolences," he says, and he leaves the room.

It is 12:35 a.m. on February 28.

life is good

the fall

gina

The morning of my thirty-second birthday, I was already looking forward to dinner with my parents. Dad and I shared the same birthday and Mom was making our favorite, linguini with traditional meat sauce and meatballs, to celebrate. With a name like Antoinette Valenti, you know her sauce is ridiculously good. I've yet to meet a person, regardless of how many vowels they have in their name, who can make a more tender meatball than my mother.

Bright sunlight bathed the kitchen in warmth. Two-year-old Drew had just finished eating oatmeal, and Sam was sitting in his high chair launching toys in between bites of Gerber baby cereal when the phone rang. My best friend, Colleen Schomaker, was calling with a solo performance of "Happy Birthday." She sang at hyperspeed, so as not to actually sing, and then reminded me that I am still older than her. We said good-bye with a plan to meet for lunch.

As I hung up, the television caught my eye. Smoke was billowing from one of the World Trade Center towers in New York City. I leaned my elbows on the counter to watch on my tiny black-and-white kitchen television and called Colleen back.

"Are you watching this?"

"Yeah, I know. Unbelievable."

We mulled it over for a few minutes and hung up again. By now, I had turned on the television in the family room. Sam was still in his high chair, happily being entertained by Drew as I watched a passenger jet explode into the second tower. My body recoiled with every replay of the plane entering the building. I sat on the coffee table in stunned silence and began to feel nauseated. My soul ached at the sight of incomprehensible suffering. With the rest of the world, I was riveted to my television on this otherwise gorgeous September day, helplessly watching America wounded and bleeding.

It took my husband, Matt, several hours to return home from his downtown office at the local NBC television station in Detroit. When I heard the garage door go up, I ran to meet him. We held each other tightly, still in a state of disbelief. My parents had already arrived. Time was standing still as we came together to watch the horror unfold. Around five o'clock I walked outside to clear my head. The late afternoon sun was blinding. I felt like I had been in a tunnel all day. My body ached from tension. It was surreal, and it wasn't even happening in our state. It was, however, happening in our safe country, in a city we had visited many times, and in a place where people we knew and loved were living. It was happening to people just like us. It was happening to us.

Dinner was quieter than usual, although the kids helped keep things light. The world may have paused, but Drew still had spaghetti sauce on his face, and Sam was still throwing things from his high chair. There wasn't much conversation aside from expressions of deep sadness, gratitude, and a strong sense of unity with our fellow Americans.

I took an hour tucking the kids into bed that night, snuggling, reading, and saying prayers. What kind of world had I brought them into? I walked downstairs and collapsed into Matt's arms. The television was muted and we sat quietly watching the images on the screen.

"I have a present for you," Matt said.

"For what?" I asked and then remembered it was my birthday. "I don't feel much like celebrating. How about if I open it tomorrow?"

"Okay, but you have to read this tonight." He handed me a letter.

9/11/01

Gina:

Especially today, with the enormity of current events, I want to convey to you again, how much you mean to me and how proud I am to be your husband. The hard work that you are engaged in right now is exhausting, invisible and largely thankless in the short term.

But honey, please know that buried at the core of this tedium is the most

*noble and important work in the world — God's work; the fruits of which you
and I will be lucky enough to enjoy as we grow old together. Watching these
little guys grow into men is a privilege that I am proud to share with you, and
the perfect fulfillment of our marriage bonds.*

You are a great mom.

You are a great wife.

You are my best friend.

You are very pretty.

Happy Birthday.

— *Matt*

Matt's generosity restored my hope. He made me feel safe and loved
and purposeful. In his own adorable way, he even made me feel beautiful,
which every mother of young children knows is no small task. At a time in
our lives when careers and kids were creating loose threads in our marriage,
and on the worst day in our nation's recent history, Matt gave me a renewed
perspective about our life together and our future. His letter was like a stitch
in the mending process. It was the best birthday present I'd ever been given.

A few months after 9/11, we celebrated our tenth anniversary in California. We planned the trip several months prior to our actual October
anniversary, mostly to accommodate schedules. We rented a convertible
Porsche Boxster in San Francisco and made the leisurely drive south to Big
Sur. Matt was in his glory. Evidence of God surrounded us. The Sierras
to our left, crashing surf to our right, and a little black sports car beneath
us. Heaven. We looped around the Seventeen-Mile Drive and took in all
the sights. The Lone Cypress Tree, tall Spyglass palms, and sea otters serving themselves a dinner of abalone on the rocks as they languished in the
Pacific. We twisted and turned a bit farther south on Highway One until
we arrived at the Ventana Inn and Spa, a quiet, romantic resort nestled
in the cliffs at Big Sur. Pulling into the resort we noticed smiling people
meandering around in white robes. Before the bell captain could open the
car door, Matt leaned into me and whispered, "Resort? Or insane asylum?"

"Either way, we'll fit in," I replied with a laugh.

Ventana was quite a contrast from our everyday world. It was an
extremely quiet, romantic escape. There was a bit of culture shock, but it
didn't take long to adapt. Fifteen minutes after we mocked the crazies in the
white robes, we were donning our own monogrammed terries with matching white flip-flops, sipping a delightful Napa Cabernet on our leisurely

stroll to the Japanese hot baths. We giggled like kids who were getting away with something. We had only two days to luxuriate, so we made the most of them, eating extraordinary cuisine and taking deep breaths of the night-blooming jasmine.

After dinner we sat on the terrace of our bungalow overlooking the tranquil mountains. I rested my head back and felt the tension in my body melt away. When I opened my eyes, there was an open jewelry box with a beautiful pair of diamond earrings sitting on top of a Ventana notepad with a handwritten note:

> Here's my big idea. When the time comes, we give one to Drew and one to Sam as "down payments" on engagement rings. Then, we go get you two giant rocks! I love you. — M

I hugged him around his neck and we kissed. He got it right. The earrings were perfect, but most of all, I loved his big idea. He considered five people in giving this gift. It was for me, our boys, and their future wives. His thoughtfulness would touch people he didn't even know.

"Try 'em on," he said, smiling. He knew he had me. Matt had been buying me jewelry for years, but much of it sat idle in the jewelry box. I had never been one to wear much jewelry, mostly because I was hyper-aware of the fact that I had it on, and I tended to fidget with it. My discomfort, however, did not stop my persistent salesman husband from buying it. Now, after ten years, he had found the perfect gift, elegant and understated, with the perfect message.

"Thank you," I whispered. "I can't wait until our boys can understand this about you."

Matt hit play on the CD player on our nightstand, and we listened to a complimentary CD titled *Going to California*. The CD was an acoustic guitar tribute to Led Zeppelin. I liked my rock-and-roll, but this mellow CD worked with the robes-and-slippers mood. It became the soundtrack for a perfect weekend getaway.

Back home, the week of our actual anniversary in early October, Matt and I were not feeling pressured to buy gifts or plan an elaborate night out. Great memories of our California trip lingered, but we were glad to be home in Michigan this time of year. The autumn chill was beginning to creep back into the air, which meant sweatshirt weather, football games, and spicy chili. Everything smells different when the leaves begin to turn. Their yearly morph releases a burnt perfume that sweetens the air.

The vibrant colors and crisp temperatures make me feel like I could run a thousand miles, although after the first two, I'd rethink that idea. Autumn arouses all of the senses like no other season, perhaps because we can feel the beginning of the end, nature's grand finale.

Matt was upstairs showering and Sammy took his morning nap while I molded Play-Doh with Drew. I took notice of the leaves that hung just outside the window. The chartreuse green was giving way to hints of vibrant red, orange, and yellow.

"Gina!" Matt shouted to me from our bedroom. I walked to the bottom of the stairs to see him wrapped in a towel, dripping wet.

"Feel this," he said as he pushed his finger into his thigh. At first I thought he was being funny but quickly realized that his tone was more serious.

"What is it?" I asked, rushing up the stairs.

"I don't know. It feels like a marble in my leg, like a tiny tumor."

I stopped moving and glanced up at him with a confused look.

"A tumor? Who says that?" I said half sarcastically. That thought lingered in the air a moment until I realized, a *Kell* says that. While the average person does not jump to the conclusion that it's a "tumor" before considering every other possibility, Matt's family, given the genetic history on his dad's side, tended to assume the worst. We continued feeling around his thigh. The marble was very deep in the muscle. Matt and I agreed that he would call his dad's oncologist.

A few days later, on the day of our tenth anniversary, I was in our bedroom and saw our acoustic Led Zeppelin CD from Ventana. I realized that the timing of our trip had been less about logistics and more about a divine plan. As Matt lay in our bed recovering from surgery to remove a tumor from his leg, I pressed play. The last two songs on the CD were "Babe, I'm Gonna Leave You" and "Stairway to Heaven."

Autumn had arrived.

CHAPTER 2

mullett lake

michael

Cold spring waters run over the small rocks at the far end of Grandview Beach, providing the only sound to the predawn stillness on Mullett Lake in Northern Michigan. The perfect crystal surface rests, motionless. In the distance, at the first break of light, a lake perch stretches up toward the tangerine sky just enough to gulp a breakfast of fallen mayflies, then disappears quietly below the surface. The silent ripples on the water glide toward the now-smoldering horizon. As the sun begins to wrestle the darkness into retreat, I wish the world could remain this perfect for just a while longer.

As I wallow in the calm, the moment quickly becomes bittersweet with the realization that, in the blink of an eye, this perfect tranquility will surrender to the sound and fury that accompany each new day. Cars and boats, people and noises, busyness and bills to be paid, and all of the blessings and curses that occupy the space between dawn and twilight will soon be upon me. In the end, the silent bliss that is morning on Mullett Lake is friend and foe alike; a beautiful and cruel Shakespearean device that each day seduces me with its promise and then shatters me with its heartbreak.

For my wife, Cathy, this was a unique and spiritual place. Her parents, Larry and Jill Lutz, owned a cottage on Grandview Beach, a pretty stretch of sandy shoreline at the far end of the lake, and Cath spent many summers there. One of the largest and deepest inland lakes in the U.S., Mullett Lake seemed to call out to her each time she stayed away a bit too long.

She became a different woman when she was up north. (That's what the locals call it; when one goes to the lakes in Northern Michigan, one goes "up north.") Along with flip-flops and waterproof sunblock, Cathy put on a new self when she was there and it looked good on her. Her slender frame seemed taller than the 5'6" listed on her driver's license. Her summer hair caught just enough of the sun's magic to brighten with highlights. Her skin, fair and pink for nine months out of the year, grew deep brown, making her teeth piercingly white when she smiled. Being at the lake agreed with Cathy.

While she and I were still dating, I had to be dragged there. "Come to my parents' cottage," Cathy pleaded.

I wanted none of it. I was strictly concrete. I loved the city and was never going to be a "happy camper." Roughing it for me was when room service stopped serving at midnight. Plus my only notion of a "cottage" came from the dreadful visits to Wisconsin where my dad had taken my three siblings and me in order to get a little outdoors in us.

"You'll love it," Cathy insisted.

"I will not love it," I said, channeling Woody Allen. "Crappy fishing shanties and deerflies the size of Volvos ..."

"It's not like that," she said. "Besides, we need a nice getaway."

"Getaway has words like *Hyatt* in it. *Spas* and *tee times*. That's a getaway! The only thing we'd be getting away from up north would be indoor plumbing and twentieth-century dentistry."

Yet, as we all know, love makes you do the occasional foolish thing. So I packed a case of SPF 90 and a five-gallon canister of calamine lotion, and we drove north out of Chicago.

As soon as we arrived, all of my fears of outhouses and backwoods banjos were put to rest. It turned out that her parents' "cottage" was actually a beautiful and well-appointed lake home with four bedrooms and two bathrooms. Being a top salesman in the furniture industry gave Larry Lutz not only access to the finer things but a taste for them as well. Their home was spotless, with a clean, contemporary style and a touch of up-north charm. The meticulous white walls remained free of any clutter, except for three large framed photographs that Larry himself had taken and hung prominently in the great room. They had more than one hundred feet of lakefront and all the water toys you could desire: ski boats and pontoon party boats, flotation devices of every kind, and even a SeaDoo to ride.

Nearby I discovered a golf course called The Secret—a fabulous little semi-private track carved out of the virgin pine forest that always seemed to have an opening on the first tee whenever I asked. The people there were great and the course not too difficult. I soon developed a love/hate relationship with the par-five eighth hole, which always taunted my ego into going for the green in two, though there was a well-placed pond in front. This diamond in the rough (all puns intended) was the deal *maker* for me with Mullett Lake. I began to look forward to going up north as much as Cathy.

Eventually I mustered the courage (brains really) to ask her to marry me. As I waited for her at the altar on our wedding day, I looked around the church at the countless friends and family gathered. My dad caught my eye and smiled a wedding smile at me and then turned toward the back of the church. Just then Cathy appeared, glowing at the end of the aisle. Dad wheeled around and caught my eye again. This time, though, he appeared dazed by the vision he'd just seen. I understood. Cathy had that effect on people.

It was her smile that took me captive the day we met, and never once let me go. There was an authentic quality to her smile that made people stop and look; a basic human truth that seemed to emanate from deep within her and naturally find its way upward and out. Like the magma flow from Vesuvius, there was simply no stopping Cathy's smile. It could freeze people where they stood and hold them there, sometimes forever.

That's what happened to me anyway.

CHAPTER 3

skyline

gina

Matt was first diagnosed with cancer the week of our ten-year anniversary. For several months it felt like I was watching smoke billowing from the first tower on 9/11. A tragedy was occurring in our lives, but it seemed distant. I knew what I had to do, and like a rescue worker, I sprang into action to assist and save the life of my husband.

We visited the University of Michigan Cancer Center and MD Anderson in Houston, armed with stacks of research and Matt's family history. The doctors we met at both hospitals were longtime colleagues who seemed to be in agreement on everything regarding Matt's case except one detail. It was known that radiation and chemotherapy could result in his type of cancer spreading more quickly, but only one doctor believed the benefits outweighed the risks. In his words, it was a "fatal mistake" not to have chemo. It was a "damned if you do, damned if you don't" situation, and the only thing we knew for sure was Matt's family history.

I spent much of my youth indifferent to the subject of history and, regrettably, have remained ignorant into adulthood. Though I might still fail a pop quiz on the Revolutionary War, I knew one thing for sure: "Those who cannot remember the past are condemned to repeat it." Traditional chemotherapy had never worked on leiomyosarcoma in the Kell family.

This big, scary word pronounced "lie-oh-my-oh-sarcoma" is a rare form of cancer that had already claimed the lives of Matt's dad and several other members of the Kell family. They all died young, accompanied by a toxic chemo cocktail that was "the best we've got to offer" by the medical community.

Highly intelligent specialists disagreed, but history was clear and we were determined not to repeat it. The medical profession is driven by the need to do something, even when that something has the potential to cause greater suffering and ultimately end with the same outcome, give or take a couple months of misery. Matt was clear about how he wanted to live with cancer, and it was going to be free of traditional chemo and doctors with blinders.

For seventeen months we were in watch-and-wait mode. Matt had routine CT scans and checkups, but our lives were not dramatically altered. He was mostly healthy and life was mostly normal. I became the Martha Stewart of living with cancer, trying to make our home and life perfect, but it wasn't. Matt spent much of the first year grieving himself in subtle ways. I could feel the pull between us. The boys and I represented a painful reality to Matt, so he gravitated toward things that felt good: work, food, and drink. Unfortunately, there weren't enough blue cheese–stuffed olives in the world to alleviate his anguish.

I sat slumped on a stool at the kitchen counter staring at the digital clock on the microwave, blinking 4:14 p.m. back at me. The house was unusually quiet. My head felt heavy and my hot tea had gone cold. Looking down at my calendar, I crossed off a bridal shower, a benefit dinner, and our family vacation to Naples, Florida. In place of those events I inked in Matt's lung biopsy, appointments with cancer specialists at Sloan Kettering and Dana Farber, and an appointment with Dr. Nicholas Gonzalez, a holistic doctor in Manhattan.

"Where are the kids?" I thought. This is not a question I usually have to ask. I realized quickly that Sam was still napping, but it took an extra few seconds to account for Drew. Suddenly, I remembered. I was thirty minutes late picking him up from preschool. In a panic I ran upstairs and grabbed Sammy out of bed. I practically threw him into his car seat, grabbed a sippy cup off the car floor, shoved it in his lap, and sped off. I could feel myself beginning to unravel. Midway through my apology to the school office staff, I began to sob. It felt like the second plane was slamming into the World Trade Center, and this time, I was in the building.

Forgetting to pick up my four-year-old from preschool was the first sign of the grief that quietly grabbed hold of me earlier that week when Matt received a second cancer diagnosis. He had another routine CT scan and minor outpatient abdominal surgery to remove what we suspected was a tiny lipoma, which is nothing more than a hard lump of fatty tissue, usually found just beneath the skin. I had driven Matt to the hospital for the procedure and waited alone with my book and cell phone to keep me company.

It was a familiar routine until the oncologist called me into a small room adjacent to surgical waiting. As I gathered my things, my hands were shaking. I was being called into a "doom room." I knew the skyline of my life was about to change.

"Is anyone with you today?" he asked.

"Just Matt."

He hesitated, as if not wanting to tell me.

"I can handle it," I said calmly. "We've been dealing with this for a year and a half."

The surgeon leaned in and I watched his hands as he spoke, subconsciously wanting to see how steady they were.

"We removed the lipoma from Matt's abdomen, but we found another tumor hiding behind it. Pathology confirmed it is leiomyosarcoma. Also, the CT scan shows lesions on his lungs and liver that could also be sarcoma. We'll need a lung biopsy to confirm."

I could feel my heart beating in my chest. I couldn't reconcile why I felt shocked, so I remained stoic. He never said the word "terminal" but it was there, lurking in the subtext like the cowardly hidden tumor.

Two weeks later, Matt had a lung biopsy to confirm what we already knew. This time I wasn't alone. Eighteen friends and family sat with me in the waiting room. When the official word came, the room erupted in tears and wailing. The first unofficial wake for Matthew Kell was taking place.

When I finally went back to see Matt, he was still groggy but reached for my hand.

"It's what we thought, right?" he asked.

My eyes welled up and he knew. He pulled me closer.

"It's gonna be okay," he said.

I wanted to believe him, but the towers were beginning to fall and I couldn't run fast enough.

Our entourage of family and friends left the hospital, only to return the next day to rally around Matt. They needed to talk to him and be near him. I remember thinking how blessed we were to be surrounded by people who were not afraid to draw closer to us at a time when stage 4 cancer was barreling down the tracks. Many people flee the scene at times like this, but not our friends. They put their own lives on hold to move in closer, giving Matt the strength he needed to turn cancer around.

A nun came into the room and offered to pray with Matt. A small group of us gathered around him and held hands while she prayed for healing and comfort. As we were about to let go, Matt asked if he could say a prayer. I saw on the faces of those gathered a sense of "Good for you. Way to be strong, Matt! Pray that you beat this thing, because you can!" We bowed our heads once again and Matt began to pray for the nun and her ministry. He prayed that God would watch over her and guide her work. Not one word of his prayer was directed to himself. This was the moment when Matt's focus turned outward. Cancer had done all the damage it was going to do. His body was weak, but I had never seen him stronger.

CHAPTER 4

mushroom cloud

michael

The modest bungalows and decaying brownstones of Chicago's West Side provide a stark contrast to the gleaming architectural hubris of its downtown skyline, and illustrate a uniquely Chicago blend of cynicism and hope. Growing up there meant learning quaint aphorisms that seemed to be passed down generation to generation: Maybe the next mayor won't be quite so corrupt. It's possible it won't be as cold this winter. Perhaps this year the Cubs will make it to the World Series. Right. Pull this leg and it plays "Jingle Bells."

No doubt about it, I was a cynic, but at least I came by it honestly. The Chicago of my youth could well be called Skeptic Valley, given the number of hypocrites, quasi-authoritarians, and just plain lapsed faithful running around the place. This rich region of doubt was fertile ground for cultivating a generation of cynics who were comfortable challenging old-school conventions. My grape was a 1962, a pretty good year: John Glenn, Cuban missiles, and white-tie dinners at the Kennedy White House. The Beatles released their very first record and Oswald was still nothing more than a punk on the corner passing out leaflets.

I was raised Catholic but, like so many, left the church long ago. My cynicism for all things religious was nurtured by a turn as an altar boy. My father, mother, uncles, and oldest brother were all graduates of Catholic education and they spoke freely about its blessings and curses. So I felt comfortable when I made my thoroughly informed decision to leave. As I've said many times, I always questioned "them." I've never once questioned Him.

As a kid the only true authority for whom I had unwavering respect was my father, Richard Spehn, aka "The Boss," a self-imposed but deserved title. Dad was the boss at work and he was the boss in his home. He seemed to be the boss, or at least very much in control of things, just about everywhere he went. People naturally gravitated to him and followed his lead. My two brothers, my sister, and I certainly followed his orders. "TB" he would sign notes to us. "Make sure the grass gets cut today. TB." The Boss.

Dad was never really called Richard. For most of his life he went by the diminutive Dick. In later years his grandchildren were too young to enunciate "Grandpa Dick." They could only muster "Gucka Hoke." Later that was shortened to simply Hoke.

He loved kids and kids loved him. Though he always had the highest expectations of them—be polite, mind your manners, pick up that garbage on the ground—those same kids adored him. He loved games and was a master at making up new ones to play. We were never bored waiting for food to come at a restaurant because Dad found a way to make a game out of sugar packs and saltshakers.

To us kids the worst thing in the world was disappointing him. Not only because he was our father and we wanted to impress him like any kid does, but also because we knew that he had such high standards. If we earned his praise, we must be doing something right. His role was teacher, protector, provider, but also arbiter for all that is worthy and good in the world. If Dad said, "Well done," that was the gold standard and nothing else came close.

As we kids became young adults and began to make decisions on our own, I think Dad's own view of his role in our lives confused him a bit. He still roared like the old lion he was, but the other lions in the den no longer regarded him the way they used to. This aggravated him to no end. I think the scariest thought that crossed my dad's mind was that he might someday become irrelevant. He preferred conflict and acrimony to disregard. He didn't mind if you thought he was an SOB; he just didn't want you to consider him irrelevant. For The Boss, that was simply unacceptable.

When I was ten, my Uncle Jack died suddenly. He was my father's brother and best friend, and Dad immediately felt a profound sense of duty to take care of Jack's family. My Aunt Peggy was left with six kids and they needed a father figure. My brothers and sister and I just wished it didn't have to be ours.

A sense of duty was very important to my dad. Responsibility came before everything else.

"It's about honor," he said.

No matter what "it" was, it was always about honor. Dick Spehn never served in the Marine Corps, but by God, he lived semper fi every day of his life. He did in fact serve in the army and was proud of it. He was stationed in Cincinnati during the Korean War. When we joked about his lack of combat experience, he always answered back with the same line: "You'll notice that at no time during my service did the city of Cincinnati ever fall into enemy hands."

So out of duty, nearly every weekend he started going to our cousins' home in Barrington, a beautiful lake-strewn suburb northwest of Chicago. He checked on his nieces and nephews, did little chores around the house, arranged Peggy's bills, and made sure the life insurance money was well invested. Quickly this became a significant source of tension in our home. My mom and dad began to argue, the kind of arguments that nobody ever wins.

Being ten, I didn't care much about the human dynamics of it all; I just wanted to be with my dad. Soon I figured out that if I wanted to spend a lot of time with him, I'd better be willing to get in his car and go to Barrington. It became something of a ritual for him and me, and I found a way to enjoy it.

The long car rides provided a lot of time when we could talk to each other and get to know each other's take on the world. He taught me about Tony Bennett and Luciano Pavarotti on those car rides. I taught him about the Eagles and Don McLean. He schooled me on how to make a sale, talk to a cop when he pulls you over, tell a great story, and ask out a girl. I told him why we should get a new game called Pong. Those car rides taught me something else too: sometimes everything you know to be true really isn't.

On a Saturday morning at the corner of Lake Cook Road and Route 12 in an unincorporated section of northwest Chicago, my father tested the first Spehn family nuclear bomb.

"You know that your mom and I will probably split up someday, right?" he said to me during one of our drives.

The air rushed out of my lungs. It felt as if I was in a plane at thirty thousand feet and someone had just opened the door. He was taking my temperature, gauging my reaction. He had me alone in the car and completely ambushed me.

I knew my parents fought. I had been in the middle of those classic uncomfortable moments at the kitchen table. He's tired, she's unappreciated, and nothing in life is turning out the way they hoped. I got that, even at ten. After a while the arguing almost became a lifestyle. No longer the exception or something to be shocked and horrified by, it was simply their life. And mine.

There wasn't abuse. They weren't throwing punches, or dishes, or knives. Their slings and arrows came verbally and relentlessly. The really hard part for me was their tone. Like two new siblings, sarcasm and scorn had come to live with us. I grew so accustomed to the din of tension that it all sounded like just another plane flying overhead. In reality it was the *Enola Gay* coming to drop the big one. *My* mom and dad were going to split up? That was a nuke.

I turned toward Dad in the car and gave a halfhearted, "Yeah, I know."

What I wanted to do was scream, "Are you out of your mind? And by the way, even if you are going to split up someday, keep it to yourself until it happens. I'm ten! I don't want to hear about it. I want to ride my bike, play with my friends, and pretend that we have a normal family."

I didn't say those things, of course, and I hated myself for it. I turned away from him and looked out the window and watched most of my ten-year-old world disappear in a mushroom cloud.

CHAPTER 5

win-win

gina

I met Matthew Christopher Kell in my sophomore year at Michigan State University while working together in retail advertising sales at *The State News*. He was a natural leader with the intellect to back it up. I couldn't help being impressed with his sales talent and high-energy work ethic, but his overconfident, bordering on arrogant, attitude didn't match up well with my feisty yet insecure personality. For two years, if we weren't ignoring each other, we were taking shots at one another. By senior year, with a little maturity and a lot of humility, we grew into each other and I was proudly celebrating with my new boyfriend when he was named MSU's Advertising Man of the Year.

Less than a year after graduating from MSU, Matt proposed to me via a ten-second television commercial that he produced at WLNS, the CBS television station he worked for in Lansing. As "Groovy Kind of Love" played, the words "Gina, will you marry me?" flashed across the screen. As I said "Yes!" the *Arsenio Hall Show* was starting, and we were hugging and kissing to the "Woof, woof, woof" of the Dogpound.

We originally set our wedding date a year out, but decided we couldn't wait to be together, so we gave ourselves six months and got married that October.

Matt and I worked in several arenas of the ad business, from copywriting to network cable sales. Eventually we landed at competing television stations in Detroit and enjoyed all the perks that our careers afforded. His instincts and performance earned him a reputation as a hot young executive. As I was exiting the business to stay home with our firstborn, Matt's career hit the management fast track and he was named general sales manager of the local NBC station before his thirty-fourth birthday. His success was made sweeter by the fact that his closest friends were also in the ad business. The real fun of entertaining clients in suites at major sporting events and concerts is the added benefit of cronyism.

One of the most intriguing qualities about Matt was the ease with which he honored and maintained unconditional, long-standing friendships. His inner circle of six appeared to be just another group of guys talking sports, business, and politics, but at the core was a tight-knit group of men who lived the same values and weren't afraid to be challenged by one another to live up to those values in every facet of life. The stereotype of men's relationships being a mile wide and an inch deep was turned on its head by Matt's "band of brothers."

Matt, Mike, Marty, Red, Doc, and Jeff were six distinctive men, imperfect and forgiving, who formed a bond of friendship that was rooted in faith and held together by integrity and a willingness to be open. They worked hard and played hard together. Every interaction between them was a natural extension of who they were and hoped to be.

Matt and Mike were the nucleus of the group. The connection between them began in middle school at St. John Lutheran in Rochester, Michigan. As kids, they were an unlikely duo. Mike Schomaker was a skinny, WASP-y kid, who could physically and verbally run circles around his peers, most of whom towered over him. He had a literal mind and a need to study long and hard to earn good grades. Matt was an Italian-Syrian-German mutt with dark hair and olive skin. He was tall and lanky with big glasses to match his smile and ego. He was a straight-A student who didn't need to study, and didn't mind saying so. His smarts and creativity were surpassed only by his not-so-quiet confidence.

Matt and Mike attended the same schools for ten years. They watched, played, and debated sports together ad nauseam, followed similar career paths, and married two women, Colleen and I, who became like sisters. We teased our husbands because they functioned like an old married couple. Matt would get exasperated with Mike when he asked inane questions like "How do I set the margins on a Word document?" And Mike was repeatedly frustrated with Matt for his petty laziness, the kind usually attributed to teenagers. Matt would rather freeze than take an extra thirty seconds to grab an overcoat from the closet. They gave each other gray hairs, but they put up with the quirks because what was below this superficial banter meant so much more.

In college, following the sudden death of a mutual friend, Matt and Mike relied on each other to make sense of it. For the first time in their Lutheran lives, everything they had been taught to believe was being challenged. They searched for understanding and answers at a time when what they knew to be true was colliding with the confusion and emotion surrounding their loss. Their need for healing set off a quest for truth that became the catalyst behind their coming-of-age decision to make a leap of faith without a cord attached.

Believing God, and the lessons they were taught, prepared them to survive and even grow through the next ten years in life's trenches: Both of their fathers died within seven months of each other. Mike's second child, Tommy, was born with a severe congenital heart defect. Matt was diagnosed with terminal cancer. Each time the enemy seemed to advance, these brothers stood strong on the front lines armed with faith.

After Matt was diagnosed with cancer, his brothers were a daily support and presence in his life. Each brought something unique to help him see beyond the disease. In the weeks following Matt's lung biopsy, our friends were with us regularly. Life felt normal, except for the 800-pound gorilla in the corner named Sarcoma.

The snow thawed and the first buds were beginning to appear on the trees. It was an early spring day in Michigan when temperatures unexpectedly reached the midseventies. Matt and I were preparing to visit cancer centers on the East Coast and our friends came over to give us a send-off. As the evening lingered on, it was getting close to bedtime for the kids. I carried Sam upstairs to get him into his pajamas. At three years old, and supposedly past the terrible twos, he still had an uncanny ability to worm his way into the cracks of my parenting skills. Professionals call it oppositional-defiant. I call it, "His Dad has cancer!" His sweet young life had been surrounded by the turmoil of this evil disease since he was twenty months old. No matter how hard we try to protect our children, or convince ourselves that they don't understand, we cannot shelter them from what is happening right before their eyes. Cancer was shaping their character. It came into our home and quietly took hold of all of us. But not my babies, please, leave them alone.

"I don't want jammies, Mom."

"Look, Sam! Buzz Lightyear!" I said, trying to sound excited.

"No jammies!" he said more defiantly.

I needed to redirect. "Let's read a book, then we can get changed."

"No, no, no!"

Our conversation escalated. Regrettably, this wasn't the first time I had allowed my three-year-old to engage me in battle, but this night Sam reached the point of screaming and flailing around wildly. The windows were open, and certainly everyone downstairs could hear the racket. I was humiliated, feeling like a parent on *Supernanny*. Finally, Matt came to my rescue.

"What's going on?" he said firmly, startling Sam.

I moved aside and Matt took over where I left off. I was embarrassed and angry, a dangerous emotional cocktail. As I watched them, it occurred to me that I couldn't do this alone. The 800-pound gorilla sat down on my chest. My husband was sick and dying and I would be left to raise two boys alone, as a damaged wife and mother. As soon as Sam was headed back downstairs happily wearing his Buzz Lightyear pj's, I began to weep uncontrollably. We sat on the floor next to Sam's dresser and I buried my head in Matt's chest.

"How will I do this without you? Please don't go. Don't leave me alone."

In my shameful tantrum, I unleashed all my fear, anxiety, and grief, without regard for the fact that I was victimizing the victim with my selfishness.

Matt wrapped his arms around me, kissed my head, and let me cry. When I quieted down, he lifted my shoulders and spoke words that I will never forget.

"G," he said. "This is a win-win situation."

Long pause. Confusion. Win-win? How could he say such a thing?

"Please, hear my words," he whispered.

I took a deep breath. He continued, "If I am cured of cancer, that is an obvious win because I will be here and we will have a great life, raise our boys, and grow old together. But it's also a win if I die."

He spoke with a level of controlled enthusiasm that was strangely comforting. His gratitude filled the air.

"Regardless of how much time we have here," he said, "I know that we will be reunited in heaven. We're only on this earth a short time relative to eternity, and we'll all be together in the end."

I sat for a moment, stunned. He actually meant what he was saying. This wasn't a line or a quote. This was his heart. He was challenged to believe his faith, and by doing so, he put death in its proper place. I had never considered the idea that death was a win, at least not outside the context of Easter Sunday. It's a paradoxical truth that Matt had embraced and wanted me to hold on to with him. Give thanks in all circumstances. Really? Yes. My dying husband was teaching me.

Matt continued, "I don't know what's going to happen, but if he's calling me home, I need you to walk me to the water's edge. I don't want to leave you, but I have to trust that he will take care of you and the boys. You belong to him, not me."

Listening to Matt made everything all at once harder and easier. That he could say this and believe it was a gift. Pure grace. I still wanted to argue or fight or scream, but there was nothing more to say. We were going to live with cancer fearlessly, hoping for life and believing that even death was a win. My heart ached, but Matt's confidence soothed me.

"I promise to walk you to the water's edge, unless you have to walk me there first," I said tearfully.

We tried not to get too far ahead of ourselves, but made promises to each other to trust God and make decisions without regret. We planned to be honest with our kids, but not so honest as to scare them. We agreed to be strong for each other, and when we couldn't, we would call on our friends and family.

In preparation for our East Coast trip, Matt spent several hours a day online, delving deep into cancer research and clinical trials. He compiled his data in a folder labeled "Cancer World Tour." We hit several cities on our tour and met a cast of characters along the way. The doctors all began to sound alike. Even the dismal setting of each location was the same, with one of two color schemes: mauve and gray or bluish-green and taupe.

Matt's mom and sister were part of our entourage for the East Coast leg of the tour. At times, under the pressure of constant waiting and anticipation of the expected drone of nothing new, we would begin to crack and rely on moments of levity to maintain our sanity.

Wearing the "Sarcoma Sucks!" buttons given to us at U of M, we were waiting in the office of another specialist who would have nothing new to say. "Welcome to Sloan Kettering" scrolled across the monitor in the office, and Matt started tapping his foot on the floor. In his best Tony Bennett show tune voice, he snapped his fingers and began singing the words, "Welcome to Sloan Kettering." Snap. Snap. Snap. Then he added, "Where cancer won't kill ya," snap, "Cuz you're gonna die waiting." Snap. Snap. Snap.

Well, that was it. We burst into hysterical laughter. Matt coined one irreverent death jingle after another and the laughter became a little too loud for a cancer center. When the doctor and nurse practitioner walked through the door, they were pleasantly confused by what they were seeing. This was a first for the doctor, who had been seeing cancer patients for seventeen years. Our laughter was infectious, and before the chart was opened and the drone could begin, the doc and the NP shared a laugh with us.

From Sloan Kettering we made our way to the offices of Dr. Nicholas Gonzalez in Manhattan, where we heard refreshing new perspectives and ideas that energized us. There were no guaranteed cures or threats of making a "fatal mistake," but the Gonzalez program allowed Matt to proactively build up his body rather than passively tear it down. It was his plan to live healthy with cancer. He effortlessly made extreme sacrifices and never once complained. Rather than feeling stripped down and devoured, he was empowered and purposeful. It freed him up to live and to pursue clinical trials to further research, and ultimately he used his energy to share his testimony of faith.

Journal Entry, Matt Kell, April

Facing the prospect of terminal cancer has finally switched my priorities. I switched off a show on the NCAA Tournament. I'm laughing when I try to read Car and Driver. *I'm out of new cars (used my allotment anyway). I was thinking about next year's MSU team and realizing I might not be here to see them. The shame is it took a very sketchy future to get me to loosen the temporal, ridiculous ties to materialism and the pursuit of happiness. Last night, I tried to loosen even deeper ties, with my children. I must trust that the author of the universe is capable of raising Andrew and Samuel without my help. It's his will, not mine. They are his boys, not mine.*

I'm now in the biggest test. What appears to be the end-of-life. Who will I touch? How will I be perceived? Do I really believe the promises? Can I experience peace and joy (not comfort!) in my trials to come? Can I reflect eternal life in the face of earthly mortality? I have been given a gift. If I can be a positive witness as a 34-year-old, father of two young boys, husband of a vibrant young wife through cancer, that would be in accordance with his will and be held as a credit to me.

just get it done

michael

My dad was the original Nike ad. "Just get it done" was a phrase we heard often in our house. At those times, to Dick Spehn, the ends *for sure* justified the means. There are moments in life, he taught us, when nothing else matters. Just get it done.

In many ways this prepared me well for marriage. When Cathy and I were first married, we had a loft apartment in a 1920s-era building on Chicago's North Side. Exposed brick and a 180-degree view of the skyline made up for the fact that it was a third-floor walk-up with no elevator. The Lincoln Park neighborhood is a place that's "cooler near the lake," and not just the temperature. Folks there know the difference between deep-dish and stuffed pizza, and kids can calculate the wind chill factor before they can do long division.

On a particularly long cold snap where the mercury didn't rise above zero degrees Fahrenheit for nineteen straight days, Cathy came home from work, climbed the stairs to our loft, and stated, "We're moving to California!" Being a newlywed, I thought she was simply tired and cold from a hard day's work. It turns out she was quite serious. Apparently I should've known this from her tone.

There is a tone that all married women possess. All married men know of what I speak. It is a pitch, an inflection that every wife seems to have. Mothers must pass this down to their daughters on the wedding day, or perhaps it was something we registered for at Crate & Barrel when I wasn't paying attention. I say this because I hadn't heard this voice prior to being married. This small but potent lilt tells the husband, "We *are* going to do this." It was a voice with which I would become quite familiar. Cathy didn't use it often, but when she did, rest assured, it worked. At those times, I knew my job was to just get it done.

Six weeks later we packed up everything and moved to California. My dad had relocated there years earlier, and so this pleased him very much. He saw our move as an opportunity to be close to what would soon be a new set of grandchildren. My oldest brother, Rick, had three boys whom my father treasured. But they lived in Chicago and Dad had to be content with once- or twice-a-year visits. Now, however, he would be able to see a new set of grandkids actually grow up close by.

Cathy and I found a home in Orange County. On the high end of affluence and brimming with diversity and culture, it was also a place where God did some of his best landscaping work. Take a drive along Pacific Coast Highway past Laguna Beach one evening at dusk and you'll know just what I mean. Although we loved our life in California, Cath and I both maintained our Midwestern roots and quietly acknowledged to each other that there might come a time when we would return to the old neighborhood.

In the meantime, I ran a franchise-consulting firm with my dad. Our company had one primary client: a Michigan-based franchisor that operated children's retail stores throughout the country. Our job was to provide services to store owners on the West Coast. We sold the franchise to them, trained them, found the locations for their stores, negotiated the leases, etc. It was fairly successful throughout the nineties and my dad and I actually got along pretty well. He had always been "The Boss" to me and now it was literally true.

As time passed, however, Cathy's longing for the familiar ways of the Midwest grew stronger with the births of our three children.

Charlotte was our first. A nearly perfect baby, she was special from the minute she was alive. Named after my father's mother, she had blonde hair and the fairest complexion. Small freckles dotted her nose and her piercing blue eyes looked as though they could see into people's hearts. My mother used to say that Charlotte had an old soul. Cath hated that, but I think she just meant that this little girl always seemed to "get it."

Jack was next. We were wishing for a boy, so I was thrilled when the ultrasound technician told us we'd put the stem on the apple. Jack was a golden child, and not just because of his downy blond hair. He was a straight-A student and you could see it coming a mile away. He always had a "please" and "thank you" for everyone, and not in the Eddie Haskell kind of way either. I called him Captain Literal because if you told him to do something, he would do it precisely. There was very little nuance to Jack. He just loved life and the people in it.

Danny was last to join us. With a big smile that broke hearts from the instant he was born, he became the funny one. The most physical of the bunch, he loved to hold both of my ears when he would crawl into bed with me and Cath around five o'clock each morning. He looked like a three-year-old version of Bill Murray and drank his milk the way Bluto from *Animal House* finished off a six-pack.

We did have one experience that was heartbreaking during these years. Cathy miscarried in her fourth month of a pregnancy. We were devastated. On the drive home from the hospital we were startled by a bright, full rainbow that hung low in the sky, filling the Saddleback Valley with a horizon-to-horizon heaven-sent message: Our baby girl was home with God, and she was all right. From that moment forward, whenever Cath and I saw a rainbow, we would give each other a knowing look. It brought Cathy much-needed comfort to know that *all* of her babies were okay.

Cathy had a marvelous way with children. She had an innate understanding of the rhythm of kids. Kids, especially those under the age of ten, have a pace, a psychological gait. If you can recognize it and go with that flow, you can accomplish almost anything. You can get them to eat their vegetables, say please and thank you, and even go upstairs, brush their teeth, and get into bed. You really can.

That rhythm was sacred to Cath. To her, if Jack wanted to tell her a story, well then, the dishes could wait. She'd get onto the floor, put Jack on her lap, and listen as if each word carried the secrets to life itself. To Cathy, reading a story to the kids always took precedence over chores. A full heart was more important than a tidy house. Smiling kids were more important than shiny counters.

She was on the floor a lot. Many people just don't understand how important the floor is to kids. They play there, read there, watch TV there, love to wrestle and be chased there.... They *live* there. Furniture is for adults. If you want to gauge how comfortable someone is with kids, pay attention to how much time they spend on the floor with them.

Growing up, Cathy was the only child of a rather proper couple. Larry and Jill Lutz were German Lutherans with a strong sense of duty and propriety. Both worked hard their entire lives, spending decades in the same professions. The life Cathy knew at home was a sedate and well-planned one. Yet as she grew older, she dreamed of a big noisy house filled with loud kids, hearty laughter, and made-up songs sung out of key.

She also wanted her kids to have the blessings of Mullett Lake. So we settled on a kind of compromise. Each year at the end of June, Cathy and I packed up the kids and flew to Michigan. I returned home after a week's vacation to get back to work while the family spent the balance of the summer at the lake. By late August, I came back to the lake for one last long weekend. I'd swim, stop at The Secret to make a donation of balls to the pond in front of the green on number eight, and fly home to California with everyone.

September meant back to school for the kids and back to a work routine for me. For Cathy it meant the beginning of the long count of days until we could once again return to Mullett Lake.

Things were reasonably good with a full life that included kids, our own business, and friends and family. Although I was agreeable to thinking about moving back to the Midwest, I likened it to turning a large ship. We couldn't just drop everything and go. We would have to make a wide turn that might take years to actually complete. Although we'd been in California for more than ten years, Cathy told me she'd be patient, but she was adamant about changing our course.

After many years of working together, Dad decided he wanted to "step back" from the day to day of the business. Since I'd taken over many of the daily tasks anyway, I was perfectly fine with this new arrangement. Companies all over the nation spent the nineties bringing technology into their businesses, and all of that work had fallen to me in ours. I was even featured in a cover story in *Inc.* magazine about intranets in small businesses. The retail market was strong and money was flowing. Hot products like Ty company's Beanie Babies were flying off the shelves and making a lot of us retailers look smart.

However, the new millennium saw a shift in financial trends, and several things happened nearly at the same time. The first was Dad stepping back. He never stepped back from anything in his entire life. Leaving the business and having nothing much to do each day was, to say the least, difficult for him. So he tried to keep his hand in the business just a bit, and often this clashed with my ability to manage things.

Around the same time, the dot-com bubble burst and retail dollars flowed a lot less freely. Layoffs hit manufacturing companies and home values started to pull back. Several of the hot sellers, like the aforementioned Beanies, fizzled after a good long run. Many a retail budget was rendered obsolete when products like those no longer generated throngs of customers queued up for hours. Then 9/11 happened and businesses everywhere saw revenue take a downward turn. Including ours.

"Excuses," Dad said. "Just get it done."

He grew impatient with my inability to perform in spite of market conditions. He disagreed, and was downright angry, with many of my business decisions. At times that reaction was perfectly correct, as I made more than my share of boneheaded moves. Further complicating things were his random appearances in our office. He went weeks without coming in, and then, out of the blue, he'd show up and start asking questions. Not surprisingly, my answers to those questions either confused him or made him mad. He lacked the day-to-day context of why certain things were being done. So I became defensive, he became angry, and the others in our office would duck for cover. In so many ways it was just like being back in grade school. I was still answering to TB.

We both knew it would be impossible for us to continue this way. Something had to change.

lost valley

gina

Matt was a sports fanatic, although I am proud to say he never resorted to face painting. He had a mind for the science and strategy of athletics, and appreciated the corporate side of sports, but it was the energy of a packed stadium that satisfied something primal in him. He loved to be in the presence of the game, whether player or spectator. Throughout his life he was privileged to attend many major sporting events. As a kid he watched his Detroit Tigers win the '84 World Series with his dad by his side, from seats just behind the dugout. He attended the Olympics, a Ryder Cup, several NCAA Final Four and NBA Championships, and countless regular season games for every sport from kids' leagues to the pros. Regardless of who was playing or what thrilling last-minute play won or lost the game, one thing was consistent: Matt always had his best friends, Mike, Marty, Red, Doc, and Jeff, by his side, and now the group was expanding to include his sons, Drew and Sam.

When Matt attended the 2004 Major League Baseball All-Star Game with Drew, it gave new meaning to knocking one out of the park. They flew to Houston on a private jet owned by one of Matt's best clients. Even for a seasoned and well-traveled sports fan like Matt, this was a rare treat. With his son by his side, this was his version of the American dream: baseball, hot dogs, apple pie, and private jets.

After a two-day whirlwind trip, Matt and Drew burst through the door in a flurry of excitement, wearing ticket lanyards around their necks and carrying bags of souvenirs.

"Sam!" Drew called to his brother. "The American League won nine to four! Look what I got for you!"

He handed Sam an All-Star T-shirt and dumped a bag of merchandise on the kitchen floor. Sam, who was only three years old, was immediately caught up in the fever of their infectious excitement, happily celebrating the AL victory and proudly wearing his new gear.

Drew breathlessly continued, "The players walked right by our seats. Dad took pictures. Derek Jeter, Pudge, and Roger Clemens walked right by me! And I got to sit in the cockpit with the pilot and I ate a whole foot-long hot dog by myself!"

He couldn't show and tell about the trip fast enough. His happy green eyes and little-boy voice made me smile.

"Mom, do you know how many times Pudge Rodriguez has played in an All-Star Game?"

"Ah, lemme guess. Fifty?"

"No, Mom! Eleven. That's a lot!"

Matt plopped on the couch with a happy, tired look on his face that I hadn't seen in a while.

"I couldn't take my eyes off Drew," he said reflectively. "He was so wide-eyed. I don't think I even watched the game. I wish you could have seen him."

It was clear that this wasn't just another baseball game that would fade into the blur of so many others. This was one for the ages. I was basking in the glow of their *Field of Dreams* moment when Matt switched gears.

"You know, G, you've got to plan your ranch trip with the boys," he said genuinely. "Don't put it off."

He knew that I'd wanted to take the boys to Lost Valley Ranch in Colorado since before they were born. This was my equivalent to private jets and all-star games.

"I would love to. But only if you're coming with us," I said.

"You know I don't do horses unless there's an engine and four wheels involved. You should have Colorado with the boys."

Matt wanted me to experience the same joy with our sons that he felt in Houston, but he had no interest in joining us in Colorado. We did make plans to travel to Disney World as a family, but I was disappointed that I couldn't convince my city-slicker husband to spend a week with us at a dude ranch. He was perfectly content giving his spot to my mom. I booked our trip to Lost Valley a year in advance, secretly hoping it would be enough time to convince him to join us and anxiously anticipating that cancer could potentially alter our plans.

The months leading up to our ranch trip were eerily calm, but it felt as if the barometric pressure of our lives was dropping the way it does before a storm. My everyday life of sticky countertops, teaching moments, and groceries provided a break from the heaviness of cancer that loomed.

At the same time, my best friend, Colleen, was dealing with the uncertainty and stress of having a child with a serious heart defect. Since the time Tommy was born, he had four open-heart surgeries. His fifth surgery was scheduled two days after our return from Lost Valley Ranch. Colleen and I didn't try to bear one another's burdens, but our mutual understanding of life-and-death issues left us well positioned as guardians of each other's hearts. We vented and processed, offering understanding and mutual reassurances. We leaned on each other, heavily at times, to make sense of it all.

Despite my attempts to manage our lives and maintain balance, the stress ultimately found its way into my lower back. I had things to do and people to care for, and absolutely no time to slow down and deal with the nuisance of my own aches and pains. Motrin and my busy pace made it easy to deceive myself for a while, but years of being a runner and the constant ebb and flow of emotions left me vulnerable.

I sought chiropractic care and started taking Pilates classes, thinking I could fix it on my own, but when sciatic nerve pain became constant and standing up straight was no longer an option, I turned to the long process of physical therapy, which eventually made a difference.

My role as caregiver to Matt and mom to the kids remained demanding. Matt continued following Dr. Gonzalez's holistic program, which forced him to make dramatic life changes, especially to his diet. He swallowed literally hundreds of nutritional supplements each day and eliminated all sugar and white flour from his diet. He gave up bread, pasta, desserts, pizza, and his beloved Coke. He drank only water, green tea, or fresh carrot-apple-beet juice that we made in our new industrial-strength juice maker. The rules and rituals of this holistic regimen would have seemed impossible at any other time in Matt's life, but this wasn't just another fad diet that deprived him of the foods he loved. This was a means to an end. Matt was liberated by the positive impact this program was having on his body and his life with cancer.

His effortless letting go of things he loved was met with moments of white-knuckle clinging, mostly to God, but sometimes to the world. Matt's career was his pride, and being at work gave him a sense of control. This was one part of his life he was not willing to let go. As much as he could be in the office, he thrived. Through treatments, extreme pain and side effects, and suits that no longer fit, Matt held on to his identity as a successful businessman. But his other full-time job of managing cancer was beginning to interfere.

Outwardly he appeared healthy, but looks were deceiving. For every visible sign of health and hope, we were privately met with equal losses. Prominent tumors, trips to Ann Arbor for clinical trials, and days off of work were gradually increasing, as were our faith and trust in things unseen. Everything moved at a slow and steady pace, which gave us time to right our ship each time it listed.

Two days before our trip to Lost Valley, I reached up to put a plate in the cupboard and felt a twinge. Sudden pain shot through my back and into my legs. I dropped to my knees. Six months of physical therapy and I was back to square one.

I took it easy for two days. Aside from setting clothes in suitcases, I didn't lift a finger. Matt handled everything. I was frustrated but determined. I knew I wouldn't ride a horse all week, but I was not going to disappoint the boys. They were looking forward to this and they deserved it. They were surrounded by the cancer life. I wanted to give them Lost Valley Ranch.

Long airport lines and stiff coach seats increased my pain hourly. On our ride from the airport, my head pounded from the deafening sound of our rattle van, I mean shuttle van, reverberating off the washboard gravel road that, in some places, was wide enough for only one vehicle to pass. The last nine-mile winding stretch leading to Lost Valley Ranch was referred to as Shelf Road. It earned its nickname due to the absence of guardrails and the abundance of cliffs. Drew and Sam were unfazed as the old van bounced and shuddered and the rear wheels slid on the loose red dirt that gave Colorado its name. They excitedly asked endless questions about every new sight. They never knew it, but pain was beginning to consume me.

For seven years, every time I crossed the cattle guard at Lost Valley Ranch, it was like entering a new world. The vibrant blue sky and the first whiff of horse were like "welcome home" signs. Being at Lost Valley was like taking a step back in time. Nothing was familiar, but I felt at home. The air was sweetly perfumed with pine. Horses milled about in the afternoon sun. Porch swings creaked back and forth and the icy Goose Creek trickled by like a soundtrack for the ranch. Majestic mountains served as a backdrop to every activity. I loved my quiet time sitting at the small chapel nestled into the side of a hill.

This time, as I arrived at the ranch with Drew and Sam by my side, relentless pain obscured my senses. I was at Lost Valley, but I was not fully present. For four days I suffered in a cabin, watching my sons go to and from their next adventure. I couldn't eat, sleep, or be still. I read Psalms and wrote in a journal when I could. Mostly, I writhed.

It hurt to breathe. Muscle relaxers and Vicoden only added to my misery, making me sick to my stomach. For months I arrogantly denied that I would ever allow a scalpel near my spine, but I was no longer in a position to argue with the reality of impending back surgery. I left Drew and Sam behind with my mom to enjoy the rest of the week at Lost Valley, and was driven two hours to a hospital in Denver.

I desperately wanted to go home, but I was trapped by circumstance. Throughout the week I began to understand Matt. Having just a small taste of his isolation was enough to draw me closer to God and open my eyes to the biblical definition of peace. I wasn't dying, but I was alone in my suffering. For perhaps the first time in my life, I was physically and emotionally broken. This changed me. In the short term I had no choice but to stop fighting for control, but I also came to understand the powerful blessing of yielding.

I was lying in a hospital bed at Denver Presbyterian, thoroughly enjoying my Demerol high, when Matt appeared in the doorway wearing a cowboy hat.

"Do my eyes deceive me?" I slurred. "Whoooo! Look at you, cowboy!" Matt smiled, amused by my drug-induced happy talk.

"What are you doing? Aren't you supposed to be hiking or something?" he asked.

I suddenly felt weepy. "You think we can make up a good story to tell?" I said, squirming in diluted pain.

"I don't think this one needs any embellishment," he said, giving me a hug.

"Well, there's one good thing, I finally got you out to Colorado."

"I had no idea how far you'd go! All you had to do is ask!" he joked.

I felt like one in a dream, a helpless spectator to my own life. I was walking in my own lost valley. I had reversed roles with my husband, and although I was not cancer stricken, I experienced the isolation of pain and the gift of suffering that draws us near to God. As a caregiver, I had started to believe I was invincible, needing to be strong and in control to care for those around me. My experience, while painful and somewhat traumatic, breathed new life into me and offered a renewed perspective and source of strength for the days yet to come.

i'm home

michael

I developed a severe case of "Sunday Syndrome." I was anxiety ridden each Sunday afternoon knowing that on Monday morning I'd have to go to a job that I hated and was no longer very good at. If I had been more self-aware, or perhaps self-confident, I would have quit years earlier. But with three kids at home and a father whose retirement depended on my continuing the business, I felt trapped.

Cathy remained firm about moving back to Michigan. She could see the toll the job was taking on me. I was almost never home, and when I was, I was short-tempered with the kids and paid little attention to her. My cell phone rang constantly and I always seemed to be putting out fires instead of moving our company forward. The real coup de grace came when our bread-and-butter client started dropping hints that they wanted out of their contract with us. At that point both Dad and I began to think about exit strategies.

That summer, I initiated talks with a third party to buy out our company. I wanted to leave, and with revenue down, our main client wavering on renewal, and the economy still reeling from 9/11, it was clear the time had come to move along. Although outwardly Dad supported this plan, I think it scared him. It meant the end of the business he had built as well as the formal start of his retirement and the ultimate fixing of his income. It might also mean, and I'm certain he considered this, that Cathy and I (and his grandchildren) would move to Michigan.

Dad and I did have one unexpected distraction from our anxieties that year: our beloved Chicago Cubs. That summer the Cubs won ninety-six games, clinched the NL Central, and were expected to roll through the preliminary rounds of the playoffs and play in the World Series for the first time since 1945. (They hadn't won a Series since 1908!)

The regular season was wrapping up and everyone picked the Cubs to go all the way. I got a call from Dan Pelekoudas. He and I had been best friends since grade school. A skinny, dark-haired kid of Greek stock, Dan and I met in a fifth-grade basketball league. As I sat with my dad watching some of the other kids play one Saturday afternoon, he pointed at Dan out on the court and said, "Look at that kid. If you want to be a ballplayer ... play like that guy."

My old man had an eye for talent, especially on the court. My new friend grew up to be co-captain of the University of Michigan basketball team, an outstanding corporate attorney, and, most importantly, my best friend in the world. Playing ball has its rewards.

"I have some very good news," Dan told me. "I have twelve, count 'em, twelve, tickets to the World Series at Wrigley Field."

I was stunned. "Which game?"

He couldn't contain himself. "Every game!"

Dan had a family connection within Major League Baseball and he got us the tickets. Twelve of them! To each home game if they made it to the World Series. Unbelievable.

We talked about this for a moment and soon our giddiness gave way to practical planning. The first order of business was deciding who would go. After doing some math in his head, Dan concluded that I could have four tickets. One for myself, my dad, my brother Rick, who lived in Chicago and hadn't missed a Cubs opening day in twenty-five years, and likely my Uncle Mel. I couldn't wait to tell Dad. Given the tensions and uncertainty that were a part of each day lately, this would be a welcome distraction. I called him immediately.

"Hey, Dad, how'd you like to go to the World Series with me?" I said.

The words sounded like a dream as they came off my tongue. I was going to take my dad to the World Series at Wrigley Field. That was as good as it gets. Cue Kevin Costner, bring up the music from *The Natural*, soften the focus, and tell Norman Rockwell he needs to sketch just one more for the ages. There would be joy in Mudville today, ladies and gentlemen, for the boys are going to Wrigley!

Dad was elated. Soon he began telling all of his friends that he was going to the Series, if only the bums ... I mean the Cubs, got there. We all began making plans, arranging flights, and anticipating this trip of a lifetime.

About four or five days later, however, things began to get a little odd. Dad started asking about additional tickets for his friends. "Real Cubs fans," he called them. "The guys who have been with them since the days of Kiki Cuyler and Goo Goo Gulan." It seems that our good fortune was infectious and some of his old buddies wanted in. He wanted my friend Dan to come up with another two or three tickets for them. I informed him that receiving four tickets to three games of the World Series was extraordinary and we shouldn't expect any additional. He asked about the others who would be coming to the games with us.

"Actually, Dad, the others are mostly Dan's family. His sister and a couple of cousins, I think."

The next day I got another call from Dad and his tone was a familiar one. Short, prosecutorial, on a razor's edge just waiting for me to say the wrong thing. Within minutes, of course, I fulfilled that promise.

"Look, I'm calling to find out, once and for all, if there will be tickets for my other guys. It doesn't matter if there will be or there won't be, just let me know."

I was stunned. "Dad, I'm letting you know ... there are *no more* tickets available to us."

"I don't understand," he shot back. "You and your buddy keep screwing around with all of this crap. I mean really ... I've never met two more selfish people in my entire life. We've got people here who have been going to Cubs games since before you were born, and you two idiots are going to tell me who can and cannot go to these games?"

I was on the phone listening to this for more than an hour. In the other room, Cathy was getting the kids ready for bed. She would peek her head around the corner to check on me at five-minute intervals. She knew the look on my face all too well. As I listened to my father rant, yet again, about how one of his children had failed to "honor thy father," I realized I'd reached my limit.

I couldn't for the life of me understand how we messed this up. This was the most basic thing in the world. My dad and I were going to the World Series at Wrigley Field. Slam-dunk, special moment. Well ... not so much.

Since he was raised in the Depression, nothing was ever given to Dad. Nothing. Not even very many outward expressions of love — the hugs-

and-kisses kind of love, that is. His parents provided food on the table and clothes on their backs but not really much more than that. This was recounted to us, his kids, almost on a daily basis throughout our childhood. I could never figure out whether this was something that brought him pride or shame. Either way, he told us about it a lot.

On the other hand, we got lots of love from Mom and Dad. That was definitely one difference from their parents. They showered us with hugs and kisses and games and play and fun. Plus a lot of discipline. They worked hard to give us the types of opportunities they never had. Like living in a big house in the suburbs in a safe and clean neighborhood. Good schools too. Public schools, mind you—nothing fancy—but good ones, with lots of different experiences.

But there was always a struggle that lurked just beneath the surface with Dad. He cloaked it with the premise that he wanted his kids to fend for themselves. He was conflicted by the notion that he should *show* his kids a better life but not actually give it to them. This seemed admirable on the surface, but this conflict got the better of him sometimes.

There was a paradox to Dad's generosity. He was always there to help in times of crisis or genuine need. (And when it came to his grandchildren, he adored them and spared no expense in buying them gifts or paying for travel.) When dealing with his own kids, however, a struggle raged within him, and you could never anticipate the expression of that struggle on any given day.

On the occasion of the World Series incident, Dad just couldn't reconcile that a couple of "punks" (in this case a forty-year-old father of three —me—and my best friend, a Newport Beach attorney) would tell him who, among his Greatest Generation friends, could go to the games and who couldn't. This left them, the old lions, completely out of the decision-making process. Again, unacceptable to TB. If anything, he thought we should have the decency to step aside and let those guys take all the tickets. After all, that would be the honorable thing to do.

As fate would have it, the Cubs lost the NLCS, and this generation got its very own Billy Goat Curse when a schnook named Bartman just couldn't resist reaching for that foul ball. There was a certain cruel irony in all that expended energy and acrimony for a trip that would never happen anyway. I felt like Jack Nicholson at the end of *Chinatown*. "Forget it, Jake, it's the Cubs."

I called my brother Rick and vented to him about it all. He was calm and let me get it all out. Then he gave me the words that I needed to hear. "If I were you," he said, "I would leave skid marks on the pavement getting out of there."

He was right. My wife wanted to go. I wanted to go. Now smart people were telling me to get out while I could. In November of that year, Cathy went to Michigan to look for houses. She took the kids over the long Veterans Day weekend and stayed in Rochester with her parents. She connected with a real estate agent there and arranged to look at more than fifty properties. Cathy sent me photos of more than thirty houses and I didn't like a single one. She became discouraged.

On the day they were to fly home, little Danny developed a fever and Cath didn't want him to fly with an infection. She called her real estate guy and told him she was staying one more night.

He said, "Well, there is one more property that just came on the market. I could take you there in the morning if you like."

The next morning Cathy called me while I was at work.

"Hi, love," I answered. "How are you today?"

There was a long pause and then she said just two words.

"I'm home!"

There was that tone again. She was calling from the front yard of the house she loved.

"Seriously, MJ," she said excitedly. "I just love it!" She sent me digital photos and I was impressed.

I pressed her for confirmation. "Really? Is this your house?"

"It's perfect. I could live here for the rest of my life," she said.

Before the end of the day we purchased Cathy's dream home. In a matter of a few weeks, we also sold our home and our business. Though it was exciting to actually be going through with this, it wasn't easy. As it became clear that we were really moving, my dad withdrew completely. He wanted nothing to do with us and it became too painful for him to even speak with me. We had a few bits of final business to take care of and some brief and barely polite conversation. During our final few weeks in California, our relationship pretty much shut down. It broke my heart.

By the time I pulled the minivan out of the driveway and pointed it east toward Michigan, I hoped that time and distance would help ease the tension between Dad and me. I had no idea that it would take quite a bit more than that.

freight trains

gina

The morning sun beamed through the classroom windows, illuminating dust particles and generating just enough warmth to give the air a stale odor. My eyelids felt heavy under the bright glow of sunshine that clashed with the cruel fluorescent lights overhead. It's the kind of light that throws shadows across a woman's face, making her look and feel every bit her mother's age.

I volunteered regularly in Drew's first-grade classroom at St. John Lutheran School. Located next to the only hospital in Rochester, St. John had a sixty-five-year history of educating kindergarteners through eighth graders in the community. This modest school sits in the shadow of a large church, which serves as its provider and protector. What it lacks in size and aesthetics it makes up for in longevity and substance.

At the end of a long morning in the classroom in late October, I was feeling particularly appreciative of teachers. No training can prepare a first-grade teacher for what amounts to wrangling cats. Their work is exhausting. After just a few hours with twenty-two six-year-olds, I had a notion of being carried out to my car.

By the end of the first month of school, the first graders started realizing that the good old freewheeling days of kindergarten were over. There would be no more cuddles and aimless wandering. Their teacher, Mrs. Nelson, was all business. She had a reputation for preparing her students to read and write, handle conflict, and become independent thinkers. This year, however, the kids were in for more than a purely academic education.

Mrs. Nelson had a few obstacles in her path that distracted from the usual curriculum. In the category of minor hurdles, she had her own son in class. This was the least of her worries. She also had three other students with real life-and-death issues occurring in their homes: Matthew Schomaker, Tommy's older brother, was surrounded by the ongoing turmoil of his younger brother's heart defect; Connor Larkin, whose father, Tom, was battling cancer; and my son Drew, who started first grade as his father started hospice. It was clear this was not going to be just another first-grade class with kaleidoscopes and cleanup songs. In varying degrees, brutal realities were being foisted upon these unsuspecting, tender babes.

Unbeknownst to Drew and his younger brother, Sam, a fully loaded freight train carrying some of life's heaviest cargo was headed straight for them. At home the distant whistles of that train could already be heard as Matt was beginning a video diary for his sons, something he avoided doing for nearly three years.

Since Matt was first diagnosed, he created an outline of all the topics he wanted to cover. We went to Best Buy and equipped him with a top-of-the-line camera. Everything was planned and ready, but we had not considered one important detail: this project required the emotional courage to actually press the record button. The idea of creating a video to encapsulate and preserve Matt's life experience, wisdom, and humor made sense on paper. Pressing that little red button, however, was not so simple.

Sitting down in front of the camera would mean saying good-bye. Saying good-bye would mean giving up. Giving up meant dying. Dying meant not being there for the boys. Unacceptable. Such is the origin of an incomplete video diary.

Making a video seemed to be an admission that Matt would not be here for his kids. Even though he had accepted that reality, the next task was cruel and unnatural. It was impossible to convey every hope and dream he had for our sons and teach them every life lesson about becoming a man and surviving this world without a father. God designed parenthood to be a teach-as-you-go program, not a DVD crash course.

Selfishly, I wanted Matt to make a series of videos. Regardless of cancer, I could have benefited from such information. As a woman in a household overflowing with testosterone, I'd be happy to take a peek behind the

Y-chromosome curtain. Unfortunately, the catalyst for making the videos was a terminal illness, and that took all the fun out of it.

Secretly, I wanted to make my own video too, but it was a sensitive subject and I didn't want to trivialize the process. It's easy to do in good health, but few people ever consider it. If we eliminated the morbid stigma associated with making a video diary, it would no longer be a depressing task representing the final good-bye, but rather an exciting new way to share life lessons, tell stories, and preserve memories. Ya know, just in case we actually die.

I have a crazy vision of infomercial guru Kevin Trudeau in a three a.m. time slot, imploring us all to get VD. Preying on our fear of death, or at least our narcissistic tendencies, Kevin would hawk Video Diary do-it-yourself kits, or personal VD Kits, complete with script suggestions and musical interludes. The initials "VD" would take on a whole new meaning in the world and, with the proper marketing spin, would become as popular as Ginsu or Snuggie. The "As Seen on TV" kits would become so common that Bed, Bath and Beyond (emphasis on Beyond) would carry them on an end-cap display with a sign that read "Death happens. Get your VD first! (Down comforters half off with every purchase.)"

While my twisted infomercial fantasy will likely never see the light of day, I prayed that Matt would follow through and press the little red button. I believed that making a video diary would be therapeutic for him, and life changing for those of us watching it. Healthy people rarely contemplate their own mortality. Life is busy and we don't have time for such nonsense. Unless the clock starts ticking out loud, there is no time or reason to make a video diary for our kids. Life is happening and trains always run on time. Tick-tock.

life is good

michael

Cathy had a great sense of "as it should be" and through the years, taught me a lot about that. While I had spent much of my life looking for perfect, Cathy showed me how to look for what was right. It was effortless for her. She believed that God had a plan for us and, while we may not know it, want it, or agree with it, it was real, and most of all, it was right.

I learned to trust Cathy's instinct on the morning of September 11, 2001, the day our son Dan was born. When the sad events of that day became apparent, it occurred to me that my new baby would be tarnished with this God-awful event forever. "Day of evil" the newspapers called it, and it would follow my son on every birthday for the rest of his life. As I drove back to the hospital later that morning, I came up with a plan.

"I think I can fix this," I told Cathy when I arrived. "I'm sure Dr. McClellen will agree to my plan."

Cathy was calm as ever. "What plan?"

"Danny was born only an hour into the day. I think I can convince the doctors to change his birth date to September 10."

Cathy never flinched.

"No, MJ," she said firmly as she held our newborn son in her arms. "This boy is the only good thing that happened today."

I thought she didn't understand me, as though her being in the hospital kept her from knowing the full awfulness of what was going on. "Cath, they're calling this the worst day in American history!" I was adamant. But I was wrong.

"I do understand," she said, holding Danny just a little closer. "If he is the only light that came into this world on a very dark day, then that is what's meant to be. I don't know why God chose to send him to us on this day, but I do know that we aren't changing a thing. This isn't our plan —it's his."

That was her gift. Cathy could see the righteousness in imperfect things. I wanted to fix it. Fix God's plan! Can you imagine? She saw the folly in that. Although this plan of his wasn't perfect to us, she was certain that it was right.

Moving to Michigan was another example of Cath knowing what was right for us. By almost any standard, this was a dumb idea. People don't actually move *into* Michigan. The economy was in the tank, education was mediocre, and there was no real culture to speak of. (Unless you consider throwing a dead octopus onto the ice during a Red Wings playoff game a cultural experience.) The new house was nice though, and the neighborhood was great.

On our first night in town, as the moving van was pulling away, two neighbor families showed up with pizzas and drinks. They even had paper plates and napkins for us. They simply came over and said, "Welcome."

Spending so much time in California (where few people even know their neighbors' names) had an effect on me and I was immediately suspicious of these people, who, less than an hour ago, were complete strangers. Heather from across the street was pouring Cokes for the kids. Susan from next door was handing out slices of pizza. Their husbands, Ed and Jim, smiled and offered me a beer. I turned a cynical eye to this group and started a dialogue in my head.

"Who are you and what are you doing in our home?" I ask with raised eyebrows.
"We want to be your friends," they reply.
"But why?" I insist.
"Because we're your neighbors," they say.
"FREAKS!"

As all the kids made their way downstairs to play in our basement, the adults continued getting to know each other. Inside my head my distrustful inner dialogue played on.

"Cathy," I say. "This must be a part of a subversive plan. All of this food and

kindness nonsense is likely nothing more than a diversion. I'll keep them occupied. You go and hide the valuables."

"But we don't have any valuables," Cathy says with a smile.

"Then what do we do?" I ask, completely lost now.

"Maybe we should just relax and enjoy their friendship," she tells me.

Of course she was right. Still, I kept this daydream going most of the night, with various plotlines and subtexts. In one version I caught one of them secretly implanting a listening device into the fur of our dog, Maggie. In another, the pizza had lethal concentrations of Iocane powder. (Yes, Iocane powder only exists in *The Princess Bride*, but I loved that movie and this was *my* daydream.)

Cathy saw the look on my face from across the room. She could tell I was confused by it all. I mean, I loved it, but I was taken aback by it too. Not her. She just smiled, bit into a slice of mushroom and sausage, and with one look told me, "We're home."

In the end, no one was hurt or became lost in the fire swamp that night. (Seriously, rent the movie, it's great!) These people would indeed become our close and trusted friends. Their children would become our children's friends. And this place would someday become my kids' "old neighborhood."

A couple of years went by. Cath and I settled in. Life in Michigan was just about everything we'd hoped for. Just about. My relationship with my dad ... well, I had no relationship with my dad. It was excruciating for everyone. I heard from my sister Lynn that Dad had become "kind of lost."

"He's just a sad guy now," she told me. "Like he has no love anymore."

It is a difficult thing that exists between fathers and sons. I missed him completely. Even at age forty, it seems a son needs the approval of his dad. The irony was that I had finally carved out the life I always wanted for myself and now I couldn't share it with him. I had a wife who loved me, a happy home filled with dear friends and lots of kids. I had a good job with a large franchising company, we were close enough to drive to Mullett Lake, and I was now coaching basketball at the local high school. I realized the only thing missing in my life was a relationship with my father. And that was a pretty big thing to be missing.

Our estrangement hurt Cathy as well. She adored Dad and he always considered her his second daughter. This rift between him and me ended their relationship too, and I felt awful about that.

One afternoon I watched Cathy as she stood in our kitchen unpacking the day's haul from Target and directing the chaotic traffic of kids and friends and dinner. She looked great. Content. It had been a long journey to this place, but she finally made it to where she wanted to be. I came up behind and wrapped my arms around her. As I did, I noticed a couple of T-shirts on the kitchen island that she had bought for herself. One, a simple green tee with a hand-drawn stickman on the front, had three words on it that caught my eye.

"Life is good."

connections

gina

Daylight filled the St. John atrium and illuminated the scuffs on the plain white walls. Entrances, stairways, and hallways all led to this large open space connecting the school to the church. Glass doors and windows extended from the floor up to the thirty-foot ceiling on both ends. There were no seats, yet it served as a rest stop for people coming in and out of the building.

An information counter sat unoccupied most days, though you could pick up last Sunday's church bulletin or a school hot-lunch menu from the racks. Generally, it was a place to lean your elbow or set your Starbucks cup while you caught up on the latest church and school gossip. Yes, gossip is sinful, but thankfully we have forgiveness, because even we church-goers love dishing the dirt. Wherever there is community, even one of like-minded folks, you inevitably have squabbles, and with those you can count on some tasty gossip. Conveniently, the Christian community creates acceptable loopholes, springing from good intentions like, "I shouldn't be telling you this, but I know you'll pray about it." In a place where the *700 Club* meets *All My Children*, prayer seems to justify gossip and God's will becomes semi-malleable in the hands of flawed humans. The atrium echoed with colorful stories of the people who continuously flowed through it, but thankfully, while everyone passed through, no one hung out long enough to get into much trouble.

I had planned to meet Colleen in the atrium to make a kid-handoff. The daily relay was in full swing and I was maxing out on logistics. I was bringing Tommy home for a play date with Sam, and later Colleen would pick up Matthew and Drew from school and bring them over to our house for the late-afternoon reset. This was the period of time after school when the kids needed to decompress with big hugs, plenty of snacks, and the occasional meltdown. We've all been there.

I arrived a few minutes early with Sam in tow and used the time to peek in on Drew just long enough for a quick hug and kiss. Before we could leave, Mrs. Nelson suggested that the class do an impromptu performance of the Tootie-Ta dance, and the kids were giddy with delight. Sam and I joined in for "thumbs up, elbows out, feet apart, knees together, bottoms up, tongue out, eyes shut, turn around and sing, a tootie-ta, a tootie-ta, a tootie-ta-ta!" I was certain that this ridiculous dance could become the next wedding sensation. I mean, people can't Hokey Pokey forever! To my surprise it was the perfect midday tension break.

As Sam and I made our way back toward the atrium, we walked slowly past room 6, peering in for just a moment. For more than twenty-five years it had been the classroom of Mr. John Schaffer, who was Matt's favorite teacher when he attended St. John. In a few years, Drew and Sam would have the privilege of becoming the second generation of Kells to be taught by Mr. Schaffer. As I looked around the room, I imagined that it hadn't changed much since Matt was a boy. Painted off-white, the sterile cinder block walls were covered with student art projects, posters of presidents, and Bible verses. There were four rows of desks facing the chalkboard and a simple, hand-carved wooden cross hanging above it. Three chess sets sat at the back of the classroom and a coatrack held two neckties that Mr. Schaffer kept for his male athletes to wear on game days when they forgot their own. For a moment, I wondered if Matt ever wore one of those ties, but quickly remembered two things: Matt would never forget to wear a tie. He liked to dress up, even back then. Plus, the ties weren't Joseph Abboud, so it wasn't even a conversation.

Mr. Schaffer liked kids. I don't think that's true of all teachers, or even all parents. He had an infectious demeanor that ignited his students' desire to learn. He set the bar high and his students worked hard not to disappoint him. His excitement and energy for educating earned him the love of his students. He taught religion as a subject for one hour every day, but that hour was more like a syllabus for the way he lived rather than just another lesson plan. Whether it was religion, math, or history, the kids learned by his example, which was the real secret of his success.

John Schaffer epitomized St. John. My husband grew up within that culture and seemed to carry it forward effortlessly throughout his life. It was the simple fulfillment of expectations. In his midtwenties, Matt received a time-capsule letter in the mail that he had written to himself as part of an eighth-grade school project. It read, "Dear Matt, How are you doing? Take a look at yourself. Are you where you want to be? Who is the center of your life? I sure hope God is." The values he was taught at home were consistently reinforced at school, and those were the same principles he was living by into adulthood and now passing on to his children. Matt's roots ran deep at St. John. The relationships he formed there were built upon a cornerstone of Christian beliefs and played a significant role in keeping him grounded throughout his life. He was born and raised a conservative Lutheran and was an active member of our church. Yet Matt respectfully maintained a position just outside the confines of the provincial Lutheran bubble.

Sam and I caught the eye of Mr. Schaffer before we could quietly pass by his classroom. Without a second thought, he stopped what he was doing and popped out into the hall.

"Hey, Sam!" Mr. Schaffer said, offering Sam a quick high five. He always made time for kindness. "How's your daddy doing today?" He glanced at me for an indication.

"Dad's at home," Sam replied. I pressed my lips together against my teeth with half a smile and Mr. Schaffer seemed to understand.

"Barb and I are praying for you," he said, giving me a bear hug.

Sam and I were now officially late to meet Colleen. As we hurried into the atrium, I saw her talking to a woman I didn't recognize. I stood back for a moment, not wanting to interrupt. The woman was slender with fair skin, soft blonde hair, and heartbreaking blue eyes. Her clothing was typical Rochester mommy, Gap style. For a moment, though, I found myself staring at her. I often see qualities in other women that I seek to emulate. Sometimes it is confidence or style, other times it's athleticism or intellect. From a distance, I had the conscious thought that this woman exuded grace. I didn't even know what that meant. It is an elusive and indescribable quality, yet I knew this woman possessed it.

"Hey, we were just talking about you," Colleen said as she waved me over. The woman looked at me as though she knew me. I smiled and looked at Colleen for a little help.

"Hi, Gina. I'm Cathy Spehn. I went to school with your husband. Actually, Mike, Matt, and I all went to grade school, high school, and college together," she said, extending her hand to me.

As we shook hands, my brain scanned the archives. "Oh, it's nice to meet you," I said, trying not to stare. I knew many people from Matt's life before me, but I was certain that we had never met. She proceeded to introduce me to her son Danny, who was clinging to her leg, and she further connected the dots between our many mutual friends.

"I can't believe we haven't met before today," I said with surprise. Together we easily came up with a list of ten people we had both socialized with and knew well. I even discovered that her father had been Matt's coach for one year.

Cathy's smile was noticeably radiant. Her voice was soft, and her personality, sweet. I almost hated to characterize her that way because it implies sugary. That, and there were girls in high school who were sweet, but never believable. In our five minutes together, I knew that Cathy was unassuming and without pretense. Genuine kindness was evident in her smile and in her manner of speaking.

The conversation, as most of mine did those days, shifted to cancer, and I could tell that Colleen had already filled in Cathy on the latest details. Colleen was my buffer in the world. She ran interference for me, dodging questions and protecting me from the burden of the cancer spotlight. The irony was that she was in her own spotlight with Tommy. Sharing this unenviable position together had taken our close friendship and turned it into a marriage of sorts. We had love beyond love, and laughter in places some would find irreverent. Without a person to laugh with in the pit, life becomes a very dark place. Colleen's husband, Mike, nicknamed us the Oprah twins because we supported each other relentlessly. Just as millions around the world collectively chant, "You go, girl!" to every word Oprah says, Colleen and I support and defend each other with an instinctive fidelity, for better or worse. We were just a couple of skinny white mamas from Detroit, but we always had each other's back. Three snaps up and one very loose neck roll for my sista.

For more than two years, I was in the unique position of having people constantly extend themselves to my family. The same had been true for Colleen in the years since Tommy was born. Our perverse form of celebrity exposed us to outreach in all its forms. The "Nikes" don't offer to give help, they just do it. They show up with a meal or come over and look around the house for something they can do. They take out the trash or water plants or call from the grocery store to see if you need anything. They do, without asking, and they seem to know the lines not to cross. Family members, close friends, or ballsy acquaintances usually fill this role.

The "Thingtimes" offer to help with "anything, anytime." But really, they aren't sure what they can do or exactly when they should do it. Most people fall into this category. Some want you to call them, but most hope you won't. For the ones who do, it's best to keep these people in your back pocket for when you are really in a pinch.

The least intrusive helper is the "Snailer." Opening the mailbox to find cards and notes of encouragement is of vital importance. The written word is the perfect form of support. It's personal, safe, and far more meaningful than email. While incredibly comforting, the mail also can become a measure of the severity of your situation. Ask any mail carrier; too many cards in the mailbox can be a very bad sign.

The "Mirror People" are the ones who, every time they look at you, all they can see is themselves. Filled with good intentions but in the end needing more help than they actually give, they want to go right past your experiences and tell you about their own. Or their brother's. Or their brother's ex-girlfriend's. How she had the same thing and she died after she thought she had it beat. You find yourself consoling them, and for an odd moment it feels good not to have the spotlight on you. Then you think again and realize how strange all of this is.

Now Cathy was caught standing between Colleen and me. She didn't know who to offer help to first. The poor thing expressed her genuine desire to help both of us but without overstating her intentions. Despite all of our connections, past and present, Cathy was just another victim of the "Thingtime" curse for now.

She waved as she headed out the atrium doors into the warm afternoon sun with her son Danny in her arms. For a moment, I envied her.

bibles and basketballs

michael

If you're ever in Detroit, Michigan, turn left at the urban blight and drive north on I-75. There you will find Rochester, a quiet bedroom community fitting nicely into the fabric of affluent Oakland County. Towns like Bloomfield Hills and Birmingham bring the median income of the place up just enough to offset the likes of Pontiac and Hazel Park. Rochester's people aren't stinking rich, but they are comfortable enough to fill their finished basements with plasma TVs and give generously to the more than twenty churches around town. It is the kind of place that looks great in brochures. Tree-lined streets, bike paths through sprawling parks, a quaint Main Street with local shops, and even a cider mill on the edge of town help present a Thornton Wilder kind of place. Imagine *Our Town, the Sequel: Revenge of the Strip Mall*, and you're well on your way to understanding Rochester.

Just down Walton Avenue sits St. John Church and School, where Cathy attended as a little girl. I was invited to join the weekly basketball open gym there on Saturday mornings. Ingeniously called "Bibles and Basketballs," the first twenty minutes consisted of a Bible study of sorts and then two hours of hoops, winners stay on.

A passage from the Bible was read and we were supposed to discuss what it meant to us. I was never much for PDF (public displays of faith), so I often tried to time my arrival to coincide with the end of the Bible reading. Many Saturdays the group actually started late and I was forced to participate anyway. My cynical mind told me they were just trying to catch us heathens sneaking in without paying respect to the Lord. In any event, there we were: fifteen or twenty middle-aged guys sitting around doing our best to read the Bible and then "share."

At some point during the prayer portion of the morning, almost without exception, one of the guys would ask the group to pray for someone named Matt Kell and his family. I didn't know this name, but I bowed my head reverently and counted the minutes until we could start playing.

I shared this once with Cathy. "It seems we always have to pray for some guy named Matt all the time.... I just want to lace up the shoes and start pulling muscles." She clued me in. Matt Kell was a classmate of hers from St. John and Lutheran North High School, and was now in the late stages of cancer. He also had two young sons. I took this to heart. A young guy with a young family, Matt sounded a lot like me. It made me begin to rethink my haste during the prayer portion of Saturday mornings. Perhaps, I thought, I should count my blessings.

I was still a little awkward at the Bible reading stuff. I hadn't had a church home since my youth in Chicago. When Cathy and I were in California, I found a new house of worship when I wandered out onto the jetty at Big Corona del Mar State Beach. A watery entrance hall to Newport Harbor, the jetty is not much more than a group of large rocks in a line stretching from the beach out into the ocean, providing a distinctly calm channel for boats entering and exiting the harbor. Many come to this spot to watch the sun set each day. It is an amazing sight to see. Countless vacation slideshows finish big with the photos taken here.

What most people don't know, however, is that God does two shows a night in Newport. There is the sunset, which is breathtaking. Then, for those patient few, about half an hour after the sun retires for good, the sky begins a glorious twilight encore. Pinks and purples and gradient blues that can't be reproduced by man gently paint the wisps of clouds lingering on a heavenly canvas. In a few moments the flicker of starlight contrasts perfectly against the blackness of night. As it unfolded I'd just breathe it all in until it was no more. Turning my head straight up, then left, then over my right shoulder, I'd watch the last few sailboats glide in silent silhouette through the no-wake jetty toward their final moorings for the night. In the distance, the only sound was an occasional sea lion sounding his barbaric yawp at the waves.

I found much comfort out on those rocks. I found peace. Which is different than quiet. I looked for God's Word among the tide pools, and his admonitions in the crashing waves. I stared in awe at his magnificent stained-glass sky. I talked to him and hoped that someday he might whisper something back. It was a nice arrangement. No Latin chanting. No collection plates. No hymns that only people over seventy understand. Just the two of us, and the rocks.

When the next Saturday came, I showed up a little early to Bibles and Basketballs and helped my friend Mark set up. Together we set up the chairs for the guys and placed a Bible on each one.

"How's Matt Kell doing?" I asked.

"Not good," Mark replied. "I was at their house last week and talked with his wife, Gina. I don't think he's going to make it."

I paid just a little closer attention to the Scripture verse that morning. I had never actually read the Bible before. I thought I knew what was in there, but I never read the words or studied their true meaning. I always thought of Holy Scripture a little like some consider chicken soup when they get sick: it's possible it won't help, but it can't hurt. Hearing about Matt Kell and his family, and seeing the effect that prayer seemed to have on his friends, made me rethink my attitude.

Once the basketball started, I demonstrated my extreme athletic ability, schooling the other men on how the game of basketball was supposed to be played. Translation: after two hours of having my eighteen-year-old brain argue with my forty-year-old body, I dragged my sorry self out to my car in pain.

I loved playing ball again. Basketball was my game. I was never all that great at it; I just had a passion for it. After high school, my playing days were relegated to pickup games and driveway shootouts. Not everyone understands the "past his prime" athlete. Even a game in an open gym at the local church can become intense. Not because we are so delusional as to think that this game really matters in the grand scheme of things. It's just that the sights and sounds of the game seem to get our endorphins running high again and we simply can't do this halfway.

There are certain sounds in sports that only athletes really appreciate: the rattle of a Titleist dropping, like a hollow ice cube, into the cup on the eighteenth hole; the crisp snap of a baseball into the pocket of a well-oiled glove; or my personal favorite, the squeak of gym shoes on a perfectly polished gym floor. It's magical to me. It calls to me. This is not the sound of winning or losing. It's not the sound of three-point shots or

ESPN highlight-reel, fast-break dunks. It is simply the sound of playing, of basketball players *playing the game.* The next time you're in a gym, close your eyes and listen. It really is glorious.

As I drove home after playing at St. John, every part of my body hurt. My eyebrows hurt. I felt like pulling into the Walgreens drive-thru and ordering a trough of ibuprofen, but reaching for the turn signal caused me to cramp up. Somebody help me ... I'm old!

As much as I wanted to lie on the couch when I got home and allow my seizing muscles to battle it out with the Advil, I had to survive our son Danny's fourth birthday party. I was late and Cathy was waiting for me to bring juice boxes.

"Please, God, give me green lights," I mumbled aloud to myself as I drove a little too fast along Rochester's winding back roads, treating every stop sign as if it were merely a suggestion. With any luck, the few squad cars that do exist in our town would be busy chasing down someone's cat and not just around the next bend waiting to raise my insurance point total. Cathy was waiting patiently with a house full of preschoolers and I was their sugar supplier. A few minutes either way can make all the difference in the life of a four-year-old.

When I got home I rushed in to find the typical noise and clutter of a Spehn birthday party. Danny was in his glory, since, as the youngest, it's rare that everyone's attention is turned to him. In the crowd was a little boy I didn't recognize. Cath placed both hands on his shoulders and introduced him to me as Tommy Schomaker. "He's in Danny's preschool class at St. John."

The first thing I noticed about little Tommy was his bright big smile and ruby red lips. I put up my hand to give him a high five and he slapped it hard. "Ohhh," I pretended, holding my hand as if the little guy had injured me. "Don't hurt me, don't hurt me!" I kidded. Tommy smiled and went to do it again. This time he put all thirty-five pounds into it and hit my hand even harder. He and I both had a big laugh and then he went back to his friends.

Cathy whispered, "That's Mike Schomaker's boy." She saw that this meant nothing to me so she tried again. "I went to school with Mike." Blank stare. "Mike and Matt Kell are best friends...." I remained unimpressed with these nuggets of mommy database information, and it showed. Finally Cath offered up what should have been the lead. "Tommy was born with a congenital heart problem. He's had five open-heart surgeries."

This staggered me. Sometimes you hear something that hits you like a wet washcloth across the face. "This kid?" I said. "This kid has had his chest cracked open five times already?"

"Uh-huh," she said, still trying to connect the dots for me. "The Schomakers are best friends with the Kells ... Matt and Gina Kell ..." It was beginning to sink in.

"Matt Kell? You mean the guy I pray for on Saturdays? The guy who has terminal cancer?" I asked.

"Now you've got it," she confirmed, relieved that she was going to find a way out of this conversation. "Tommy's mom, Colleen, just told me that he is going to need a heart transplant soon."

It was all slowly washing over me. I was spinning. I looked over and saw Tommy Schomaker looking up at our pantry with a big smile on his face. He stood almost in silhouette as the afternoon sun poured into our kitchen, but I could tell that his imperfect heart was beating just a little faster taking in the sight. We Spehns love our snacks, and on this day the pantry was full up—no vacancy. Chips and cookies and sugary cereal as far as the eye could see. It looked like Willy Wonka's distribution center.

"You want something, Tommy?" He half turned and nodded big. "You can have anything you want," I told him. "Take two." The smile got wider than I thought possible, and for a moment, I smiled too. When you feel really helpless, you tend to lean on the healing power of an Oreo cookie.

I thought a lot about the Kells and the Schomakers. All week long I couldn't get them out of my mind. I was struck by just how different our lives were from theirs, even though we all lived just across town from each other.

The next Sunday we were driving home from church. The kids liked it when I timed our arrival at home precisely with the ending of the song on the radio. It was one of dozens of little games we've made up to pass the time in the car. Only occasionally did I get it just right, but when I did, the kids went wild.

With Train's "Drops of Jupiter" only in its first verse, I knew I had to stall, so I went the long way, missing our usual turn into the subdivision, and drove slowly while the kids sang along. Turning in on the street behind ours, I suddenly stopped singing. There, on the front porch of a house, was a red cooler.

In our subdivision, when people got horribly sick or died, the neighborhood women organized meals for the family. They placed a red cooler on the front porch and the women took turns filling it with that day's meals. To me, the notorious red cooler became a tragic symbol, like a death flag waving mortal surrender on the front doorstep. I mentioned this once to my neighbors, Ed and Heather, and we made inappropriate jokes and shared an uneasy laugh. Truth was, I hated the red cooler. I understood the sentiment behind it, but I imagined being a kid in that family who, every time they came home from school or turned their bikes into the driveway, saw the mark of death on their front doorstep.

I drove slowly past the house with the red cooler while the kids sang along to the radio, oblivious in the backseat. I looked over at Cath.

"We have been so lucky. You know? We have been so blessed."

It was all I could muster, but it was enough. She knew exactly what I was talking about. Without saying a word, she just looked out the window and nodded.

'tis the season

'tis the season

gina

Journal Entry, 11/16

*it seems to me
that time is standing still
no longer making memories
only waiting
for everything to change
matt is missing
only glimpses these days
life as i know it
as my children know it
is about to become
the great unknown
fear grips me
and yet i move forward
hoping for some semblance of order,
joy, peace
but not stillness
b/c then reality molests me
and i am overcome with grief*

Matt's eyes were sunken and wide. His face, thin and jaundiced with sharp angles. Skin draped his bones like a mask. I hadn't realized the severity of his appearance until we started having more frequent visitors. Their expressions made me painfully aware of how much he had changed.

Matt was lying in his usual spot on the couch and I was kneeling on the floor beside him. I held his soft hands and studied his face in the quiet of morning before the phone and doorbell started ringing. This was my favorite time of day, our chance to exhale before family, friends, or the occasional celebrity stopped in for a visit.

In the weeks before Christmas, Matt's friends and colleagues from the advertising business arranged for two hometown sports heroes to visit us. The first was Michigan State University head basketball coach Tom Izzo. Since graduating from MSU, Matt followed his beloved Spartans around the country for the NCAA Tournament. Having his alma mater represented by Tom Izzo, an iconic coach with class and a stellar reputation, was a source of pride for Matt. Having that coach in our home was like a dream come true, despite the nightmare circumstances that made it possible. Matt was grateful for the memories that his sons would grow to cherish and deflected the bittersweet shadow cast by cancer.

Coach Izzo arrived bearing gifts, including an NCAA Tournament basketball with a handwritten message and signatures from the team.

"How are you, Matt?" he asked with concern as he entered our home.

"Well, I thought cancer was my problem, but since you showed up, I think my heart may give out," Matt replied, instantly putting Coach Izzo at ease.

He stayed over an hour and graciously signed piles of memorabilia. He probably would have signed an empty milk carton if we put it in front of him. Cameras quietly rolled and clicked, and memories of a lifetime were made. Without fanfare, Tom Izzo gave my family "One Shining Moment" that two soon-to-be fatherless boys would grow to appreciate far more than a visit from a National Championship coach. This was a life lesson in giving back.

Ten days later NBA All-Star Chauncey Billups from the Detroit Pistons came to our home. Like Coach Izzo, he kindly signed autographs and smiled for photos. He even followed the kids into the basement to see their Fisher Price basketball hoop. They shared a big laugh at the sight of the real Chauncey standing next to his 6'3" image on a life-size poster that hung on our wall. It was the epitome of life imitating art.

At the end of another full day of sports heroes and excitement, Pastor Karl Galik stopped in for his weekly visit. Since the first time they met,

Matt and Karl sojourned together through the spiritual side of cancer. As his friend and his pastor, Karl gave Matt permission to go to dark places when he needed and used the Scriptures to guide him out. Their conversations were long and meaningful. Matt grieved his children, confessed his sins, and thirsted for comfort. In response, Karl painted verbal pictures of God's promises and the magnificence of heaven. His words repeatedly brought the refreshment Matt needed.

To give them time alone, I joined the kids outside in the dark to build a snowman in the glow of the Christmas lights. When I peeked in through the bay windows, I saw Matt on the couch and his friend in the chair across from him.

Both men were asleep.

December 22—Journal Entry

Today it began. Memories began flooding my mind. I've lost him. He's here, but he's slipping. His sharp, witty, brilliant mind is fading to black. It makes my heart ache to see the process. They call it "actively dying." This is awful. He is being called home. He has asked me repeatedly to take him to the water's edge, and I will walk my beloved there and I will say goodbye to all that is his and his alone. Knowing one day we will be reunited again is my only comfort now.

Since the time we signed on for hospice, Matt was determined to attend Christmas Eve worship at St. John. He didn't want to let cancer break a thirty-six-year tradition. Before having kids, we attended the midnight candlelight service. There is something stirring about choirs softly singing "Away in a Manger" and harmoniously shouting "Joy to the World," but when the worship culminates at midnight with "Silent Night" being sung a cappella by five hundred people holding candles in a dark sanctuary, I am moved to tears by the magnitude of what we are celebrating.

The day before Christmas Eve my folks arrived around five to pick up Drew and Sam. The boys were excited to sleep in their "cowboy room" at Nona and Papa's house. My parents designed a bedroom for the boys complete with rustic Colorado pine bunk beds and dressers, and a scenic mural of mountains and aspen trees covering the walls. The artist used metallic gold and yellow paints for the aspen leaves, giving them a realistic glow. A big floppy moose and a big brown bear sprawl across the beds and flop over the pine rails of the bunks. There is also a cuddly raccoon in honor of an encounter my dad had with a local critter that may have involved rabies shots. We don't discuss it.

The cowboy room also had a secret. The walls were filled with Scripture verses that were now hidden behind the aspen trees. When the artist was prepping to paint the mural, he lightly wrote a series of verses on the walls, including "Let the little children come to me, and do not hinder them, for the kingdom of God belongs to such as these." Knowing Scripture verses adorn the walls beneath the mural makes my heart smile. It reminds me that we may not see God, but he is always present.

With Drew and Sam away for the night, the house was quieter than usual. Their mere presence gives the house life, even when they are asleep. Before starting Christmas chores I checked on Matt. I barely stepped in the room before his eyes opened and darted, and he began to sit up, much like he did when he would spring out of bed for the workday. Before his illness Matt rarely had trouble getting out of bed in the morning, and he liked to taunt me with his Robin Williams spastic cheerfulness. I typically woke up cranky and unwieldy, more like Robert Downey Jr. after a bender.

Matt winced in pain trying to sit up. "I have to use the bathroom," he said, letting his leg fall over the side of the bed. We straightened out his oxygen tubes so he wouldn't trip as he staggered to the bathroom. As a matter of routine, he picked up a *Car and Driver* magazine and sat down on the toilet. I knew he wasn't reading it because he was holding the magazine upside down. It was simply his pattern of doing things and he didn't miss a beat. I turned the magazine around for him and he glanced up at me and smiled. I giggled to myself because his smile was telling. The magazine was his pacifier. I got that. I sat on the edge of the tub and waited.

"Time for meds," I said, referring to a spreadsheet that helped me keep track of twelve different medications, each taken at different intervals throughout the day.

"Thank you for taking care of me," Matt said in a childlike voice. Whenever he thanked me I'd get a lump in my throat. By letting me care for him, he was actually taking care of me.

"That's my line," I said with a smile that held back my tears. I plugged in the baby monitor and headed downstairs to wrap presents. "If you need me, just say my name and I can hear you."

I turned on *Letterman* to keep me company. I was missing the last-minute help and the surprises Matt would show up with in the eleventh hour. He always found a special something to give the boys. After I spent two months making lists and shopping, it was Daddy's last-minute gift that had the boys screaming with joy.

Before I realized it, *Conan* was on and then a rerun of *Oprah*. The Susan Lucci infomercial was my cue that I had stayed up into the early morning hours of December 24 tending to Matt and getting organized for Christmas. He called me regularly on the monitor to get him a drink or help him with bathroom breaks. If he had a coughing fit, I'd rush upstairs to bang on his back to help loosen the gunk in his chest. Other times he just wanted me to be near. I was torn between making Christmas special for the kids and simply wanting to lie down next to Matt. The rituals of Christmas seemed trite and insignificant. But in the eyes of Drew and Sam, it was everything, especially this year. This was going to be their last Christmas with their father. I did everything I could to preserve their joyful anticipation.

After four hours of light sleep, I woke to Matt watching ESPN. This was our big day. He was going to attend Christmas Eve worship. To start the day right, I served breakfast in bed: narcotics, nerve blockers, and anxiety meds with a side of eggs and toast. He picked at the food while I took a long shower to shake off the cobwebs. As I stood under the water, I could hear Matt coughing continuously. After a minute, I stepped into the bedroom dripping wet and saw Matt standing next to the bed trying to balance and fumbling with his oxygen tubes. His breathing was labored as if he had walked up the stairs. I grabbed a towel and ran out to help him.

"What happened?" I asked with panic in my voice. "Why are you up?" I took the oxygen tubes from him to untangle them.

As he struggled to get his breath and get back into bed, he couldn't answer, so I began piecing things together. At first it didn't click, but then it hit me. "No way did you go downstairs when I was in the shower!" He nodded yes.

"What were you thinking? You could have killed yourself on the stairs! And you took off your oxygen? Oh, geez, listen to you breathe!" I was exasperated.

Matt's eyebrows went up and a smirk crossed his face. I was yelling at a dying man that he might kill himself and he found this amusing. But I wasn't going to let him off the hook that easily.

"You're like a human Weeble! You just can't go downstairs without me. And we agreed that today you would stay upstairs until we left for church! What did you need that couldn't wait?" I demanded.

"Football pool," he replied through labored breaths. "Sorry, G."

I wanted to scream. Stupid, stupid, stupid man.

"I could have done that for you."

"I had to make my picks before noon," he said before having a painful coughing fit. He lay back in bed until he slowly resumed normal breathing, which was still heavy and labored. I was angry that he'd made a boneheaded decision, but football pools were like *Car and Driver*. It's what he does.

"Did you save enough energy to shower?" I asked with a hint of sarcasm.

"Yeah, but I might need help shaving." Matt couldn't stand long without pain radiating into his lower back.

"I'd love to give you a shave! I've never done that before."

"No one has ever given me a shave," he said, rubbing his chin with his fingers.

After the hard work of taking a shower, Matt sat in a comfy chair in our bedroom. I filled a stainless-steel bowl with warm water for rinsing, grabbed shaving cream, and attached a new blade to Matt's heavy silver razor. I thought the weight of the razor would help me feel like I had more control.

Giving Matt a shave turned out to be an unexpected gift to me. After thirteen years of marriage, we were sharing a first. He removed the oxygen tubes and I applied a thin layer of shaving cream that smelled fresh and masculine. His stubble was long and soft. Matt tilted his head and closed his eyes as the razor glided along his face.

"Ow!" he said.

I gasped and pulled the blade back quickly.

"Gotcha!" he beamed.

"See what you did? Now I'm nervous!"

"No, you're doing great. This feels good."

The sound of stubble meeting the blades relaxed me. It felt good to have this time with him; this touch. It was a private, even romantic exchange that brought forth memories of the intimacy cancer had stolen away. When his face was smooth, I rubbed the tops of my fingers along his face. He reached up to hold my hands and pulled me close. We gently kissed. I had almost forgotten how it felt.

When it was time to get dressed, Matt chose the only suit that still fit and a dress shirt big enough to cover the tumor in his neck. I stood in the bathroom doorway watching him slide a tie back and forth around his neck, preparing to make the knot. As he straightened up to look at himself, I wondered if he recognized the man in the reflection. It was like looking into a broken mirror.

"You look incredibly handsome," I said, reaching my arms around his frail body. We held each other for a long time.

"Let's celebrate Christmas," he said.

Matt's close friend Red spent every Christmas Eve with us, and this year he did not break tradition. He arrived early to help Matt get to church through the bitter cold and snow. With Red on one side and Matt's mom, Susan, on the other, Matt shuffled through the empty space in the garage that once occupied his beloved Infiniti G35. He'd generously let a family in need borrow it. Given Matt's love of cars, I considered it to be a symbol of his ability to live in the balance between acceptance and hope.

Matt and I held hands in the backseat. We couldn't wait to see Drew and Sammy. My stomach was in knots, and I took several deep breaths because I really couldn't believe we had made it this far. I could have used a hit of Matt's oxygen.

As we pulled into the parking lot, Mike Schomaker rushed over to usher Matt out of the car and into a wheelchair. There was a buzz in the air. My parents arrived with Drew and Sam, and I greeted them with big hugs. With his sons by his side, Matt was wheeled to the front of the sanctuary. As we turned the corner to enter the transept, we saw the entire section filled with our family and friends. Matt placed his hand over his heart and his eyes smiled as he connected with all those around us whom he loved. Many had tears in their eyes. He took my hand to find his seat and continued looking around and waving. He tweaked Drew's ear and gave Sam a poke in his "bacon belly."

While the pre-service music played, the youth pastor came alongside Matt, placed his hand on his shoulder, and whispered, "God bless you, Matt."

Matt placed his hand over the pastor's and replied, "He has, he has."

At four o'clock the Christmas choir began to sing at one church in Rochester, Michigan. As "O Holy Night" echoed through the sanctuary, I was moved by the thought of millions of voices around the world joining together to honor and celebrate the birth of a baby more than two thousand years ago. The sounds of age-old Christmas hymns being sung about a child, born for the purpose of our eternal salvation, were pure and radiant, as if I were hearing them for the first time. The message of Christmas resonated deeply within me.

As the service came to a close, I locked my arm around Matt's. "You did it," I whispered with excitement. Before the last song ended, we slipped out a side door waving to friends and family who had gathered to worship with us. Walking into the parking lot with Mike and Red on each arm, Matt became weak and wobbly. Without warning he doubled over and began to vomit. After being sick three times, he made it to the car and recovered, but he wasn't quite the same.

"You okay, Mattie?" Mike asked.

"Yeah, better now."

Mike reached in and grabbed Matt's hand. "I'm proud of you," he said, not letting go. "Thanks for the memory of this day. I love you."

"I love you too."

As we backed out of the parking spot, several people we knew were pouring out of the building. Some tried to catch us before we departed, but we were on our way. I felt like everything was in slow motion. I waved to Mike and Colleen as we drove away from the church. Slowly, family began to fill our home to go through the motions of Christmas. We ordered Chinese food, a long-standing Kell family tradition, and forced ourselves through a gift exchange.

The evening was like a high-speed replay of the past several months, with people flowing in and out of Matt's room, each sharing their good-byes. No one walked away from his bedside unmoved. Being aware of the nearness of death brought forth purity and humility in each conversation. The most profound moments came when Matt asked for something. By simply asking, he was giving a gift, and a means of remaining alive in their hearts.

I stood outside the bedroom door and overheard Matt talking through labored breaths and crying with his sister, Meghan.

"You're going to be okay, Megs," he said, wiping her tears. "I'll be okay too. I'm not afraid."

"I know," she replied through sobs. "You're so strong. I love you so much."

"Take care of my Peach and make sure she keeps laughing."

"I promise." They held each other for a long time and whispered a few more words before I slipped into the room. Matt's mom, Susan, followed closely behind carrying a Christmas present. She handed it to Matt, left the room, and he handed it to me.

"What's this?" I asked.

"Mom helped me pick out a present for you," he replied weakly.

It was beautiful necklace with three birthstones representing Matt, Drew, and Sam.

"There's something else," he said. "I'm probably not going to be around much longer. When I'm gone, I want you to find a good Christian man and marry him."

His words startled and confused me.

"No, honey. Please don't," I said.

"Peach. It's okay. I need to say this. You're young and I want you to have a great life."

"We will, we will. I don't want to hear any more." The tears began pouring from my eyes.

"You should share it with someone. You don't have to do it alone."

"No, I can't. Please, stop." I could not stop crying.

"I just want you to know it's okay."

His generosity was devastating.

Drew and Sam, filled with excitement for Christmas morning, set out cookies and milk for Santa. They said good night to Matt and I tucked them into bed with a prayer. After everyone left, I cleaned up the kitchen, routinely checked on Matt, and set up for Santa's arrival. There was a Green Machine and a Big Wheel and a Basketball Pop-A-Shot in the basement. I ate the cookies the boys left out and walked to the top of the stairs. The only sound in the house now was the hum of the oxygen tank. I had two little boys waiting for Santa and a husband waiting for Jesus.

They were all expecting gifts, some better than others.

Journal Entry—December 24

In this life I hate it that the boys will never know so much of him. What a gigantic, cavernous void. They would have been so much better off having him here than me. He is a better all around human being. He can teach them, enrich them, relate to them and set an example for them in a way that I never will be able to. I miss him so much. I want to ask him things about what I should do about this or that, but he has no answers for me now. He doesn't care about those worldly things. He has one foot in another world and it is so much better than this place. He is easily letting go of everything now. Initially it was by force, but now, he is letting go because he wants to. He is being called home and that call cannot be denied.

CHAPTER 14

coach

michael

There is a moment, one of hundreds really, that only coaches and players know about. It happens just before the game. In the locker room of any sport, there is a culture all its own. It has its own language and characters, ambient sounds and etiquette. To an outsider, someone who has never played the game, it is all so foreign. To the inhabitants of this world, it's home.

Once in their uniforms, the players wait for me in the locker room. Sitting on plain wooden benches, they fuss and fidget with their shoes and jerseys. Mindless manifestations of the stress building inside them. Once I come through the locker room door, the boys all sit up straight and listen intently. Standing directly before them, I give them the plan.

"Okay, tonight we're going to start with Jake in the one, Tommy in the two, Rags in the three, Big Bear, you play the four, Mac in the five. We're starting in our twenty-two, man defense, help side wing, you gotta get over for the low post double—and please, gentlemen . . . let's cover the weak side boards tonight. Offensively, we are in Power to begin with, but feel free to call Arm-up, Split, or High with each trip. Gentlemen, you are the superior team tonight. The only question left to answer is, will you play up to that? You guys ready for this?"

The room erupts into "Yes, Coach!" and we all gather in close. Hands in the middle, together, as I give them just a few last words.

"I have tremendous faith in you. This is your game. Now go take it! Victory on three. One, two, three! VICTORY!"

It's hard to remember whether my coaching prepared me for fatherhood or vice versa. I only know that I hear my father's voice coming out of me every time I talk with my players. Whether it's practice or games or speaking at the year-end banquet, I'm the one moving my lips, but it's his voice. That may be why I love it. I missed him so much during those days. I really wanted him to see me coach at this level.

I loved the chess match that went on between coaches during the game. The strategy, preparation, and tension intrigued me to no end. Most people watch a basketball game by paying attention to the ball as it's passed around from player to player and eventually shot toward the hoop. Not me. I watch the coaches. I try to gauge their substitution patterns, their defensive calls, and their management of time-outs.

I loved the practices almost more than the games themselves — working with the players to perfect an offense or to correct a rotation on a half-court trap. I loved the workshop aspect of basketball practices. On game night there is an electric atmosphere in a packed high school gym. Cross-town rivals, local reporters, and maybe a college scout or two all mix together with the pep band playing the theme to *Rocky* and the student section that never sits down. Win or lose, for two hours on a Friday night, you're having fun surrounded by the sights and sounds of your youth.

As my team went through their pregame warm-ups, Cathy and the kids would make their entrance. Jack led the way; Charlotte was right behind him, then Cath and Danny walking together. Everyone had a bag of popcorn in their hands and Cathy had a couple bottles of water to share. They sat directly across from the team bench in the front row. Throughout the game I'd glance over at Cath and she would throw me a smile. From time to time the kids made up goofy dances to the pep band music playing during time-outs. It made all the difference in the world to me that Cathy was a part of this.

There are many wives who simply tolerate their husbands' coaching, but Cathy loved it almost as much as I did. After every practice she asked me a dozen questions about how it went. Some of our away games were too far or too late on school nights, so she stayed home with the kids. She made me tell her every detail the moment I came home. Without a doubt, though, my favorite times during the season were after games, at home, after we put the kids to bed. Cath would get snacks for us and we'd curl up together and watch the game film from that night. I mean, she would *make* me watch the game film from the game we just saw together! While it played, she'd ask why I did this or what I said to the ref just there.

There were a couple nights on the court when everything came together.

Four seconds to play, we're down by two points so I call a time-out. In the huddle I remind the guys of the play I just happened to show them in practice that week on a hunch that we might need it someday. I draw it up on the whiteboard slowly for them. I speak calmly and look them directly in the eyes to show them that I have complete faith in what they are about to do.

"Take your time. Four seconds is an eternity. Set a good screen, and, Bear ... take a good shot. Rely on the things you've been taught. Rely on each other and good things will happen."

The time-out is over. My guys go back onto the court. It is up to them now. Watching them walk away, I can sense that they are prepared. The shot will go in or it won't. I have no control over that. I have done my job though. I have prepared these young men.

Later at home, with Cathy and the snacks, we rewound the game film over and over to watch the three-pointer go in at the buzzer for the win. Cathy had a suggestion for me, a wish really.

"You should call your dad and tell him about tonight," she said.

"You're right. I should," was all I could muster as the smile left my face. I should.

CHAPTER 15

so this is christmas

gina

I felt a gentle touch on my arm. "Mom. Mom, wake up!" Drew was standing by the side of the bed tapping my arm. His tap had become part of a scene in a long, disjointed dream I was having. "Wake up, Mom! Did Santa come?" I was groggy but managed to open one eye enough to see the clock. Seven forty-five. Not bad for Christmas morning.

"Merry Christmas, baby," I said, reaching out for a hug.

"Can I wake up Sam?" Drew asked excitedly.

"Yes, but gently, please." Sam's not exactly cut from a morning cloth. Much like his mom, he could stand to linger in bed a while before interacting with humans, or even inanimate objects for that matter.

Matt woke up and slowly started to get out of bed. He was weak and shaky, but determined to share Christmas morning with his family. His breathing and coughing were loud and heavy. At his request, I pounded on his back a few times.

I slid out of bed and threw on a sweatshirt. Amazingly, Drew woke Sam on the first try. I'm certain that the anticipation of presents on Christmas morning alters the chemistry of a child such that REM sleep is never reached.

The boys were bouncing off the walls with excitement as Matt shuffled past them toward the stairs in his baggy pajama pants and Detroit Pistons T-shirt. I glanced at the three of them and my mind took a snapshot, momentarily freezing the juxtaposition of the loves of my life. I was affirmed in my determination to live in the delicate balance between exuberant children and a cancer-stricken husband.

I instructed Drew and Sam to wait at the top of the stairs until I called for them. I lugged the big oxygen tank down the stairs to the family room and Matt made his way to the couch, with fifty feet of oxygen tubes dragging behind, ready to watch the boys enjoy some Christmas magic.

"Looks good, G," he murmured as he observed the splendor of Christmas morning.

I ran back upstairs. "Okay, boys! Santa has definitely been here!" As they started running, I grabbed the video camera and followed them downstairs through the kitchen. They saw red and green bows lined up on the floor, but paid no attention.

It was a gray morning and the house was dark, except for the lights from the nine-foot tree, which lit the room with a warm glow. Our tree was filled with family ornaments, most of which the boys placed near the lower front section of the tree, and draped with red and gold ribbon as it has been every year since we were married. The tree was perfectly prelit, perfectly trimmed, and perfectly pine-free. It was our first artificial tree and it was entirely fake, albeit stunning, much like Christmas trees at the mall. It was one more sign that things were different. Even the smell of Christmas was missing.

The boys were quietly excited. The oxygen tank hummed and spurted in a rhythm that never quite became white noise. Christmas morning wasn't a wild screamfest with paper flying and gifts strewn everywhere. It was very quiet, almost polite. Perhaps it was our keen awareness of and consideration for the agonizing sight of our husband and daddy. Matt was sitting in the middle of the couch, leaning over his pillow, with labored breathing, able to eke out only one-word comments in response to the kids' excitement. It only took about ten minutes to get through the presents and stockings.

"Hey, guys, what about all those bows on the floor? They look like they might lead somewhere," I said, trying to drop the hint.

"Santa put these here!" Sam shouted as they followed the bows. Without a word, Matt stood up and began shuffling toward the stairs.

It was only another ten seconds before the boys were in the basement, squealing at the glorious sight of their new NBA Pop-A-Shot, complete with two baskets, digital scoreboard, and sound effects. The sound of the boys screaming with joy was my first indication that this was by far the highlight of the morning. Santa could have saved himself a few bucks and skipped everything else under the tree. Before Matt and I had made it to the stairs, the boys were shooting baskets. If it had been one month earlier, Matt would have had a Pop-A-Shot smackdown with the boys, complete with trash talk and "in your face" chest bumpin'. Instead, he sat on the stairs next to me and watched. I had been videotaping the boys shooting the first of what would be millions of baskets when Matt whispered, "Peach, can you call them over?"

As the game buzzer went off, Drew and Sam ran over to us on the stairs and instinctively slowed and quieted. Matt's voice was weak, and when he began to speak the boys leaned in to listen. Between every few words, Matt paused to take a slow, slushy breath.

"Okay, guys." Breath. "We've had a great Christmas." Breath. "So let's say a prayer together." The boys bowed their heads and Matt started: "Dear Lord ... We thank you very much for the gifts that you gave us this year ... I ask that you be with us in the next year ... that you teach us how to be even better boys ... and act even more like Jesus. In your name we pray. Amen." Tears rolled freely down my cheeks. I clicked off the video camera and thanked Matt for his prayer and for working so hard to share Christmas with the boys. He looked at me with his tragic eyes and wiped tears from my face. He leaned in so I could give him a peck on the cheek. I understood his heart. He understood my gratitude.

While the boys shot baskets, Matt turned on ESPN as a matter of course. He was awake, staring at the TV, but seemed to be looking right through it. He was uncommunicative and uninterested in eating the Honey Nut Cheerios I poured for him. I gently insisted that he eat because he needed meds. He forced down a few bites.

Drew came bouncing up the stairs and into the kitchen. "What's for breakfast, Mom?" he asked, winded from his Pop-A-Shot marathon.

"Papa's famous apple pancakes."

"Yes! I can't wait!" he said as he ran off to tell Sam the good news.

Christmas breakfast at my parents' house was more than a family tradition. It was a highly coveted culinary event. My dad started selling tickets to next year's breakfast at this year's breakfast table. He also tried to sell tickets to random people throughout the year. Of course, there were no actual tickets, but he played it up as if his breakfast had the demand of the Super Bowl, the tradition of the Kentucky Derby, and the excitement of the Final Four. The apple pancakes were the MVP and Chef Valenti would be "going to Disney World" wielding a spatula and wearing his tall white chef hat that earned him the very Christmassy nickname "Pinhead." He did a jive-turkey dance and flipped apple pancakes while Uncle Louie criticized his technique and taunted him in Italian. It was Christmas cheer, Sicilian style.

As we were waiting for the festivities to begin, Drew and Sam watched TV with Matt while I flitted around doing some last-minute cleaning, or more appropriately, straightening.

"Dad, the Pistons are playing today. Isn't that cool? They get to play on Christmas Day."

Drew tried to initiate conversation and Matt tried to respond, but the best he could do was say a few words, which completely lacked enthusiasm or even inflection. Drew became increasingly frustrated by Matt's lack of response.

"Mom, why is Dad ignoring me?" he asked. "I keep talking to him but he won't say anything."

"I know, baby. Dad is so tired that it's hard for him to answer your questions right now. Maybe we can try again later," I said, trying to comfort him.

Drew went back and sat quietly next to his dad. Matt's eyes were still pointed at the television.

"Do you want to go back to bed?" I asked.

Without looking at me he nodded. He was considerably weaker than he had been twenty-four hours earlier. He just needed more rest, I thought.

The family breakfast was scheduled to start at ten. I walked upstairs with Matt and we sat on the edge of the bed together. He struggled to catch his breath. As he began to relax, I stood up to make room for him to lie down. He squeezed my arm.

"Peach," he said, "I can't die on Christmas Day." His eyes were wide and searching.

I could feel my heart begin to race. He had caught me off guard. As calmly and gently as possible, I replied, "Well. Yes. You can. You will go when you are called. But I don't think today is the day."

He closed his eyes as I stroked his hair and the side of his face. I could feel myself begin to sweat. Was he seeking my permission to die? Did I just give him permission? I watched him drift to sleep.

I slipped away to shower and dress. I was in a bit of a fog and my body ached. I kept nudging the Moen faucet to the left. I couldn't get the water hot enough to satisfy my pain. Sheer tension and lack of sleep were taking a toll. I threw on my new green "Peace on Earth" T-shirt over a long-sleeved white tee. It was Christmassy enough, with the right message, and although it wasn't my Sunday best, I was comfortable.

I heard our families downstairs arriving at once. They were filling our house with loads of food and presents. I didn't move. I wasn't ready to show my face yet. I soaked up a few more minutes of quiet, lying next to Matt, just wanting to be near to him, touching him. I had my eyes closed for only a few minutes when I heard a soft tap on the door.

"Merry Christmas!" Susan and Meghan gently pushed open the bedroom door. That was my cue. They deserved some alone time with Matt.

It was time to shift gears and greet the rest of the family. The house smelled like all the best parts of a breakfast joint, cider mill, and bakery. Candle makers try to capture this scent in a jar, but they always forget to add the bacon scent. Apples, cinnamon, and maple syrup are nothing without the bacon.

This year, my parents converted to "Meals on Wheels" as they were known to do on occasion. One year they became famous, or at least very popular, at Beaumont Hospital when they delivered aluminum trays filled with apple pancakes to me on Christmas morning when I was admitted for preterm labor with Drew.

Everyone was bustling but stopped to make time for hugs. My sister, Tara, and brother-in-law, Bob, were cutting celery and mixing spicy Bloody Marys. Mom was pulling the foil off trays of Dad's apple pancakes. My kitchen had been taken over by a band of Christmas breakfast bandits. It was a wonderful sight. I made myself a cup of tea and walked around the kitchen, quietly observing the frenzy of activity.

The dining room table was set with my parents' traditional Christmas dishes. Powdered sugar and syrup were plentiful. Powdered sugar if you loved my dad, syrup if you wanted to hurt him. He felt that anything other than powdered sugar on an apple pancake was a crime. I always had to sneak my syrup. What's the point of a pancake, apple or not, if you do not have some good old-fashioned Aunt Jemima? Everything looked and smelled wonderful. I prepared a plate, and within two bites, Sam was on my arm.

He whispered, "Mom, I need help upstairs."

"What's up, buddy?" I asked, hoping to finish my pancakes.

"I need help with something now!" he said emphatically. Okay, breakfast could wait.

I followed Sam upstairs and into his bedroom. "See!" he said, pointing at his sock drawer. It was empty, a very urgent matter indeed.

"Okay, let's find you some socks." Sam followed me into the bedroom where Matt was resting. As I was digging through the laundry basket, Sam was getting goofy and started playfully punching me on the butt.

"What are you doing, silly?" I asked, turning around. Sam was giggling and shy. I could tell he wanted something.

"I want to say hi to Dad," he said.

I was pleasantly surprised to hear this, but I wasn't sure what to expect. Sam had become somewhat distant from Matt in recent weeks, seeming almost afraid at times. Matt's condition was frightening to adults, so I could only imagine what was going on in Sam's four-year-old mind. I lifted him onto the bed next to Matt and left them so I could check the med chart. When I returned, Sam was chatting it up about bacon, his favorite food. He was completely at ease and laughing as Matt poked him in the tummy. In healthier days, Matt would ask, "Where's your bacon?" and Sam would start to giggle in anticipation of what was coming. In his best crazy Cookie Monster voice, Matt would say again, "Where's da ba-gon?" as he pretended to eat Sam's belly. Sam would burst into the most infectious belly laugh that it was impossible not to laugh with him. He was missing that kind of connection to his dad and it ripped at my heart.

With his eyes open wide and a big grin across his face, Matt used every ounce of energy to engage Sam. In the midst of a busy Christmas morning, Sammy sought out his father for a little one-on-one time, a rare gift indeed. In hindsight, this was my second clue.

"Love you, Dad," Sam said. He jumped off the bed and bounced out of the room. His work was done.

Matt and I were alone again and it was time for the second round of morning meds. The bedroom was quiet with the din of the oxygen tank, which did a good job of drowning out the noise from downstairs. I didn't want Matt to hear what he was missing.

As we sat alone, I felt the urge to say everything that was on my heart. I wanted to convey my love and gratitude, and apologize for my failings as a wife.

"I love you so much," was all I could muster, through tears.

Matt squeezed my hand. "I know, Peach," he said.

My words were inadequate. I reached for the Bible that was sitting on the nightstand and read to Matt the biblical account of the Christmas story. He listened with his eyes closed. Before I finished the story, he fell asleep.

I had been missing in action from the family for a while. It was time to reappear on the scene and start yet another gift exchange, this time with my side of the family. My experiences throughout the day were in stark contrast with one another, from our bedroom where Matt lay dying, to the bustle of Christmas festivities a floor below. A gift exchange seemed trivial, yet it was the perfect metaphor for what Matt and I had been doing for the past three years. Our exchange became completely intangible. There were no sweaters or jewelry left to give. We exchanged the only thing left when everything else has been stripped away: love.

It was not physical or material. This love lacked inhibition and boundary. It was limitless and free of expectation or regret. It was effortless, all-encompassing love; given, received, and understood. I think it's rare in life to experience this kind of love. In any relationship it ebbs and flows, but once you've had it, you crave it like no lustful urge you've ever had. I was filled with it on my wedding day, and when I held my babies in my arms, and again when my husband was diagnosed with terminal cancer. If only we had the ability to live life as though it were so new or so close to the end that all we could do is give and show and become love. It seems that beginnings and endings teach us about this kind of love. It is in between that we tend to forget.

We began the gift exchange while the Pistons played on TV. The boys were excited about the confluence of events that seemed to revolve around them. There was plenty of laughter and fun being had by all. My dad received an engraved, silver-plated yo-yo and began reliving his youth as he demonstrated his yo-yo prowess.

"Puppy dawg!" he shouted as he extended the yo-yo to the floor and suspended it there for several seconds before snapping it back into the palm of his hand. The crowd went wild! Then with some fancy fingerwork he used the string to form a triangular cradle and swung the yo-yo through like a pendulum. Despite the stellar entertainment, I found myself focused on the sounds coming from the monitor. Throughout the afternoon, different people slipped upstairs to be with Matt. I was all at once grateful that he was not alone and selfishly resentful that I wasn't the one with him.

The house quieted down and Drew challenged Uncle Bob to a Pop-A-Shot contest. My dad assembled some toys and tried to remove others from their packaging, which required several tools and a master's degree in engineering. Tara went home with Mom so they could put together trays of lasagna for dinner. I was sleepy and finally headed back upstairs to lie with Matt.

"Did the kids get Xbox 360?" he asked as I walked into the room. Matt was not allowed to have video games when he was a kid.

"What do you mean?" I asked, somewhat surprised by the question.

"The kids need Xbox."

"*Need* Xbox?" I replied with sarcasm.

Matt's eyes closed, but his eyebrows raised and every muscle in his face shifted upward. All I could see was his beaming smile. His face said, "Yep, they don't need it, but I want them to have it." An insignificant gaming system brought out the essence of Matt Kell. Even if he couldn't have it for himself or even share it with them, he wanted it for his kids. Give 'em joyful experiences at every turn. Say yes to everything from trivial video games to having Tom Izzo and Chauncey Billups sit on our couch. Live every day to the full, always in service to God, and the joy will be abundant. This wasn't something Matt had to think about; it was his nature. I rested my head on the pillow next to him and placed my hand over his heart.

"I'll take care of it," I said. I could not stop smiling.

Over the hum of the oxygen tank, I heard the doorbell but decided not to move. Before I knew it, Karl Galik and his wife, Marilouise, were in our bedroom. Sue, Meghan, and my dad followed behind. It occurred to me that this was the first time my dad had come upstairs to see Matt.

"Merry Christmas, Kells! Please, Gina, don't get up," Karl said as he approached the bedside.

Matt began to cry and he reached out his hand to his friend and his pastor. They had shared a raw and reciprocal intimacy since the time of Matt's first diagnosis. I believe it served both men.

Matt clung to Karl's hands as he listened to him reiterate some of the conversations they had shared previously about "the journey." I felt privileged to be eavesdropping on such a conversation. Karl created verbal images of the unimaginable sights and sounds of heaven, captivating everyone in the room. He spoke of the joyful awe and magnificence of entering the gates of heaven and described what it must be like to arrive at the table of the eternal feast. His words painted a picture of the bounty and glory of heaven.

"Matt, soon you will see the face of Christ and will be dining with the Father in heaven," he said, smiling. Matt nodded yes. Oddly, I felt happy for him as tears streamed for my children and myself. Marilouise sat on the bed next to me. Using her training as a physical therapist, she encouraged me to breathe as she rubbed my back.

Matt looked up at Karl and whispered, "You keep talking like that and I might go before my time." Not everyone caught his comment, but Karl laughed quietly and shook his head.

"You still got it, Matt," he said. Matt flashed a quick smile, pleased with himself.

Karl then offered a prayer. When he finished, he moved in very closely to Matt and whispered, "If I don't see you again ..."

Matt reached his arm up to Karl's shoulder and interrupted, "I will see you again."

"Yes ... I'll see you in eternity," Karl said.

After a long pause he started the sentence that had become the tagline of their relationship.

"You know, I'm your pastor and your friend ..." Together they finished, "... and that makes you closer than a brother."

Karl leaned in to embrace Matt. They held each other for an extra moment. This was good-bye, for now.

I walked the Galiks out of the room and we stood in the hall hugging and crying.

"We're not going to Chicago this week. The time is near," Karl said with a sure and steady voice.

"Really?" I said, almost surprised. Yes, of course, the end was near. But how could he be so sure? We've still got some time, I thought. I couldn't stop crying.

"He's going to be fine," I heard myself say as I wiped my cheeks. I wasn't so sure about the rest of us.

By the time I returned, Matt was asleep. I decided not to wake him to give him meds. It was the Christmas-afternoon lull and the Galiks lingered for a while. Karl seemed to be taking time to restore the mood of the house. Marilouise used her magic hands to give Meghan some stress-relieving massage therapy. Most of us sat in the kitchen talking and snacking. Sammy peeled a juicy clementine that he grabbed from the top of the heaping bowl that sat on the table. Matt's mom had a piece of chocolate orange, an orange-flavored chocolate ball that splits into slices when you smack it on the table. Drew was hanging around having a little of everything. Almonds, chocolate Santas, and dried apricots were his favorites.

As we were giving the Galiks a send-off, my mom and Tara returned with two heavy pans of lasagna. Our continuous-loop food-fest was coming around again. Ugh.

I was not sure what to do with myself. The baby monitor had been quiet for over an hour. I debated in my head whether Matt should have his meds. I peeked in but didn't have the heart to wake him. It was rare that he slept peacefully, without coughing or restlessness. I saw his Bible still sitting on the nightstand. I grabbed it and headed downstairs.

"Mom, a couple weeks ago Matt told me that he wanted to give you a gift for Christmas," I started. "I don't think he's going to be able to give it to you today, so if it's okay, I think I'll give it to you now."

"Matt has a gift for me?" she said, surprised. "Should I wait for him?"

"Well, he wanted you to have it today," I replied. "You can go up and thank him later."

I placed Matt's Bible on the counter and slid it across to her.

She placed both hands on it and stared at it. Her mouth opened but words did not come out.

"He really wanted you to have this," I said.

"Is this his Bible?" she asked, already knowing the answer. "Oh my goodness." She opened it and ran her fingers across the tabs. "I'm honored." She quietly continued flipping through the pages. "You know, I've never read the Bible," she said thoughtfully.

"Well, you were raised Catholic," I said, only half joking. I could never resist a quick jab at my old Catholic roots.

Ignoring my snide comment, she said, "Leave it to Matt to help me take the first step."

Matt and my mom had a history of getting into religious debates that wouldn't end well. The first year we were married, we took a family vacation with my parents to Marco Island, Florida, and a conversation about Jesus, and attending church, started in the parking lot of an ice-cream shop while we were all enjoying our double-dip cones and shakes. Within ten minutes my dad was nowhere in sight, and my mom and Matt were nose to nose in the parking lot. Needless to say, it spiraled out of control and my mom was pissed at her snot-nosed son-in-law for telling her how to be a good Christian. Matt was sick-to-his-stomach regretful that he had offended his in-laws. He later apologized, but as years went by, they brushed up against the topic of religion with questions like, "Where are you going to church on Christmas Eve?" Any substantive conversations on the subject all but ceased. Everyone knows that new in-laws are the last place to ever pursue a religious debate. But what Matt learned in that one exchange taught him a few important lessons.

"I've seen how your faith has been the source of strength that has gotten you and Matt and the kids through all of this," she said tearfully.

She had said those words to me in recent months and I always found it difficult to respond. It's incredibly humbling to learn that people are actually seeing evidence of God through you. The best part is that it didn't require a conversation. It was purely by example.

"Mom, to hear you say that may be the whole point of Matt's cancer." This was a lot to put on my mom. I half regretted saying it, but Matt and I had talked about this so many times that it seemed appropriate to throw it out there.

There was a long pause. "What about the boys?" she asked.

"Matt thought of that too. He just asked that you would pass it along to them someday."

As I was returning to my chair after a long hug with my mom, I heard Matt yell from upstairs.

"Gina!"

His voice sounded strong and a bit panicked. It was unexpected and it scared me. I ran up the stairs skipping three steps at a time to find him up and on his way to the bathroom. His breathing was extremely labored. He seemed confused as he approached the bathroom.

"I think I have to pee," he said. "Gina. Help me."

He shuffled into the bathroom and realized he didn't have to go. Susan and my dad helped Matt as he staggered back to the bed. I began reviewing the med charts. What had I given him and when? There were so many drugs and so many dosages. Methodone, Roxinol, Ativan, Levisen, Cymbalta, Neurontin, Valium, Morphine, Decradon, Fentinol, Oxycontin, Oxycodone. He had rested peacefully for so long that he had been without meds longer than usual. I had to think. What was next? I had to help him calm down so he could resume normal labored breathing. I put some of the anxiety meds under his tongue and some drops of morphine in the back of his mouth. I talked him through it, trying to reassure him that he would be okay. This had happened several times before and he always came out of it. Matt was unusually restless, wanting to get up and then realizing he was unable. I gently insisted that he remain in bed; however, it was apparent that he could not lie down. His lungs were filling with fluid.

"Meghan, the number for hospice is in on my desk in the blue folder,"

I said as I tried to help Matt find a comfortable position. Through loud, heavy breaths, Matt actually said the words, "Take me home, Jesus." He knew. The time of death was upon him. It felt as if my soul was gasping for breath at the thought of that truth being revealed to him. Through my calm panic I thought, "This is not happening. He can't leave us. I'm not ready."

In one startling moment, Matt abruptly sat up in bed and violently ripped his Pistons T-shirt over his head. This stunned and terrified me and everyone in the room. He hadn't moved that vigorously in months. I was rocked to my core. Oh my God. I knew. As his shirt came off, it was wrapped around the oxygen tubes that were still in his nose. We slid his shirt down and away from his face until it was lying on the floor with the oxygen tubes still inside. Immediately Matt tried to rip out the nosepiece, but it was wrapped around his ears and under his chin, preventing him from pulling it out. He grabbed the nosepiece and pulled it taut, away from his face, with a very tight grip and determination that it would be out. My heart was racing.

"No, no, please, you need to keep that in, baby. Please." I was able to pry it from his hand and put it back in his nose.

When the shirt came off, I knew exactly what was happening.

"He's going to the water's edge," I said out loud. "He's going to the water."

My mind raced, "Oh Lord God, help me through this. Please, God, please, don't really take him. Don't do it. This is really happening."

As he struggled to breathe, I softly whispered to him, "I love you. I'm right here with you. It's okay. We're gonna be okay." Jesus, help me.

I sat next to Matt on the edge of the bed. Meghan was behind him, cupping her hands together to hold his head up. Sue was on the other side holding her son and propping pillows to make him comfortable. The reality that she had ushered him into this life, and was now at his side to usher him to the next place, seemed so unfair. How does a mother say good-bye to her child at any age? I suppose the same way a young father says good-bye to his young sons, with words of comfort and love. "Do not be afraid, because I am not afraid. I love you and I will always be with you. I'll see you soon."

Susan was the mother of that courageous young father, and I imagined myself in her position making a guttural plea, "This is all wrong! I want so much for you in this life. Your children need the example that only you can give. They are being robbed. This is all out of order!" There is no reconciling the death of your own child apart from God. As I watched Sue comfort her son, I was grief-stricken for her.

The bedroom was full of people on what seemed like a rotation. After much adjusting, we were able to get Matt into a comfortable position. I had my right arm around his upper back, helping him sit up. I gently rubbed his chest and touched his face while whispering words of comfort into his ear. His breathing was steady but disturbingly labored. He was staring at nothing.

In the midst of the struggle, the bedroom door flung open and Sammy came into the room. That sweet four-year-old child saw the scene. Daddy dying. The adults in the room were surrounding his father and crying. I asked him if he wanted to come over to say good-bye to his dad, and without hesitation he said, "Yes." He walked around to me and his Nona helped him onto my lap. He rubbed Matt's back, softly touching his dying father. I will never forget it as long as I live. He was fearlessly comforting his dad. I am convinced that Matt knew Sammy was there because he slowly began to lean into us. Sam's arm became "stuck" in between Matt's back and my chest. That made Sam a bit nervous and he pulled his arm out with my help and decided he was done. He kissed Matt and said, "I love you, Dad," and he left the room.

Drew came to mind immediately. Without much thought I decided he needed to say good-bye as well. Meghan went downstairs to find him, but he refused to come. He was afraid and confused. I had to leave Matt's side to console Drew and help him find the courage to see his dad one last time. The fear and sadness on Drew's face ripped at my heart. Before I could say anything, he was already saying no.

"Drew, do you want to come with me to see Daddy?"

"No!" he said again more loudly.

"Okay, come sit with me." My mind raced as I held him. There was no time to deliberate the pros and cons of bringing him to his father's bedside to say good-bye. Sam had done it. I thought it was right for Drew to do the same. I finally had to tell him that Dad might not be here much longer.

"What do you mean?" he asked. I could not believe it had come to this.

"Dad is going to heaven soon." I choked out the words. "You can come with me and say good-bye. It will be okay. I'll be right there with you."

Drew reluctantly agreed. I tried to be strong for my son, to give him every assurance that this was right and good and safe, but I wasn't convinced myself. I went on instinct. This would not be easy, but later, there would be no regret. Or would there? Was this the lasting image they would have of their dad? What was I doing to my children?

Ultimately I believed that I made the right decision to have him come in, but there was a moment when I was certain that I had made a terrible mistake. As I gently ushered Drew into the room, he was not prepared for what he saw. Terror gripped him and he cried and yelled, "No, Mom, no," and covered his eyes. The scene was horrific. The sound of Matt's breathing alone was enough to terrify, but add to that seeing his dad surrounded by all of the adults in his life, crying and afraid. His world was altered in that moment. Innocence gone. He clung tightly to me and I tried to offer him comfort.

"Drew. It's okay," I whispered. "It's Dad. You don't have to be afraid."

His eyes searched mine for assurance.

"I promise, it's okay. Dad can hear you. You can say good-bye."

"I want to say good-bye," he said. The fear in him subsided momentarily. I picked up my six-year-old son and carried him over to the bed. He sat on my lap.

"Good-bye, Dad." Drew leaned over and courageously kissed his father, who was lying with his head tilted back, the tumor in his neck grotesquely exposed, his chest seizing with every breath.

"I love you," Drew said. Matt was nonresponsive and this confused Drew. "Why isn't he saying anything?" he asked.

"He can hear you, but he can't talk. You did real good, baby."

Drew climbed down and left the room. "What have I done to him?" I thought. "My poor babies."

We were very near the end when the hospice nurse walked into the bedroom. It wasn't our usual nurse, and I felt bad that this woman was called away from her family on Christmas. She didn't look like the other hospice nurses, who typically dress professionally in suits or at least business casual clothing. Our new nurse wore pastel-blended nurse's scrubs. She stood at the end of the bed for a moment taking in the scene. Then she grabbed a blood pressure cuff and moved toward Matt. My brain was not computing why she even considered taking his blood pressure at this point.

"I don't think we need that. He doesn't have much longer," I said with a hint of confusion in my voice.

"Oh," she replied. "Is that a tumor in his neck?"

This was quite possibly the most absurd question she could ask given the circumstances. "Yes, that is a tumor," I said, growing troubled.

"Is that the cause of his breathing difficulty?" she asked.

This woman was distracting me from Matt, and my level of frustration was growing.

"No. If you listen, my husband's lungs are filling with fluid right now. The tumor has nothing to do with it."

She then began to defend her position, pointing out that the tumor could be placing pressure on his throat. It was clear to me that this woman was, at the very least, unqualified to be here, if not mentally ill. No person in their right mind would have the audacity to ask such questions in the midst of such circumstances.

As the nurse reached for her stethoscope, my mom looked at Meghan and through gritted teeth said, "Get that woman out of here!"

Meghan grabbed the nurse by the arm. "You have to go now," she said, pulling her toward the door.

For two months, hospice had provided phenomenal care and comfort to our family. This experience was proof positive that you want to avoid the need for medical attention on a holiday.

Matt was sweating profusely. I wiped his brow and his face with a damp cloth. It was paradoxical that his body had to work so hard in order to stop. Dying was work. His breathing was rhythmic and steady. In the quiet of the room, soft conversation and sniffles could be heard. The burden of struggle shifted and I realized that this was becoming harder for us than it was for him. Matt became calm and peaceful despite the distress in his breathing. He was being received into his new life. I began to pray aloud asking the Holy Spirit to be with us and bring Matt peacefully and safely to the other side. I had kept my promise to walk Matt to the water's edge. His eyes were open and pointed at me, but fixed on nothing. He was focused elsewhere. Heaven was in sight. He was slipping away. Gradually, his breathing became slower, quieter. I whispered, "He's calming down."

Sue said, "This isn't good, G." She picked up his right hand and saw that it was becoming bluish. I knew then that death was near. I listened to each breath. They became beautiful whispers, and my own breath harmonized with his. The softest wisps of air slipped from his lungs. His breath became my breath. I asked that the oxygen tank be turned off. The room was utterly silent but for the last whispers of earthly life seeping from Matt. There was an indescribable beauty in this moment. I was beside the quiet waters with him. We lingered in the stillness. People surrounded us, but it was just the three of us in that moment. The pauses between breaths were long, and with his final whisper it was no longer a "matter of time." Suffering and pain and cancer lost out to the applause of heaven. At the sound of one last rattle in his chest, I was struck with the grief of three years. Upon his last breath I began to cry over him, "No no no no no no! I love you, honey, I love you. Don't go. Please, God, help me. It's okay, it's okay, it's okay," over and over until I could only weep over him with groans. I couldn't let him go. I still haven't. I never will.

After I left Matt's side, I finally made my way downstairs. The hospice nurse was sitting at the table counting pills and getting ready to dump the narcotics. As soon as I entered the kitchen, she turned around with tears streaming down her face.

"Have I done something wrong? Your mother has yelled at me and told me to get out."

Inexplicably, I found myself dealing with this woman in my kitchen just minutes after my husband died.

"No," I said calmly, "it's not you. This is a difficult time and all we want is to be left alone. My husband just died, you see, and my mom is upset. I really can't worry about this right now. Please just finish your work."

After this exchange she thought it was a good time to tell me that she nearly fell down my stairs because they are so steep, and also that the front walk was icy.

"What?" I just stood across from her and stared at her, dumbfounded. "It's December in Michigan!" I said. With wide eyes and a clenched jaw, I looked over my shoulder into the family room, where my mom, dad, and Mike Schomaker were watching this scene unfold. They were laughing out of sheer disgust. What else can you do when you are aghast by such ridiculousness?

While the hospice nurse was still mulling around, a police officer arrived to confirm, "Yes, the man is dead." I don't know why, but this infuriated me. I thought of how Matt must have looked to him, shirtless, gaunt, and with tumors bulging from his abdomen and grotesquely protruding from his neck in an exaggerated way as his head was slightly tilted back. That officer didn't know Matt. For the sake of some paperwork, a total stranger had to come into my home and get a glimpse of my dead husband. I felt violated.

Before the funeral home directors went upstairs to take my Matt's body out of our home, I spent one last minute with him. He lay in our bed, his final resting place, and couldn't look at me with helpless, loving eyes, or say, "I love you, Peach." His hand and arm were cold. Just thirty minutes earlier he was sweating profusely and I was wiping his face and brow. My love was gone from this world. Oh no, where did you go, sweetheart? Where are you, honey? After thirteen years of marriage and three years of being focused exclusively on Matt's health and life, I found that my focus was gone. After holding his hand a while, observing the peace, I stood back from the bed and looked at the scene. It really happened. Everything is different. Lord, help us.

After Matt's body was taken out of our home, I had the urge to run out the door after him. Instead, I returned to our bedroom. In the place Matt had just died, the funeral home left behind a red silk rose with a gold tag that said, "Our memories are our treasures now." I don't know if it was a release of tension or the sheer absurdity of it, but I laughed out loud. The stem was cheesy fake green plastic. It was awful. If Matt had seen it, he would have laughed with me. I'm sure that others who receive that rose are actually moved by it, but this was just the kind of off-kilter thing that made Matt and me laugh. In place of my husband's thirty-six-year-old body, they left behind a tacky, fake rose with a trite message attached. A perfect memento for any grieving widow.

Before anyone left, it was decided that my mom would stay. Apparently I needed to have someone sleep over. I had no idea why. We were all a bit shell-shocked. I held Drew and Sam on my lap in front of the couch and we read two books together. Pastor Galik sat on the floor with us. His presence was soothing. He didn't get preachy or try to make the boys express their feelings. He made himself available, and that was enough.

When it came time to tuck the boys into bed, I received many offers to help, but this was the only thing I wanted to do. Comforting them was all that mattered to me. They needed to know how loved and safe and blessed we were. Both boys expressed confusion about the evening, but no fear.

Drew pulled me in close and whispered, "I'm not afraid to go to heaven anymore." After months of anxiety, he had found peace. His wonderfully tragic words brought me to my knees.

I talked with my mom for a while and walked around the house, avoiding our bedroom. When I finally did go in, I lay on the bed and wept in a way as never before. I had no thoughts. I was numb. I slept in our bed that night. I had to. I knew if I could do that, I would be able to face any situation that came my way.

And so this was Christmas.

CHAPTER 16

applause of heaven

gina

I was a living paradox. Walking through the funeral home feeling all at once famous and invisible, I was blinded by the widow's spotlight, feeling alone in a crowded room. I was completely numb, but filled with pain. Strong, but weary. I felt isolated although people from every corner of my life surrounded me. Looking at photos of Matt confused me because I couldn't remember him before cancer ravaged his body. Those who knew me best didn't know me at all. I didn't even know myself.

The thick scent of lilies smothered me. All my carefully chosen words, placed on my tongue by God I presume, told everyone in my path that I am not my grief. I refused to be defined as such. Although hundreds had come, tearfully wanting, and grieving for my family, a corner of my heart began grieving for them. I gave them Matt's gratitude, faith, and clarity because I had nothing of my own left to give. I stood next to his casket for hours and hugged so many mourners that my neck ached.

Pastor Galik sat on the floor with Drew and Sam at the foot of their father's casket and used colorful pictures to tell the metaphorical story of how their father was like a caterpillar that became a butterfly. It made sense to the kids and even a few adults.

After the second long day of visitations, more paradox. I returned to my home, which was quietly overflowing with friends and family. My girlfriends filled my kitchen with copious amounts of delicious food that was met by my nonexistent appetite. The remnants of wrapping paper and Christmas presents lay scattered beneath the tree just a few feet from the now-silent oxygen tank.

In my mind, I stepped back, as if peering in through a window. Matt wasn't sitting on the couch waiting for his meds. His voice was not calling me through the monitor. Yet friends, many of whom had known Matt longer than I did, filled the empty spaces. Their presence comforted me. I was overwhelmed with gratitude for the relationships and love that filled the room. Matt was missing, but the life he left behind was his gift to me.

Matt's funeral was held in the decorated sanctuary at St. John. He asked for a celebration of his life and I planned to honor that request. The service was reverent, but bordered on Lutheran revival, if there is such a thing. There was an uplifting children's message, celebratory music, and powerful faith testimonies given by Matt's friends, each intertwined with beautiful remembrances. As Mike recounted the night Matt asked him to take care of his sons, my heart broke into a million pieces.

The service concluded with a dramatic eulogy given by Pastor Galik that stirred souls in the congregation as he spoke of taking the journey to heaven. For several weeks, he had been painting verbal pictures of that journey for Matt, and now he was vividly revealing those steps to the rest of us who would someday take that path.

Toward the end of the eulogy, the distant sound of applause could be heard coming through the sound system. It caused me to look around for a moment, but I continued listening to Pastor Galik's words. As he spoke, the applause in the background became increasingly louder, as did his voice.

"It's just a matter of time, before the voices of this world begin to grow dim, like an AM radio, scratchy. Before the light of this world begins to fade into no light at all. It began to happen with Matt."

Pastor Galik spoke passionately. The emotion in his voice, paired with the distant applause, was captivating.

"At that point in time, with some part of self still in this world, Matt began to turn away, because in the distance there was a music, a sweet music that brought light. It began to replace damaged cells with perfect cells. It began to create life where death had been. It was a sweet song spoken of by the prophet Zephaniah, when the promises of God would be sung over him. That song began to echo in the distance. And Matt turned even further. He began to follow the familiar, the powerful, sweet harmonies, symphonies, and melodies, which were his. He turned, as the psalmist describes, toward the valley of the shadow of death, and the music was like a guide walking through it."

The sound of cheers and applause began to fill the sanctuary. Pastor continued, preaching more loudly.

"If you listened closely, you could hear the echoes of heaven begin as they waited for Matt to show. He would be drawn closer to the light, drawn deeper into the joy and into the music. Then he came upon a portal of light, in which he saw thousands upon thousands gathered around the throne, welcoming him into eternity. Because that which was lost had been found!"

With his arms extended wide, facing the altar and looking up at the cross hanging above it, Pastor Galik joyfully shouted one word at a time, "He—made—it—home!"

Hundreds in the congregation were weeping and some, applauding. As the applause faded out, Pastor Galik turned around, pointed to the congregation, and softly spoke the last words of his eulogy.

"And look. Here you come."

CHAPTER 17

not a pinched nerve

michael

I wanted to go with Cathy to Matt Kell's funeral, but Jack came down with a bad cold so I stayed home with him. Cath met up with some of her friends from high school who had come back into town to attend Matt's services. After it was over in midafternoon, she stood in our kitchen reading the funeral program.

"You would have loved the service, MJ," she said with awe in her voice. "This was not a typical funeral. It was more like a celebration of Matt's life. It was incredible."

She was genuinely moved by the experience. I looked at the program. It had the usual fare: the order of service, with hymns, prayers, etc. On the back, however, was something I had never seen before. There was a photo of Matt Kell with his family. With it were a few paragraphs about his life and faith.

"That's really nice." I handed the program back to Cath.

"You would not have believed how many people there were. I mean, they were out to the street!" She couldn't take her eyes off the program.

"That's pretty typical," I said. "When a young person dies, the church fills up."

She put the program into the kitchen drawer where we keep coupons and pizza flyers. She wasn't buying my cynicism. Just as she always did, she added her own self-effacing editorial.

"If I died they wouldn't fill five pews," she said with a smirk.

"I'll tell you what," I shot back. "If you die, I'll hire some people to come and make you look more popular."

Her experience at Matt's funeral seemed to renew Cathy's faith. She became even more determined to get us to go to church on a weekly basis. No easy task. I had not yet felt connected to St. John on a spiritual level and I only knew a handful of the people there. I made it to church about one out of every four Sundays. I did like the pastor there, although I never could remember his name. When it came to delivering sermons, he had some game. He spoke from the heart and he made the message sound relevant. As he spoke he moved around the altar and sometimes out into the crowd. This was engaging and, for me, helped make the doses of Scripture more palatable. A spoonful of sugar, I suppose. By and large, though, it had not quite become *my* church.

I resisted primarily because of my experiences as a young man growing up in Skeptic Valley. Like many, I had become so distracted by the flawed men delivering the words that I was unable to get very close to The Word. God bless her, Cathy kept trying to connect us both, God and me, without the benefit of those rocks in California.

In the weeks following Matt Kell's funeral, Cathy reached out to Gina Kell and her boys. She wrote several emails to Gina's best friend, Colleen Schomaker, trying to coordinate things. It broke her heart that there were these two young boys growing up without their father. She wanted to get everyone together.

From: Cathy Spehn
To: Colleen Schomaker
Sent: Friday, January 27 3:12 PM
Subject: Re:
Colleen

     I know you are super busy. I was hoping to get to know Gina better—and with our boys being same ages—I thought that would be nice. Maybe we could plan a play time all together. Or even a pizza dinner if Mike ever has to work late. My Michael is always gone at dinner till bed and I imagine that is a tough time for Gina too. Pizza and letting the kids run wild in my basement might be a good get together??? Have a great weekend.

                                Cathy

The three women, each of them juggling their own family schedules, never could seem to connect. Cathy vowed to keep trying though. There were kids without a parent and she wanted to help them out. I marveled at her capacity for love and compassion. I wished I had a fraction of it.

It was the end of January and I was working in our home office, making calls to franchise clients and catching up on paperwork. I heard the car pull into the garage, and I knew the kids were home from school, so I took a break from my work. They all poured into the house one after another. I didn't see Cath right away and I assumed she was talking with a neighbor or retrieving the mail from the box at the curb. She finally came in a short time later. She was holding her head and had an odd look on her face. I stood across from her at our kitchen island.

"You okay?" I asked.

"I think so. I just had the worst headache getting out of the car." She described it as starting from the back and moving forward. "It felt like a vice."

I immediately chalked it up to the headaches she typically got when her period was close. "Is your 'aunt' due to arrive?" I asked, using our code.

"No," she dismissed me. "This was weird. It only lasted about thirty seconds."

"You get migraines ..."

"No. I don't think this was a migraine." She walked out of the kitchen to move on to her next chore. As she reached the next room she touched her head lightly, and before she turned the corner she added one last thing.

"This was different."

Over the course of the next few days, Cathy's headaches went from once in a while to more frequent. We talked about "seeing someone," but really, who do you see about a headache? We thought for a time that her rotten posture might be the cause. Cathy would sit hunched over on the floor with the kids, to read her email or to watch TV.

"It's probably a pinched nerve," I reassured her, and an appointment was made with a chiropractor for that Friday afternoon. "If he can't fix you and you aren't feeling better by the weekend, we'll just walk into the ER."

Throughout the next few days the pain intensified. She tried a variety of painkillers, and some actually worked for a time. Eventually she felt the pain coming on again and it was beginning to worry her.

Friday morning was the kind of dreary waste of a day that gives mid-February its well-earned reputation. Gray and cold with freezing rain, the day looked like Cathy was feeling. She didn't get up with the kids that day. I got them off to school.

"Mom doesn't do it that way," Charlotte told me as I packed the sandwiches for their lunches. I really thought the kids would like their bread toasted. I forgot that they wouldn't be eating for another three hours, and by then the toast would be less than appetizing.

"Yeah, well, this is the way Daddy does it," I informed her and zipped up their lunch boxes.

Charlotte put a workbook in front of me to sign.

"What's this?" I asked.

"This is my daily workbook," she said. "Mom signs it every day to prove that she saw it."

I opened it to the correct day and signed my name hurriedly. I was about to hand Charlotte her book back when something caught my eye. Cathy had signed all the other days of the week. The signature looked odd to me but I couldn't figure out why exactly. I flipped to the previous pages and realized what it was. Cathy was known for her handwriting. She had a way of writing freehand that was almost perfect. She could write in a straight line without lined paper and the words all flowed beautifully together. That was the case with her signature on all of the other pages. On this current week, however, her signature began to slant downward, from the C to the y. By yesterday the last two letters were almost illegible and they were way below the others.

I handed Charlotte her book and got her and Jack on the bus. Danny was up and having breakfast and I was thinking about what to make of all of this. When Cathy finally made it downstairs, she was clearly in pain. Mornings seemed to be the worst and this was the worst morning so far. If we hadn't made the appointment with the chiropractor, I probably would have brought her into an ER right then, but since we were already planning to see someone in a few hours, we agreed to go there first.

Around two o'clock we headed to our appointment, but his office was overfull with patients. Cathy was in agony by now and Danny was starting to feel out of sorts. I finally lost my patience and we went back home. Cath went upstairs while I got Danny settled in with some snacks.

"MJ," she called to me from the stairs. I hurried up to her and saw that she was deteriorating by the minute. "I just threw up," she said.

That was it for me. I still had no idea what this was, but I knew enough that this was not a pinched nerve; we were now talking about something real. I called Larry and Jill and had them come over to watch the kids.

I drove Cathy to Beaumont Hospital in Troy, about a fifteen-minute drive away. I pulled into the ambulance bay in front and she walked into the ER while I parked the car. By the time I got back inside, she was filling out the forms. I asked her about the signature in Charlotte's book.

"Yeah, I've been having some trouble writing lately," she admitted.

A crowded ER is not a good place for someone with a headache. First of all, the industrial lights and the constant noise make it a most unpleasant place. Second, if you have a gunshot wound or your water just broke, you can expect pretty good service. If you are there for a headache ... you'd better pack a lunch because you are going to be there a while.

Four hours later, Cathy was brought into an ER bay and examined. She explained all of her symptoms to the physician and he poked and prodded in all of the usual ways. Eventually there was nothing left to do but order a CT scan.

"To rule out anything serious," he told us.

An orderly rolled Cathy's ER bed down to the lower-level CT lab. I went with them and waited just outside the door while they took a scan of her head. When they were done we all went back up to the ER.

"How long before we know anything?" I asked the attendant.

"Usually, on a night like this, about ninety minutes," he said.

I couldn't believe it. Another ninety minutes! Cathy was still in pain and trying to rest. I decided it was best to call Larry and Jill to tell them we would be awhile longer. I had just started dialing when the doctor rushed into the room with the CT scan in his hand. I immediately knew that this was bad news. He wasn't supposed to be here for another hour and a half. Only something urgent would bring him in here so quickly. I hung up the phone.

"We have your scan here and it tells us that you have a mass in the thalamus region of your brain. There is another on the right side as well, but there is a well-defined mass in a very bad part of your brain. I'm sorry to have to tell you this. It doesn't look good. We are sending you over to Royal Oak Hospital because they deal with more of this type of thing."

What? Did he just say ...? WHAT? Oh no. No, no, no! Please, no.

CHAPTER 18

gratitude

gina

Sam had the flu so we rang in the New Year quietly at home. I dismantled the Christmas tree and other decor while we watched the Detroit Lions lose another game. The fog in my head was thick. With each passing day the quiet was becoming more and more noticeable. I was going through the motions of life like a robot.

I knew that sending Drew and Sam back to school after Christmas break would be good for them, but it was harder for me than I thought. On days when Sam was in preschool, I avoided being home. Everything was out of sync. A couple of times, I started dialing Matt's office number at WDIV-TV until I remembered he wasn't there. Once, I had to call the station with a question about health benefits and Matt's voicemail answered, startling me. I couldn't decide if this was a pleasant surprise or a shot to the heart.

Journal Entry, Thursday, January 5

Nothing but drear everywhere. The sun would really be a gift. Mom helped with address lists for thank-you letters. Sam is tired—maybe still recovering from the flu or maybe just coping. Hard to tell. It's been quiet and lonely and I wonder, "What would Matt think about this or that?" Never knowing has the potential to paralyze. Time, go by so this won't hurt so much.

"Where did he go?" I asked Pastor Galik, demanding an answer. He tilted his head with a quizzical look.

"Heaven," he replied plainly.

"Of course. I understand that. But *where* is he? I know it sounds crazy, but I can't reconcile his absence in my brain. I want to go where he is."

Pastor Galik patiently did his best to answer my questions, but most of them were unanswerable. I was suspended somewhere in my leap of faith, hanging in the balance between reality and acceptance. Gone where, exactly? I couldn't bury those intangible things that were uniquely his: his humor, his energy, his mind, his voice, his soul. These reside in heaven. I ached.

Journal Entry, Sunday, January 8
I know Mike is struggling without his best friend of twenty-five years. Seeing him makes my heart hurt even more. The quiet around here pierces my heart. I love you, Matt. Will you come to me in a dream?

There was no avoiding the hours between nine p.m. and whenever I finally went to bed. Each night, after the kids' lengthy bedtime routine, I felt lost in my own home. Before Matt was sick, I would skip down the stairs, grab a bowl of cereal, and plop on the couch to watch television, but that was no longer an option. These days I stood at the edge of the kitchen, somewhere between the pantry full of cereal boxes and the empty couch. I would stare at the vacant space, then turn around and head for the office. I felt safe surrounded by Matt's books and memorabilia. To everyone else, it was just another room filled with bookcases and credenzas, but I knew that tucked away on every shelf was a piece of Matt's life and character. My comfort came from glancing at his signed baseballs and basketballs, leafing through his *Purpose Driven Life* journal, and laughing at the placement of *The Art of War*, by Sun Tzu, on the shelf right next to a copy of *Sun Tzu Was a Sissy*, by Stanley Bing. I dedicated a shelf to "Matt media," including three homemade CD compilations of the best cheesy music of our era. He called them *Burned Cheese*, *Fromage Part Deux*, and *Fromage a Trois*.

The media shelf also included several *Best of "Saturday Night Live"* DVDs, two seasons of *NYPD Blue*, his favorite movies, *Nothing in Common* and *The Godfather*, and a VHS highlight tape of his high school basketball career consisting of exactly one game, when Matt scored fifteen points in one quarter, shooting three pointers like a Larry Bird protégé. There were also three mini-DVDs containing Matt's video diary.

Journal Entry, Tuesday, February 7
Tonight I went to the funeral visitation for Tom Larkin, the second dad

from Drew's class to die in less than a month. Hugging Tom's wife was like
hugging myself. I had nothing to give her, but she thanked me over and over
for coming.

I spent the evening going through Matt's personal things, including his
laptop where I discovered an outline he had made for creating his video
diary. I reviewed it, closed the file, and logged out. I tried to distract myself
from the video diary that haunted me from the shelf. I cleaned out the
fridge, folded laundry, and attempted to sleep. I longed to see Matt "alive"
again, but I didn't know if I was ready. Sometime after midnight I gave in
to it. I grabbed my pillow, a box of tissue, and the DVDs and headed for the
family room. I sat cross-legged on the coffee table and hit play.

For nearly two hours I watched my husband talk to his sons about the
importance of God, faith and respect, pragmatism, and school. And me.
He talked to them about his expectations for how they should treat me and
regard me throughout their lives. He referred to me as a "princess" and then
he said the most selfless thing I ever could have imagined.

"The next person I want to talk about may or may not even exist. But
your mom may remarry another man. And if she does that, I want you to
know that I expect you to respect that man as if he were me.... If Mom
respects and loves somebody enough to marry him after I've passed away,
then I want you to expect that I love and respect that guy too. I know your
mom's values and if she remarries, she's gonna remarry somebody that I
approve of.... Treat him with love and compassion and like you would if
I were still alive."

I wept with gratitude. The future was unknown, but Matt's legacy of
faith and altruism would certainly define it.

Journal Entry, Wednesday, February 15
    For weeks, Mom has been tirelessly helping me create a mailing list in
    Excel from the funeral guest book. Tonight, twenty beautiful girlfriends came
    over to help me stamp, stick and seal over one thousand funeral thank-you
    letters. So glad that work is finished.

The generosity of others almost overwhelmed me. Friends from church
brought meals nearly every day, but after a few weeks I requested they stop.
I didn't mind cooking and it seemed like a waste to have so much food for
three relatively small people. My mailbox was on a steady diet of sympathy
cards so much that after the third week my mail carrier, Faye, came to my

front door and hugged me. Many of the cards I received included specific remembrances of Matt. This meant more to me than any other sentiment.

My parents, including Matt's mom, were the definition of support. Susan helped me with the boys and offered spiritual guidance and practical advice. She is an incredibly strong, faith-filled woman who already lost her husband and was using our shared experience to come alongside me at a time when she was grieving the loss of her son. She is among the most selfless people I know.

My own parents, like a steady stream of love and kindness, gave quietly and consistently in a variety of ways. The impact of their gifts was enormous. My parents are absolute "Nikes" in that they identify a need and "just do it" without overstepping bounds. Mom has laser-beam instincts about matters of the heart. Dad is her perfect partner, being more intuitive about practical matters. Together they recognize needs, emotional, physical, and financial, and find a way to fulfill them unconditionally.

On February 16, two days before Drew, Sam, and I were leaving for a family vacation to Florida with my parents, I dropped the thank-you letters off at the post office. Sending them was a weight off my shoulders. It also felt totally inadequate. There really is no way to thank people who have done so much to help you through the darkest hours of your life. The best you can do is hope to someday give back.

Gratitude. Peace. Memory. Comfort. Love.

"Jesus said, 'Love the Lord your God
with all your heart and with all your soul and with all your mind.
This is the first and greatest commandment. And the second is like it:
Love your neighbor as yourself.' "

Matthew 22:37 – 39

Dear Friends & Family,

Matt discussed *"love your neighbor as yourself"* at length on the DVDs he recorded for the boys prior to his death. He reminded us that this is what we should strive for in every relationship, every human contact. It is with immeasurable gratitude that I must tell you that your role in our lives and throughout this journey has actively helped Matt and I teach our children what it means to *love your neighbor as yourself.*

Each person receiving this letter is part of a larger body that collectively makes up the loving arms of God. Experiencing and receiving the second commandment, as it has been brought to life by your unconditional generosity and kindness, has made God's love tangible for Drew, Sam, Susan, Meghan and me. Thank you for such an outpouring. There simply is no measure of the generosity we've received, nor of the gratitude we hope to convey.

For everyone who prayed for us and continues to do so, thank you. There are many days when strength and peace are upon us despite circumstances. Without a doubt, it is the result of your prayers being offered, heard and answered.

Many have also given us the gift of memories. These are the treasures we hold on to every day. Memories will serve as the means by which Drew and Sam come to know their dad more fully. We appreciate the time and effort you have given to share and preserve our cherished memories and we gladly welcome any others you may have.

For the many who donated to the St. John Foundation, as well as other charities, thank you for your overwhelming generosity. Your donations are essentially a gift of faith that will create a lasting legacy for many generations to come.

For each person who sent a thoughtful card, took time to write a personal note, sent flowers or gift baskets, prepared home cooked meals, provided books and resources, cared for Drew and Sam, or in some small way extended themselves on our behalf, thank you for the difference you made in our journey. Each of you has brought some measure of peace and comfort to our home.

Finally, a gift from Matt to you. . . .

Matt's legacy is firmly rooted in his faith, which he continually shared with others. He would be pleased to know that his life or even his death has stirred something within you . . . a longing to know God or grow deeper in relationship with Him. I pray that you will not ignore that undeniable voice. ***"And we know that in all things* (including Matt's death) *God works for the good of those who love him."*** Romans 8:28

With love and gratitude,
Gina, Drew, Sam, Susan and Meghan

CHAPTER 19

sixteen days

michael

The dream is always the same. My point of view is that of a floating camera, like the ones they use for NFL games or concerts. My camera moves above a city I recognize, Ann Arbor, Michigan. It searches for something . . . or someone. It is a clear fall day and the camera approaches a stadium. It glides over the outside wall of the stadium and drops into the large bowl structure known as The Big House, the University of Michigan football stadium. It is filled with more than 100,000 people and is a beautiful sight on an autumn Saturday . . .

A certain chill grips you when you get into a car in an open-air parking lot after midnight in February. Some air is described as "a dry heat" or "a damp chill." February in Michigan has just one property: cold. The kind of bitter frost that seems to reach into your veins, creating an involuntary shiver that you're convinced will never stop. The body's defense mechanisms try to create warmth by forcing the muscles to expand and contract. The result is a nonstop tremble that lets the world know, unmistakably, you are freezing. Of course it was more likely that on this night, I was simply terrified to my core.

"We'll be taking your wife to Royal Oak," the tall paramedic had said to me. "Get your car and pull behind the ambulance; you can follow us there."

I drove for about a half mile in the dark cold streets before I picked up the phone and called my brother Bob. He is a "go to" kind of guy. Never married or tied down to many commitments, he always seems to be available when I need him. He lived in Southern California but came to Michigan to see us at least five times a year. He loved our kids and he and Cathy had become like brother and sister, so on this night, following an ambulance carrying my wife at 1:00 a.m., I knew Bob was absolutely the call to make.

"Hello?" he answered with ease in his voice. "What are you doing up so late, isn't it—?"

I cut him off. "Yeah, listen, something's going on here and I need to talk to you about it." My voice was starting to crack. I was going to say it out loud for the first time and I was afraid that if I did, it would somehow make it more real.

"Cathy is in an ambulance being taken to a hospital in Royal Oak. They found a mass on her brain and they think ... they don't know for sure, but they are pretty sure that it's a tumor." I was losing control of my speech while gripping the steering wheel tighter and tighter.

Bob was horrified. "Hold on, Michael ... what are you saying?"

"Cathy's headaches got so bad that I took her to the hospital tonight. They did a CT scan and they found a tumor ... what they are pretty sure is a tumor. They could not handle it in Troy so they are transferring her to another hospital in Royal Oak and I am following them right now. I just needed to tell someone what's going on."

Bob and I finished our conversation and he said that he would take care of calling everyone. "Do you want me to come out there?" he asked.

"Not yet. We need to find out what this is exactly. For now, you can stay put."

Bob being Bob, he was on the first plane in the morning.

I got Cathy settled into a bed at the new hospital. We didn't say much to each other. They gave her a load of medicines to ease her headache and allow her to sleep a little. Very early in the morning, I came home to grab some things and to tell the kids that Mom was going to be staying a few days in the hospital so the doctors could help her with the headaches. They wanted to see her immediately. I told them they would have to wait a few days so "Mom can concentrate on getting better."

The doorbell to our home rang a little too early for a Saturday morning. Bad news travels fast. It was our friends Kimberly and Tom from down the street. They came in and we sat on the couch for a minute. They apologized about disturbing me. Tom's eyes began to tear.

"We want you to know that we are here for you," Tom said. "Anything you need. Anything. The kids, the house, meals ... *anything.* We'll be here for you."

They were the first. Though I did not know it at the time, this conversation would become commonplace. I thanked them and ushered them to the door. Their intentions were designed to be comforting, and in so many ways they were. However, there are certain expressions people use when there is a crisis that are just simply startling to the listener. "We're here for you ..." "Anything you need ..." Or the mother of them all: "We're praying for you." That's the one that kills you. No one says that to someone who just won the lotto.

The next two days were blurry at best. Further tests were ordered. CT scans, MRIs, blood work. They all came back with the same thing: We think your wife has a brain tumor. They still couldn't be certain without actually going in for a biopsy, but all indications were that she had a very bad cancer growing in a very bad place in her head.

Meanwhile, something dramatic was happening to Cathy that no one was able to control. She began to rapidly lose the use of the left side of her body. She had feeling and sensation, but no motor skills, no ability to grip things in her hand, and no strength to walk. On Friday, she had walked into the hospital and filled out the forms herself. By Sunday night she was racked with pain, had been diagnosed with a brain tumor, and could not move the entire left side of her body. According to her doctors, the tumor was growing quickly and causing her brain to swell in areas that controlled the left side. This was simply unbelievable.

Cathy was transferred to a room on the eighth floor, designated and known to all as "8-South." This is the area of the hospital for cancer patients. It is actually one of the newer and nicer sections of that large facility. However, as you walk down the brightly lit hallways and pass state-of-the-art nurses' stations, you notice that just inside the rooms are people who are suffering life's most hideous reality.

I was in line at the cafeteria Sunday afternoon making small talk with the cashiers when I learned about 8-South. Considering the quality of their cafeteria food, I decided to have a little fun with the large woman sitting on the too-small stool.

"Are you guys trying to drum up more business for the hospital with this stuff?" I joked.

She gave it right back. "Well, it looks like you only picked out the bad stuff. We do have some fruit over there if you want."

"I heard they need a new wing in the gastro-intestinal department," I said. "So I'm loading up on the junk food.... You know, I'm doing what I can for the cause ..."

The large woman laughed a bit harder now. "Honey, you gotta get yourself something that's good for you and put it on that tray of yours."

"Ma'am, when I look back on the best times of my life ... *none* of it was good for me."

She began to shake a little with her laughs. She finished ringing me up. "You visiting someone today?"

"My wife. She's up in 8-South."

She stopped laughing. Her face grew more serious. She took my money, gave me the change, and as she did, she gave my hand an extra pat. Then she said it.

"I'll be praying for you, honey."

My camera/eye floats over the seats looking down at all of the people. Some look up at the camera, squinting; others simply look straight ahead as if afraid to look my camera in the eye. They don't know why, but they are certain they want the camera to keep going, past them and their friends. The camera sails all around the stadium, and after it has seen everyone, an announcer tells them they can leave. There is relief in everyone's eyes. What are they afraid of? Why don't they want to be the one?

8-South is a shrine to paradox—an awful place inhabited by wonderful people. They struggle to do God's work, spending endless days and nights stretching the limits of their human understanding to earn a victory against the Evil. Yet in the quiet corners of their own understanding, they know that the best they can hope for is a token resistance to the relentless tide that eventually beats them into submission.

Cathy's attitude through it all was remarkably fearless. We had plenty of times that we cried together but many more that we laughed together. That was the story of our life and marriage. No matter what life threw at us, we laughed together. The engraving on our wedding rings said it all: "Life, Love, Laughter." That was Cathy.

The doctors quickly began to medicate her with steroids and painkillers that helped reduce the swelling, which was causing most of her pain. She was constantly asked, "What is your pain at today?" She always answered with "I guess a six or seven." She had a growing, apparently malignant tumor in her brain that caused constant headaches and she had no use of the left side of her body ... but to Cathy, it was just a "six or seven." She never complained. Ever. It wasn't in her nature.

Once her pain was more under control, she was allowed visitors. Charlotte, Jack, and Danny were finally able to visit on February 14. They brought Valentine's Day cards that they had made in school and we put up photos of our family all around the room. It was beginning to look as though she would be in this room for a while, so we tried to make it look a little less sterile.

The kids were so happy to see their mom. Danny sat on her lap in the bed and Cath smiled big. We all ate dinner together; bland cafeteria food, but we didn't care. Cathy occasionally had to fight back tears. She knew things the kids didn't. She was so glad to see them, but she sensed that these times together were short now and there was no telling how many more she would have.

The decision was made to do a biopsy. There was a risk that came with doing any kind of surgery on her brain, but we simply had to know for certain what we were dealing with. Cathy would have her head shaved in one spot. The doctor would insert a very thin wire, carefully winding through specific areas of the brain until it reached the mass. Once there, the doctors would grab small tissue samples to examine under a microscope. Then, and only then, would they be able to tell exactly what disease Cathy had.

The surgical waiting room was a huge open space with very tall ceilings and plenty of comfortable seating for family and friends waiting for loved ones to get out of surgery. More than a dozen groups were gathered in their own clusters on couches and easy chairs scattered throughout the space that morning. At the front, a large desk staffed by two volunteers served as both comfort station and traffic control.

From time to time a doctor appeared. Hollywood gets this part right as doctors just out of surgery on-screen look pretty much the same as in real life. Surgical scrubs, sometimes their surgical "cap" in their hand, a serious but reassuring look on their face, and always, extreme exhaustion that showed with every step.

The doctors who came into the waiting room that day all did the same thing: they strode toward the patient's family and smiled a little smile. The family would stand up in unison, stern looks on their faces. The doctor would mumble a few words like "Uncle Harry did great in surgery. He will be back in his room in about an hour or so. You can see him then." Then the collective shoulders of the family would visibly relax and there would be hugs and relief. The group then gathered its belongings and walked out together.

I watched this scene unfold time after time that morning. My brother Bob, Larry Lutz, and myself; sitting quietly in our own cluster, representing what seemed like a thousand of Cathy's family and friends who, across the world, were waiting to hear the news that we would hear first. Later, it would be our job to take anything we learned today and make the phone calls either providing relief from this nightmare or confirming the worst. I thought about all of those people. At that moment they were going on with their day, working, driving, eating breakfast. In the back of their minds they knew that a phone call would come later today that would bring either peace or horror. Still they proceeded with the laundry and the emails and the demands of the day. Life goes on. Until it doesn't.

I was beginning to feel drowsy when Dr. Olsen approached us. I noticed him from across the room. He was still twenty yards away when it hit me that he was no longer wearing surgical scrubs. He was wearing his white lab coat. He had taken the time to change. I waited for him to address all three of us and say, "Cathy did great, she is out of the woods, you can see her in about an hour." Instead, he reached our group and came directly to me.

"Michael," he said in a hushed tone, "I want to speak with you. Let's go into this conference room back here so we can talk."

No. No! I don't want to go into the room. I don't want to talk. I knew that going into the room meant only one thing. Please, God in heaven, stop this now! I'm begging you with all that I am. Please!

"Just a minute," I told him.

I turned around and went back toward the others. "Larry." I waved him over to me. "I want you in here with me."

We all sat at a conference table. Dr. Olsen sat at the head of the table and Larry and I took seats across from one another. In an almost hushed tone the doctor told us, in clinical terms, what was wrong with Cathy.

"Well, I'm afraid it's not what we wanted to see. Anaplastic astrocytoma. We also see components of glioblastoma multiforme. There isn't significant necrosis there, but we could see cell division actually microscopically, which is unusual ..."

"I'm sorry, Doctor, can you speak up just a bit?" I said.

He raised his voice to normal levels, spoke plainly, and summed it all up.

"The slides confirm that it is primary brain cancer. GBM. The tumor itself is growing aggressively and it shows signs of both stage 3 and stage 4. I'm very sorry."

Larry and I sat quietly and took it all in. I had a few questions but nothing really of substance. Until the last one.

"What do we do?"

"There are treatment protocols but they won't offer a cure, just extra time, and that's only if she responds to them. You could try to get into a clinical trial, but there isn't anything proven successful out there for this yet."

It was as if he was making things up just to say something. At last he had nothing more to say other than the awful truth.

"If I were you I would be looking to make her comfortable."

There it was. The sound of surrender.

I asked the doctor if this was a genetic thing that our children would be vulnerable to.

"No. This is just a cellular anomaly. It's not passed down through generations."

"Is this very rare?" I asked.

"Well, given the type of cancer she has and the location ... The thalamus is deep in the center of the brain. This is extremely rare. I'd say this is one in six or seven hundred thousand."

Later that night, Cathy and I talked in her room. We cried quietly together. I crawled into bed with her and we held each other for a long time.

"I'm so sorry, MJ," she said. "I'm so sorry I have to leave you."

"God has other plans for you, I guess," was all I could muster in response.

She shook her head and looked me in the eye. "I just don't get it."

"What, my love?"

"I don't know why he gave me my babies," she said, "if he wasn't going to let me raise them."

Tears streamed down her face. She didn't make much of a sound. No wailing or pounding the sheets; just a torrent of tears without end.

Her question sat out there for a while. Neither of us had any answers, nor would we try to find one. There was a time in my life when I had an answer for everything, or thought I did. The longer I stayed on 8-South, the more I realized that I didn't have any answers to anything anymore.

About this time our neighbors Tom and Kimberly came to see us again. They informed us that Kimberly's father was on staff at Duke University Medical Center and was friends with Dr. Henry Friedman. Dr. Friedman was the leading authority on brain cancer in the world and he agreed to take

Cathy as a patient. To start, we were to get the biopsy results to Dr. Friedman as soon as possible. I made sure he had everything he needed within forty-eight hours.

At our home an entirely new way of life was taking shape and I had very little knowledge of it. My sister, Lynn, had come to town, and between her and my mother-in-law, Jill, the kids and the house were generally being taken care of. This allowed me to continue to be at the hospital with Cathy without worrying about things at home. Every couple of days I spent an extended time at the house, catching up on the mail and paying bills when needed. On the day after Cathy's biopsy, I found a letter in the mail addressed to her. The return address was from Gina Kell, Matt Kell's widow. I decided to open it myself. Inside was a beautifully written letter thanking everyone for their love and support during her husband's illness and ultimate passing. The letter was eloquent and personal and it impressed me. It scared me too. I tucked the letter into my top desk drawer and tried to forget about it. For now.

It was comforting to know that people who loved them were tending to the kids. Having Lynn around for a lot of this time made things easier for me. Lynn and Cathy had grown to love one another in ways that really made me happy. I used to say that she liked Cathy a lot more than she did me, her own brother. I really couldn't blame her; Cath was more lovable.

As the years went on the two of them developed a great friendship. Lynn was up visiting with Cathy on 8-South one day when an acquaintance from church stopped in to pay their respects. Cathy said hello and then turned to introduce them.

"This is my sister, Lynn," she told the other visitor.

Not "sister-in-law." Sister. This little gesture meant the world to Lynn. They were, in fact, sisters.

In an instant the stadium is emptied and fills back up again. It is an ebb-and-flow mix of happiness and dread. Each time there is a new group; one hundred thousand more. They react to my camera the same as the others. They continue to look straight ahead hoping it won't take notice of them. They dread its very presence. The camera keeps searching, drifting above them, sometimes swooping in for a moment and then turning to glance at others.

Once again, the announcer clears everyone and another group enters instantly. This happens again and again. Finally, the seventh time, the camera moves with purpose . . .

I headed back to the hospital the day after the biopsy. As I drove along

Coolidge Avenue, the sun shined through the windshield and I fumbled for the fifteen-dollar sunglasses that Cath got for me on a trip to the grocery store last summer. Finding them, I realized that there were a thousand little things in my life that were gradually being transformed from worthless trinket to treasured memento simply because she was a part of them.

I arrived at the first stoplight a couple of blocks from the hospital and waited. The light turned green, but I hesitated. Turning right would take me under the same old underpass toward 8-South. For some reason I turned left.

I was overtaken with emotion. It began to wash over me. This was real. This was bad. No, this was evil. Suddenly I felt completely alone. I was filled with the most obvious thought: I needed him.

I had not spoken to my father in almost three years. The rift between us had grown to Grand Canyon proportions and everyone in our family was resigned to the fact that we simply would not ever speak again. Now, however, I needed to connect with him. Cathy wasn't sick; she was dying. My children were about to lose their mother. There was one simple truth: I needed my father with me and everything else was just crap.

I dialed Norma's number. Norma, the woman who lived with Dad for twenty-eight years, had become an important part of our family. They met almost six years after my parents split up. Norma was well traveled, refined, and had a marvelous, quick laugh. Best of all, she loved my dad. She brought him peace in ways that no one else could. They enjoyed so much life together, and she and her family became yet another twisted branch of our weird and lovable family tree.

"Norma, it's Michael," I said into the cell phone as I drove aimlessly. Her tears, like mine, came almost immediately. I hadn't spoken to her in three years either.

"How are you?" She knew of course. Lynn had been calling Dad several times a day telling him everything about Cathy's status.

"It's not good," I said through tears. "Norma, we're going to lose her." We cried together on the phone.

"I'm so sorry, Michael," she said.

I continued making left-hand turns as we talked. From Coolidge to 13 Mile Road to Woodward and back again. I was actually lost for a while and I knew it, I just didn't care. The sun beat into the car each time I turned left onto 13 Mile. The cheap sunglasses were not up to the task. My phone battery was running low so I got right to the point.

"Can I call him? Will he allow me to call him?" I asked.

This was humiliating. Not in the sense that I was groveling or that I was somehow "losing" and he was "winning." I wasn't humiliated about reaching out to my father, but rather that it had taken such dire circumstances to bring me to this point. I regretted what I had done, and what I had failed to do, all these years.

Love atrophy. I had simply let go of our relationship. We both let it go, too far and too long. How could I have allowed things to slip into such disrepair that in the midst of a crisis, I was forced to reach out to Norma for permission to call my own father? I did not know what to expect from her, but I could tell that she was pained by the whole premise.

"I don't know, Michael, really I don't," Norma said. I was heartbroken. To me, this was the same as saying no. "I don't know" really meant "It probably wouldn't be best."

I always thought that he and I would deal with our past and with each other when the time came. Eventually we would get it right between us. I figured that all of it—the business decisions, moving away to Michigan, the good times and the bad, the arguments and the disappointments—would be sorted out someday. It was just that in the meantime I had things to do.

In the meantime I had my life to lead. I was a husband, father, businessman, and coach. I would get around to dealing with my father and all of the history between us. I would eventually get around to being a son again, but in the meantime I was busy doing other things.

What I didn't anticipate was that it would turn out to be a very long meantime.

I was crying now, the kind of tears I hadn't shed since I was a boy. I parked the car on the side of the road. Gripping the steering wheel tightly, my words came almost as if being pushed out of my mouth one at a time.

"Norma, please tell him that I called and that I hope he is okay, and if he wants to call me, I'd like that. I need that. We really need him here now."

This wasn't what I imagined. None of this was going according to script. I was being shown in so many ways that real life was not as tidy as it is in Hollywood. The movie of my life that plays inside my head had things working out differently. My wife and I were going to be ninety years old together. My children would grow up in a loving and intact home. My father would always be a part of our lives.

Instead, I was driving in circles around southeast Michigan pleading with Norma, asking forgiveness and repenting and kneeling before God himself, begging for the forgiveness and love and acceptance of my Father.

Both of them.

My pride and stubbornness and laziness and naiveté … all had kept me at a distance from him. Now, in the right lane of traffic on Woodward Avenue, I was reaching out to be closer to him. He was still here and I knew I needed him.

Both of them.

I needed his *presence*. I needed him to simply be here. Right at that moment I desperately needed his presence to change things in my world merely by his being in it.

"I'll talk to him. But, Michael, I can't promise anything," Norma said with regret.

Late in the evening the next day, the phone rang. Caller ID told me it was him. I felt the chills on my arm as I reached for the phone. My heart raced.

"Hello?"

"Yeah, it's me," he said, with the West Side of Chicago, get-to-the-point tone I had missed for so long.

Tears welled up in me. I was so thankful that he called. "Dad, thanks for calling me. You know what's going on, right?"

"Yeah. How's everyone holding up?" he asked.

"Dad, we need you here. Is there any way you can come and be with us?" For my father, knowing that he was needed was enough. He didn't hesitate.

"I'll be on the next plane," he said.

I knew he would be. He was my father and I needed him.

Both of them.

This group is the one. The camera hones in as it moves left, banks back to the right, and then gets lower, just above the crowd. Then, in the corner of its eye, it sees what it wants. It rises up, turns left to completely cross the field. As it passes over the large block M painted at the fifty-yard line, it has its target locked in.

It begins to descend and now I feel a sense of dread. In the crowd a familiar face is smiling like everyone else, but growing larger in the "lens" of the camera. No. This can't be. No! The camera glides smoothly onto its final path and begins to slow. In seconds it's there, with only one person left in focus. Cathy.

One … out of six or seven hundred thousand.

I wake up shaking.

Since the moment we arrived at the hospital, each day had become more agonizing than the last. We found hope in small but diminishing moments. Just days ago Cathy had been a vibrant, seemingly healthy wife and mother in the prime of her life. In the blink of an eye I was cheering for her because she could get herself out of her wheelchair and back into bed. A few days after that, I marveled at how great it was that she could hold a toothbrush by herself. It was amazing how adaptive my brain was to the ever-changing standards by which I judged how the day was going.

I watched helplessly as Cathy battled for comfort. The rising tide of pain and fear created a constant restlessness. It was her worst day yet. With barely the strength to open her eyes, she couldn't bear the thought of visitors and I made a few calls to wave off anyone with a notion of coming up to see her. Any commotion in the room was unsettling, so we kept the door closed and the curtain pulled. Thankfully, the drugs allowed her to drift off occasionally throughout the day.

Nutritionists and nurses stopped by to encourage Cathy to eat. She had no appetite and I simply allowed the food to sit without comment. She never was much of an eater; in fact, more often than not, she preferred a simple cold can of Coke to an actual meal. Now, under the most hopeless and painful circumstances of her life, it was senseless to prod her into eating.

The dusk outside the window on 8-South reduced the room to a dark gray. I kept the lights off, knowing that the incandescent glare from the hospital fixtures would only provide yet another assault on us both. Gradually, our eyes adjusted to the not-quite darkness.

Around 5:30 p.m. there was a knock at the door. My heart raced. I knew who it was. Cath didn't even acknowledge the sound. I pulled back the privacy curtain and slowly opened the door. There he was, standing straight and firm as ever. My dad.

In one moment everything that happened before was erased. Every disagreement, every disappointment, every exchange — good and bad, every single thing that had ever happened was insignificant in comparison to the gravity of this moment. In my helplessness, I had reached out to my father for help and comfort, and without hesitation, he opened his arms to me. Two men, who had lived with and without each other for forty-three years, stood in the doorway of a hospital room and hugged. A loving, pain-wracked, "be with me" embrace that seemed to press the delete button on our squandered past. The only thing that mattered was now. And what was next.

"Thanks for coming, Dad." My throat was tight and my voice strained.

As we finally released our embrace, I could feel his massive hand wrap around the back of my neck to hold me in a way he hadn't since I was a young boy. He looked me deeply in the eyes and without speaking told me that he was indeed here with me.

"Wait right here; Cathy needs a minute." He understood and took a step back out of the doorway.

It took a moment to rouse her. "Cath, there is someone here who really needs to see you for just a minute."

"No, MJ. Not today," she pleaded through closed eyes.

"It'll be okay. Just very quickly, he won't stay long. He has come a long way and just wants to see you for a minute."

"Okay, then," she said.

My father moved deliberately, slowly entering the room as I held the door. He stepped to the end of the bed, taking in the sight of it all; the photos and the poems from the children; the IV and the tray of uneaten food; the frail shell of a woman who had once staggered him with her beauty at the end of the church aisle, and who now lay helpless in bed. As he moved to Cathy's bedside, I turned on the small reading light on the side table.

"Hey, kiddo," he said. Cathy opened her eyes and saw her father-in-law for the first time in more than three years. Her eyes went wide and a smile arrived at the same time as the tears. She raised her head and shoulders above the pillow for the first time in thirty-six hours and beamed as she wept, reaching out her right arm, her only working limb, to touch the face of the man she adored so much.

"You look good," he lied.

"You like my new barrette?" she said, pointing to her scar and the visible staples in her skull.

"Yeah, I love it," he said, playing along. He got closer and knelt on one knee next to the bed. He knew about hospitals. He knew that there might be something under the covers that should not be sat upon; a tube, a monitor cord, or even a limb that needs to rest in exactly that position. He knew that until he got the okay, he should not simply sit on the bed. This was the things that most people missed about my father: his simple, quiet understanding. "Respect," he would call it. But for me it was even deeper than that. He got it.

"They treating you all right?" he asked.

"Oh sure," Cathy shot back. Her speech was getting stronger. I could even see the color coming back into her face.

I noticed that they never let go of each other. They held on to each other's hands and arms and never lost contact. At one point he gently stroked her forearm. I had forgotten about his tenderness. Cathy was simply overjoyed that he had come.

After making some bad jokes and promising to hurt anyone on the hospital staff who didn't take good care of her, Dad wanted to get serious for a moment. He was a man who could move mountains for the people he loved. Now there was a member of his family who seemed to need whole tectonic plates shifted. Dick Spehn was ready to do the job.

He leaned in close and asked quietly, "What can I do for you?"

"You've already done it," she replied through tears.

He nodded to her. Tears streamed down his weathered face now too. Perhaps for the first time in his life he understood that sometimes you move mountains by simply showing up. His presence was the only thing that was really needed now. There were no more jobs to be done. This simple woman taught this powerful man a most fundamental lesson: Just show up. Don't try to run my life, or even save my life. I only ask that you be *in* my life.

As I watched these two living souls connect in such a profound and intimate way, I noticed there was something else in the room with us: a perceptible, indescribable element that affected everything and everyone for those few moments in the half-light of the space. I have only recently come to understand what it was.

Grace.

In the days that followed, Cathy's condition became stable for the most part. The hospital transferred her to the rehab ward so she could learn a few tricks like getting in and out of a car, brushing her teeth, etc. The rehab ward was an awful place. Old tile hallways, low ceilings, and several patients to each room made it uncomfortable and depressing. I found myself missing 8-South. Cath hated it there and we made plans for her to accelerate her rehab training so we could take her home. There was little else the hospital could do for her now.

It had been only sixteen days since Cathy walked into the ER and began this spiral into hell. Sixteen days. Yet it felt as if we had lived through a lifetime. In a way we had. We were crossing over from one season of our life into another and it was happening in a blink of an eye.

We heard from Dr. Friedman at Duke. He was kind enough to call personally one morning when I was home. He agreed with the treatment plans set forth by our doctors at Beaumont. He talked us through several different scenarios and possible clinical trials. His tone had a sound of resignation to it, so I asked him point blank.

"What's her prognosis?"

He had only one word.

"Lousy," he said. The sound of his voice just hung in the air.

I asked him how long she had.

"If she responds to treatment, maybe a couple of months. If she doesn't, it will likely be quite a bit shorter."

Shorter? I thought. What's shorter than months?

CHAPTER 20

five balloons

gina

It was mid-February and I was grateful to my parents for offering to take us out of town. The Michigan winter was beginning to suffocate me in my malaise. The warmth of Florida sounded like a welcome opportunity for rest and deep, cleansing breaths for my soul. Coincidentally, the Schomakers and two other families from St. John were heading to Florida later in the week, vacationing less than an hour from us.

The night before our trip, while folding laundry and packing, Colleen and I had our final checklist phone call. She was on speakerphone and the television was on mute as I watched Conan O'Brien, with his lanky body and floppy orange hair, wildly gyrate across the screen during his monologue.

"How much packing do you have left?" Colleen asked, knowing that I usually stay up into the wee hours the night before a trip.

"Not much. I'll get to bed before three," I replied. Without Matt, going to bed early made me feel vulnerable, but I chose not to admit that.

Colleen chastised me for staying up too late and I defended myself while watching Conan dance in and out of the frame with hysterical expressions and movements, causing a smile to creep across my face.

"Did I tell you that I saw Cathy Spehn's husband today at school?" Colleen asked. "He looked rough."

"Really?" I replied, half distracted.

"Yeah, I heard that Cathy was still in the hospital, so I was surprised to see him. He was trying to keep his head down, but I went over to him."

I stopped folding laundry and turned off the TV. "She's still in the hospital? What's wrong with her?" I asked.

"Well, he didn't give details but he said it isn't good."

"You gotta keep me posted. Maybe I can do something."

"I'll call you if I hear anything."

The Schomakers were scheduled to arrive in Florida the day after Sam's fifth birthday, which meant he would have two birthday celebrations. He was excited to celebrate with Tommy in Florida, but he was also keenly aware that this was his first birthday without his dad. He talked about it throughout the week and in his journal he etched out, "I miss Dad," in his best preschool handwriting.

I blew up five balloons and set them around Sam's room before he was awake. He came out an hour later, still sleepy and holding a big red balloon, and curled his tiny body in my arms. I softly sang "Happy Birthday" to him. He and Drew started bouncing balloons all over the condo while I fixed Sam's favorite breakfast: bacon with a side of anything.

The birthday boy wanted to spend his big day at the pool, which seemed like a great idea until it became painfully obvious that the crowd at the pool was all fathers and sons. There were no other moms in sight. I kept scanning the deck to make sure it wasn't just my imagination. Drew and Sam stood in the shallow end watching one of the dads, who had a booming voice, line up all the boys for a game of diving catch. With each throw he gave praise and advice. Drew joined in, but Sam couldn't swim so he stood on the deck and watched. Although it was apparent to me, I wasn't completely sure if the boys recognized the imbalance. By the time we left the pool, things leveled out, but it felt like a cruel joke.

The duffel bag full of small toys I brought from home sat untouched as the boys made up endless games with the ten-cent balloons that I had shoved into my purse as an afterthought.

The fun ended with a bang when one balloon landed on a plant and popped.

Sam began to cry, "I want it back! I want the balloon back!"

I tried to console him, reminding him that there were four other balloons.

"But I'm five!"

"You're right," I said. "Look, I have another one." I quickly blew up another balloon to make the number five again.

"No! I want that one!" he said, pointing at the red pieces of popped balloon stuck in the plant. "I want it back!"

For thirty minutes he lay in my arms and sobbed out loud. This wasn't a temper tantrum from a spoiled child who lost his balloon. This was grief. Three years of watching his father slowly die before his eyes came to the surface all at once. I couldn't stop his crying and I didn't want to. I had a twinge of relief that he was expressing some of the confusing pain that stirred in him, but it pierced my heart. Drew sensed Sam's pain and tried to offer comfort.

"It's okay, Sammy, see!" He tapped a balloon into the air. "We can still play."

But Sam continued weeping over his missing balloon, repeatedly saying, "I want it back, I want it back."

"Sammy, I think you want Daddy back," I said through tears. "Daddy is like that red balloon. He's gone and I can't bring him back for you."

I wanted to take this pain away from my children, but instead, I was the one who needed to guide them toward it. We lay together for a long while and Drew and my parents joined us. We began talking about Matt and his favorite things, and soon our memories brought laughter. The grief didn't cease, but as we huddled together, Sam understood that he was not alone.

CHAPTER 21

february 27

michael

9:00 a.m.

As usual I was running a little late and driving a little too fast. Cathy had been transferred to the physical therapy ward and today she had more treatment scheduled at 9:30. I needed to be with her to learn what would be necessary once we got her home.

There was an odd sense of routine returning to our world. My father left early in the morning to catch a plane back to California. He declined my offer of breakfast and mumbled something about picking up a snack during his three-hour layover in St. Louis.

The kids were at school, even Danny, who would be picked up by Jill at 11:15. Our neighbors Heather and Tonya were due at the house any minute to begin turning our master bedroom into an "apartment" suite that Cath could live in while she received treatment. They were bringing a fresh new color of paint and frames for family photos and many other touches to turn our room into a sanctuary for their dear friend.

My brother Bob and sister, Lynn, both returned home to try to catch up with their own lives. Across town, Larry was in his home office as well, spending much-needed time on his paperwork and other minor but necessary chores. As I drove, I considered what lay ahead; the start of Cathy's chemotherapy was scheduled for later that day. A sobering thought. Then in two days we'd actually be able to bring her home.

I made good time and arrived exactly at 9:30. The physical therapist was running a little behind and I was relieved. I wanted to spend a few minutes with Cathy. When I got to her bedside, however, I could see she was in distress. Her hand was up against her head and she wasn't opening her eyes. As I had done countless times during the last seventeen days, I asked about her pain.

"What's it at?" I asked.

"Nine," she was able to mutter.

"Nine!?" I exclaimed. "You have never been above seven! Did they give you anything?"

"They gave me something a few hours ago, but they said I couldn't have anything else for a while," she said through blinding pain.

I rushed out to the nurses' station. "My wife needs pain meds now," I demanded.

"Your wife can have more in about two hours," the nurse on duty said, checking her chart.

"No, she needs something right now and she's going to have it," I said in a flat matter-of-fact tone. The nurse recognized my seriousness and went into the room to check on Cathy. She returned and said she would get her something. I decided to be patient for a few moments and returned to Cathy's bedside.

"Hang in there, love," I said.

My head was starting to fill with strange thoughts. What is this? What can be sending her deeper into pain?

The physical therapist showed up but left immediately after seeing Cath in such distress. At 9:40 the nurse hooked up an IV and started a morphine drip. As she left the room she assured us that this would do the trick.

It didn't.

10:00 a.m.

I went back to the nurses' station and told them Cathy's pain was not getting any better. After some hand wringing about it, the nurse came and gave Cathy an IV push of 2 milligrams of morphine. This is meant to speed the effects of the morphine and bring immediate relief.

It didn't.

At 10:40 I went back to the desk. "She is racked with pain," I said. "She needs something else." The nurses could not believe it. These were really great nurses, but they were really great *PT ward* nurses. Whatever was happening to Cathy was getting into an area that they didn't deal with on this ward. I insisted they call her doctors. Suddenly I was missing 8–South very much.

They received permission from Dr. Annak to administer 1 milligram of Dilaudid in an IV push. Dilaudid is a powerful drug administered only in extreme circumstances. After administering the meds, the nurse left the room. Within moments Cathy opened her eyes and half smiled. I sat on the side of her bed and held her hand.

"Hey, there you are. Are you doing better?" I asked.

She nodded and said, "It feels so much better."

Then she held my hand tightly and looked me straight in my eyes and said, "Thank God for you, MJ."

Before I could say anything, Cathy's eyes rolled back into her head and she fell back onto the pillow.

"Cath! Cathy?" I panicked. *Is she dying on me right now?* "Cathy! Can you hear me?" I shook her and rubbed her arm trying to get any response. I put my thumb to her eyelid and opened it. Her pupils were rolled up and fixed. I took off on a run to the nurses' station. Screaming in the halls now, I shouted, "I need help now!"

One nurse came out from behind the desk and moved toward the room. She tried to wake Cathy but couldn't. She tried to stimulate her by pressing and rubbing hard on her chest but got no response.

Then the alarm bells went off.

11:00 a.m.

Dr. Annak rushed in. Then the people with the cardiac crash cart came in. Several other nurses arrived next. Someone asked me to leave but I ignored it. I moved all the way to the back of the room to allow them to work. Cathy was hooked up to the cardiac monitor and they frantically tried to get her to respond.

"Mr. Spehn, you have to leave and let us work," one of the nurses said again, more insistently.

"Do your work. I'm out of your way. I'm not leaving this room, so if you want me gone you better go get a gun." She returned to her work and no one mentioned it again.

No one could figure out what was causing Cathy to be unconscious. She was breathing but her vital signs were way down and she appeared to be in a coma. The nurses and doctors looked at her charts, talked to each other, and were basically scratching their collective heads. The doctor in charge ordered 10 milligrams of Decadron thinking that they needed to reduce swelling in her brain. Nothing changed.

The doctor asked about what medications she was on. The chart hadn't been updated because everything had been happening so fast. Again, everyone looked around and said very little. Finally, I couldn't take it anymore. I spoke quickly, but firmly.

"She had a morphine drip about one hour ago, then a 2 milligram IV push of morphine about 40 minutes ago. Fifteen minutes ago she had a 1 milligram IV push of Dilaudid and now you guys have just put 10 milligrams of Decadron into her."

As soon as the doctor heard the rundown of meds, she knew what was needed. "Give me an IV push of Narcan," she called out.

"What is that?" I asked, moving closer to the bed now.

"Narcan," the doctor told me as she injected the IV tube with the drug. "It'll basically erase all of the drugs we've given her so far."

Within moments Cathy's eyes opened and she looked at all of us. She squeezed my hand. The doctor asked, "Do you know where you are?"

"Beaumont Hospital," Cathy responded.

"Do you know what day it is?"

"Monday," she said.

Everyone breathed a little easier, for the moment. Inside though, I knew things had changed. Cathy almost died on me and I was desperate to get control of the situation.

Within minutes it was apparent that, yes, we had gotten her back, but now, with all the medications "erased," the pain was back with a vengeance. At 11:20 a CT scan of Cathy's head was ordered. I demanded to go with her. I wasn't going to leave her side today.

She was rushed to the CT lab. The nurses didn't wait for an orderly to come and wheel her down to the lab; they simply took her, "stat." We didn't run, but very quickly walked down the hall and into the elevator, down several floors to the lab, and out of the elevator again. They stopped me just outside the door.

"She'll only be a minute," she said. "It's not safe for you in there."

It only took ninety seconds or so to get back to the PT ward, but by the time we arrived, I noticed Cathy's oncologist, Dr. Margolis, waiting in the hallway.

"Michael, come with me; I need to talk with you," he said. Cathy was wheeled into the room. Dr. Margolis and I went into a small office adjacent to the nurses' station. He wanted privacy. I hated that.

"I have the CT scan here. Cathy has developed a bleed," he started. "This happens frequently with brain tumors. It is one of the reasons they are so problematic. This is really ... not good." There was a resignation to his voice.

He continued, "As a result of the bleeding, there is significant edema (or swelling) and as a result of the swelling, she is developing hydrocephalus, which is basically water on the brain. The brain has millions of electrical impulses that occur each second. As a result, fluid is produced as a byproduct of the impulses. That fluid has to drain downward through ventricles or tubes in your brain. These ventricles carry the fluid away from your brain through the spinal cord and eventually out. The swelling is squeezing one of Cathy's ventricles and fluid is building up and causing extreme pressure.

"So she has bleeding, swelling of the brain, hydrocephalus, and of course, the primary brain tumor, which is growing very quickly. Any one of these things is fatal and she has all four going on at the same time."

"What do we do?" I asked, knowing the response I was about to get.

"If it were my wife, I would be looking to make her comfortable," he said.

"What about her treatment?" I asked. "They are ready to start that anyway. Is it worth trying?"

"You can try anything," he said. "I don't think that she will respond. But certainly you can try." He explained how her treatment might actually make her worse in the short term, but he remained understanding of what we were facing. "I will do whatever you decide," he told me.

I wanted to talk with Cathy about this. First, though, I picked up the telephone on the desk in front of me. It was time to let others know about what was happening. I called Larry.

"Well, hello there, what's going on?" he answered casually.

"I'm at the hospital up on the PT ward. Get here right now."

He recognized my tone but wasn't convinced.

"You need me to bring anything?" he asked, looking for any kind of relief to what was sounding like an emergency. I offered none.

"No, you need to get here now. Right now." I didn't wait for any response; I simply hung up the phone.

Cathy was now in intense pain and no longer able to open her eyes. She lay upright with the head of the bed propped up, and her right arm was against her forehead. I sat next to her on the bed. I spoke in a half-whisper and stroked her hand. I leaned in and put my cheek next to hers. I had to tell her the truth.

"Cath, you have a bleed in your brain. This is causing it to swell and that is why you have so much pain right now. Do you understand?"

She nodded.

"Margolis is telling me that there is nothing more they can do for you. They don't think that they can fix this. Sweetheart, he wants you to stop fighting."

She nodded again.

"They can give you your treatment, but they don't think it will help. It may even hurt more because the radiation can make your brain swell even more."

She was nodding through all of this. Quick, short little nods.

Our faces remained together. Warm. Soft. One. Maybe for the last time. *Please, God, do something to stop these awful words coming from my mouth!*

"I'll get them to do anything you want," I continued.

She stopped nodding.

"I want to keep fighting," she whispered.

"Are you sure? It's going to be so hard for you ..."

"I want to keep fighting," she said firmly.

Incredible. But not even a little surprising. She needed to fight for her babies.

"I'll make it happen," I said. "I love you."

I went back into the hall and saw that Dr. Margolis was still there. I told him of our decision. His look told me we were making a mistake. He never flinched, though, and immediately got to work arranging everything. She would have a radiation treatment as soon as possible. Then later they would begin the chemotherapy.

I knew in my mind that we were spitting into the wind. Nothing, not the tests, not the consultation of the leading brain tumor doctor in the world, not the advice of the learned men who were treating her or the obvious symptoms that were presenting, not even my own forty-plus years of life experience told us that doing this was worthwhile. But my wife had spoken.

"I want to keep fighting," she had said in a tone I knew all too well. It was the tone that told me we would be married. It was the tone that told me we would move to California. The one that told me I would not be "fixing" my son's birth date. It was the tone I'd heard only about five or six times in my life with her, but one I recognized so clearly.

"Just get it done," I told Margolis.

Dr. Margolis recommended that we be transferred to the MICU, a specialized intensive care unit where Cathy could receive very special care during treatment—though I didn't know exactly what this meant. I was just glad to be getting off the PT ward.

12 NOON

Larry arrived and met me outside Cathy's door. I quickly brought him up to date. I tried to be as matter-of-fact as possible. He said hello to Cathy, then came back out to consult with Dr. Olsen, her neurosurgeon who had shown up in the hallway.

There was a quiet desperation to my voice. This man represented our last hope. He was the court of last resort here on earth for my wife, my children, and myself. What he said in the next five minutes would determine our whole lives.

"Where do we stand?" I asked, knowing, but needing to hear him say it.

"It's not good," he said.

Then he reviewed everything we just heard from Margolis. I looked for anything that could be considered hopeful. There was nothing. I grasped at the very last straw I could think of.

"What if we asked you to operate anyway? What if I signed whatever you need me to sign to indemnify you and the hospital and I told you, 'Go get the tumor'?"

"What do you mean?" he asked.

"Would she have any kind of life? Would she recognize her kids or a sunset? I don't care if she can walk or even speak. Would she know her family?"

The doctor was gentle with me but unequivocal.

"No respectable hospital in the world would allow anyone to operate on your wife in that manner. Such a procedure would be actively killing her and, frankly, barbaric. I would never allow such an operation to take place here and I don't think you would find anyone who would agree to that. She would die on the table within minutes."

Larry and I took a breath. It was over. Surrender had begun. We may have a few more skirmishes ahead, but the white flags were being raised. God help us all.

Larry and I held on to each other for a minute in the hallway. He went inside and sat with Cathy. I went down the hall to try to find a quiet place to call several people and deliver more bad news.

"Bob?" I said after dialing my brother in California. "Cathy has taken a turn for the worse. It looks like she may not live more than a few hours. I need you to find Dad and have him come back."

This staggered him. I gave him a brief update on the morning's events and again told him I needed him to call Dad.

"I am pretty sure he is flying Southwest and has a layover in St. Louis. Turn him around and get him back here for me."

Bob said it would be done.

I returned to Cathy's room and they were ready to move her to the MICU and begin her radiation treatment. The brutality of the day was only beginning.

1:00 p.m.

The MICU is a cold and secluded place. To enter the unit you must show your identification to a video screen and someone unlocks a large double door that slowly and automatically opens to reveal a sterile, quiet place that serves largely as a waiting room for God. Cathy and I were led into the room at the farthest corner, where two halls meet. The room had even less warmth than most hospital rooms; nothing more than a bed, several monitors, a single armchair, and a window that looked out onto the colorless world of late February in Michigan.

It was here in this lifeless room that we would meet an angel who would shepherd us through the next few hours. A physically nondescript young nurse in her midtwenties, she moved with the confidence of a veteran who knew exactly what she was doing. It was her voice, though, that stood out the most. Gentle and firm, it was oddly familiar and provided a surprising comfort. It had a quality that put me at ease the moment I heard it; like a favorite song from a long time ago.

She was competent and honest throughout our time there, and most of all, she was kind. She told us to call her Christina and she immediately recognized my need to be fully with my wife. Christina not only allowed it; she offered ways that surprised me and gave me peace.

The first opportunity came not long after we arrived in the MICU. We were only there a half hour before they came to get Cath for her radiation treatment. It was her desire to "keep fighting," and this would be the first step in that fight. The orderly came to bring her down and they needed to move her from the room bed onto the gurney that would transport her to the radiation lab. Christina and the orderly got into position, but before they did anything, Christina gestured for me to help.

"Take the sheets on the other side of Cathy and hold tight," she said.

I was so pleased that I could participate in my wife's care, if even for a moment. On the call of "one, two, three," we all gently moved Cathy onto the gurney and went down to the radiation lab.

The lab reminded me of an underground government control room you'd see in movies. In fact, there was an actual control room with video screens and monitors and very darkly lit stations where technicians sat and conducted these treatments. Inside what looked like a fortified room was a platform about two feet wide and six feet long. It could be raised and lowered on hydraulics and it was surrounded by odd-shaped lights attached to an ominous-looking machine.

Christina seemed to clear the way for me to not only enter the control room but also go into the radiation room itself. By the reactions of those who worked there, it wasn't their habit to allow the spouse of a patient to breach this inner sanctum.

We all repeated the process of moving Cathy gently to the platform. The nurses carefully strapped her in and left the room. Cath was in terrible pain but she was determined to go through with this. Christina whispered to me that I could watch from the control room where it was safe for me.

"Come on, Michael," she said. "They have video monitors in there. You can see Cathy clearly." I liked so much that she called us by our names.

We went into the control room and they closed the massive door behind us. I saw Cathy on the video monitor. She looked like some Frankenstein experiment, strapped to a platform and being subjected to harmful doses of radioactive material shot into her skull. It was gruesome.

"How long does this take?" I asked.

"It's done," came the response from the technician in charge.

We went as quickly as possible to Cathy's side and gingerly moved her again back onto the gurney for the ride back to the MICU.

2:00 p.m.

The day was getting worse.

After radiation treatment, they had us wait in the hallway of the ward. There was a "code" emergency with a patient nearby and they needed everyone to stay put. Cathy's pain was increasing by the minute. She seemed to go in and out of lucidness. At the same time, it seemed that the end of the road became visible to us both. Clearly she wasn't going to get any more treatments. That had been a mistake. There was nothing left to do now. It was there, in the empty hallway of the MICU, that she and I would begin to say good-bye.

Cathy was the embodiment of the phrase "pain and suffering." Most of her left side was paralyzed. Her right hand, which had spent most of the morning up at her eyes covering them from the light, now lay still on the bed. I was the helpless man at her side. There was very little to do and almost nothing to say.

I actually thought about her funeral for a moment. We never really talked much about those things. We were young and so full of life. We never really had a serious discussion about what each other wanted. We should have. Now here we were, in this moment, with me yet again looking to the woman I loved to guide me.

I stammered, "Should we talk about ... what you want?"

Cath was confused. "What do you mean?" she asked.

"Where ... um, where do you ... I mean, where do you want to go?"

"I'm going to heaven," she said without hesitation. She was calm. Matter of fact. She was sure of it. Incredibly, so was I.

"I know, babe, I know," I said. I let it go.

She seemed to want to talk now. "Make sure that Charlotte grows up to be strong. Make sure she's a strong woman, MJ," she said.

"I will," I promised.

She was stroking my hand now. Actually telling me what to do and comforting me. "Tell the boys how much I love them," she continued through the pain.

I was crying now. "I will, my love, I promise."

"Make sure Charlotte knows that she is the best little girl I could ever hope for."

"I will." I promised everything she asked for.

She rested for a few moments and held my hand as best she could. She told me that she loved our life together and that she loved me.

"I love you back," I said.

"I'm going to tell the angels about you," she said.

We cried and I held her in my arms. The love of my life was slipping away and all I could do was watch.

3:00 p.m.

They allowed us back in the room. Cathy began vomiting, though there was no actual food to spit up. Christina had told me to expect this. Outside the window, the dull gray sky was showing the long light of the afternoon and I wondered if my love would see another dawn. She was in and out of coherence and that was a blessing. Her pain was continually a 9 out of 10. The vomiting was just another insult. From time to time she could drift into a type of sleep.

Out of the blue, without opening her eyes, she said to me, "Call Gina Kell."

"What?" I said incredulously. I knew the name. She was Matt Kell's widow. I tried to dismiss this.

"Call Gina Kell," Cathy insisted. "She has two boys and they will need to learn basketball. You're a coach, you can help them."

I wanted to completely change the subject. This was making me very uncomfortable. This was not what I wanted to talk about at this moment. Yet it seemed so very important to Cathy.

"Cath, please. I don't want to talk about these . . ."

"Michael," she stopped me. She opened her eyes and squeezed my hand. "Call Gina Kell," she said firmly. "She'll help you, too."

This was the last time I would hear her use that tone. Don't argue; just trust. Unbelievable, I thought. She is dying and all she can think about is other people who might need help.

4:00 p.m.

As Cathy and I dealt with an endless cycle of vomiting, intense pain, and discomfort, followed by a brief period of quiet as she "slept," we were left relatively alone by the staff. I attended to Cathy the best I could, but this was primarily her struggle alone. I have never witnessed anything like it. The clash of two giant forces: the firestorm of glioblastoma assaulting her body, and Cathy's indomitable will to live and see her babies grow up. To stand by and watch this happen to your wife is a certain private hell requiring its own strength and faith. For me, I simply became caught up in the tasks of it all. Making certain to wipe her mouth, fix the sheets, offer comforting words or some ice chips. I found myself fixating on the monitors, which announced the slightest changes to Cathy's vital signs. I had become knowledgeable about the basic numbers needed to sustain life. Cathy's were inching lower and outside the range of the required values. Her heart rate in particular was alarmingly low. It wavered between 30 and 35 beats per minute. I felt powerless and, once again, inconsequential.

Until he walked in the room.

Clearly a doctor (although we had not seen this guy before), he wore a white coat and he had an authoritative manner. He got right down to business as he entered Cathy's room.

He extended his hand to shake as he introduced himself to this near-death patient. This was awkward as Cathy could neither see him nor raise her hand to shake. He picked her hand up off the bed and placed it into his to complete the shake. I watched from the foot of the bed and began to sense that something was wrong.

The doctor looked at the monitor, noticing the vital signs, and began to do a cursory examination.

"Are you feeling better today?" he asked.

Cathy didn't respond, of course.

"Have you had anything to eat today?" he continued.

What did he just say? This was getting bizarre. Did he not know what Cathy was going through? Could he be confusing her for another patient? Or was he just an idiot?

"Don't worry about a thing, dear; we'll get you better in no time," he said finally. That was it. I could take no more.

"Doctor, may I see you out in the hall?" I said. We walked together about twenty feet into the hallway. Before I could say anything, he spoke.

"Is your wife a long-distance runner?" he asked.

I was floored. "What!?" I said. "What are you talking about?"

"Her heart rate is amazing. Does she run marathons?" he asked with a straight face.

I was astounded. I had been warned about such fools all of my life by my father. He had prepared me for just such a moment. *"Protect your family."* His voice rang in my ears as I squared off with the doctor.

"You haven't read her chart, have you?" I challenged.

"Of course I . . ." He tried to respond, but I was livid.

"If you had read her chart, you would have known that she is in late stages of glioblastoma multiforme and has already received one dose of radiation treatment. She has hemi-paresis on her left side and has been in and out of consciousness all day. She is moments away from hospice and her heart is shutting down."

I began to turn in frustration when I caught the eye of Christina, who was speaking with another nurse down the hall.

"Christina, can you come here, please," I called to her. She recognized that I was agitated and she came quickly.

"What's the problem?" she asked.

I pointed to the doctor and addressed her directly. "I want you to make sure that this piece of garbage never sets foot in my wife's room ever again."

The doctor attempted indignation. "Hold on a minute. I don't appreci- ate th—"

Christina cut him off and took a half step in between us. "You should move away now, doctor," she said.

"Just a minute," he tried to continue.

"You really should step away now, doctor." Christina stood firm.

The doctor paused for a moment to take this in. A nurse was publicly standing up to a doctor. He looked at me and considered the consequences of taking this to another level. After a beat, he simply walked away.

I looked at Christina, my new friend.

"I never want to see that man again," I said.

"You never will," she said.

5:00 p.m.

Cathy's mom and dad were with her at her bedside. I left the room to let them be alone with their daughter, and I slipped away to a private place within the hospital to make a couple of calls.

Once again, my first call was to Bob. I asked him if he was successful at reaching my dad. He told me yes, Dad was on his way.

"You should try to tell him that we are not in the same room anymore. We're in a completely different part of the hospital—I don't even know where—and they only let you in with proper ID."

Bob said, "Don't worry, it's Dad. He'll find you."

I hadn't talked to him in several hours. He needed to know how Cath was doing. "It's over, really, Bob," I said. "We're just saying good-bye now."

I asked him to tell everyone. "Please make the calls for me now. I have to get back in."

He assured me that he would. After we hung up I headed back into the MICU. As I did, Bob called our oldest brother, Rick, in Chicago. "They are saying good-bye," Bob told him through tears.

"I'm on the way," Rick replied. He hung up the phone and picked up his car keys and cell phone and walked out of the house. He went straight to his car and began driving east. It wasn't until about Gary, Indiana, that Rick realized that he had forgotten to tell Patti, his wife. He also forgot to pack any clothes or a toothbrush for what would surely be at least an overnight stay. He also realized he forgot to even put a coat on.

That was Rick Spehn. Throughout our entire ordeal, for the past seventeen days, he had waited patiently and expectantly. There would be a need for him; the call would come. Bob's call to him was his ringing fire bell. For Rick, nothing else was happening in any world anywhere. "I need to get to Michael's side," was all that he knew. He had six hours of eastbound pavement ahead of him. But get there he would.

The time had come back in the MICU. Cathy's mom and dad were just outside the room. Christina remained available for our every need. Friends and family all over the country were hearing the news. Somewhere over western Michigan a plane carrying my father back to us was on final approach. As the last light of the day cast long shadows in the room, Cathy realized that she had lost the fight.

I got as close as I could. I pressed my cheek against hers and held her hand tightly. She was in agony and I began to feel guilty. She knew she was going to heaven. But she also promised to fight. I needed to reassure her and to allow her to make another choice.

"We'll be okay, love," I said with tears streaming down my face. "You can go if you need to."

She nodded, the same quick, small nods that she gave this morning.

Cathy nodded. "I want to stop," she said.

I held her face close to mine and whispered in her ear. "Are you sure?" I asked. "Do you want them to make the pain go away?"

She nodded.

"Do you understand that, if they do, you won't ever wake up again?"

Cathy nodded firmly and knew what she was saying. It was time.

"I want to stop fighting," she said. "I want to go now." I cried, but only for a moment. My wife was in agony and I needed to relieve her pain and allow her to begin life in paradise. I got up from the bed and went to the hall. Christina was there and I motioned for her to come.

"We want to stop all measures now," I told her. "We want you to make her comfortable now."

Christina went into the room. She asked Cathy again if this was what she wanted. Cathy told her yes. Christina then placed a call to Dr. Margolis on the phone in the room. She put the phone in my hands so I could talk.

He told me that he understood our decision and he agreed with it. He said that they would make Cathy comfortable and that she would not feel any pain whatsoever. They would move her to a hospice room later, but for now they would stop all measures and treatments and they would take her out of pain.

I hung up the phone and Christina asked me if we wanted time to say good-bye. I told her to go get whatever she needed to get and do this as quickly as possible. Cathy needed to be at peace now.

Christina left the room. I realized that this was the end. Cathy and I had just a few short moments together and we were able to say a few things. Mostly, I just wanted my love to be out of pain. This had been agony all day and now, with the decision made, I simply wanted it to happen.

Christina reentered the room. She had a syringe and a bag for the IV. She asked if we were ready. I nodded yes. She was so gentle for Cathy and so loving. She reassured her that she would not feel any more pain in just a few minutes. Everything would be okay. I cannot accurately describe her voice or her demeanor that day except to say it was simply perfect. She was so comforting and compassionate. I began to believe that God himself had sent this woman to be with us.

She hung the bag and pressed the syringe. In a matter of moments, Cathy fell into a deep sleep.

6:00 p.m.

The Dilaudid, which earlier in the day had brought such panic and chaos to my world, now brought peace. Cathy was in a chemically induced coma of sorts. She would not wake up again.

People talk about the day Cathy died as February 28. I know it says that on the death certificate, but that's not what really happened. As I look at it, Cathy stopped breathing on February 28, but she stopped living on February 27. Our life together was over. I looked out the window of this very empty room and into the frozen darkness. All I could think of now was Charlotte and Jack and Dan. My God, I thought. I'm going to have to tell them.

I stepped out into the hallway and once again found Christina.

"What's going to happen now?" I asked her.

She misunderstood me. "Your wife will be moved up to a hospice floor and ..."

"No," I interrupted. "What will happen with Cathy? What should I expect?"

Her words were gentle but matter-of-fact.

"She will be kept comfortable and out of pain by the medications in her IV. At some point the edema, the swelling in her brain, is likely to get so severe that it becomes herniated out the bottom of her skull. That will press down on the brain stem and eventually she'll stop breathing."

I pressed for more. "How long?"

"I don't know," she offered. "Probably not long. I would guess that within about four to six hours you will see signs of herniation and then she will not last long at all. Perhaps another hour or two after that."

"How will we know that it's happening?" I asked.

"Her breathing will be very distinct and labored. She'll make almost snoring sounds as she gasps for air. There will be a kind of double breath that happens. It's unmistakable. You'll know it. At that point, the end is very near."

I couldn't get over how precise she was. I couldn't help but feel a little sorry for this woman. She must see death so often that she can give a time-table of what will happen.

She informed me that she was going off shift. I thanked her for her kindness. She hugged me.

"God bless you and your family."

Later I asked a nurse for Christina's full name and the correct spelling. I hoped to someday write to her or send her a gift to let her know how much she meant to me in those hours. The nurse wrote on a slip of paper for me. I stared at it and I couldn't help noticing her name as it was written. "**Christ**ina." It just stood out to me.

7:00 p.m.

Larry joined me in the room. He remained mostly at Cathy's side. I sat on the armchair near the window. We talked about nothing really; hospital small talk. I was beginning to think about going home to the kids when I heard a knock at the door. I rose to answer it, but it opened before I could get there.

It was Dad. He walked in the room and saw me. As I moved toward him, he looked at the bed and saw Cathy. The look on his face was pure pain. I actually thought for a moment about how he looked at me when he saw Cathy walk down the aisle at our wedding. This expression now was the polar opposite. He recognized a woman about to die. He knew that he was looking at someone who in fact was already gone. His face became the picture of the way I was feeling and I wrapped my arms around him.

"Oh no," he said in a resigned whisper. "Oh dear God, no." He held on to me as tightly as he ever had. I didn't want to let him go.

"You made it, huh?" I said through the tears. "Thanks for coming back. I just really needed you to come back."

"Oh, Michael James," he said. "What happened?" He moved to Cathy and stroked her hand and kissed her face.

I told him the story of our day. I told him that Cathy had made the decision to stop fighting and that we were going to be moved to a hospice room where we would wait for the end to come. He and Larry stood arm in arm together. Stunned. Two men who had lived a combined 140 years and thought they had seen it all. Silent and bewildered that this ... this ...! could be happening. And they had no power to stop it.

8:00 p.m.

I decided I should go home and see the kids and tuck them into bed. Cathy's Aunt Di and Uncle Dave were spending the night at our house. Although they had everything completely under control, I needed to see the kids; to touch them and to pray with them and hold them.

Stepping out of the hospital and into the darkness, I was hit with a cold and bitter wind. I stood at the curb and put my face directly into it. I stood motionless for a minute and then began slowly to walk across to the parking lot. Everything was different now. The man I was just eleven hours ago no longer existed. Someone strange and different got behind the wheel and drove back down Coolidge Avenue toward home. Awaiting me were children who were different now too. They just didn't know it.

I arrived and was greeted by a chorus of "Daddy!" I hugged Di and Dave and exchanged knowing glances without tipping off the kids to what was transpiring.

I tucked them in just before 9:00 p.m. We had many bedtime routines back then—all of them fun. The kids always pressed me for more at bedtime: more jokes, more stories, more funny voices. On this night, I indulged them a little extra long.

Finally we said good night. I was so sad but tried hard not to show it. I knew how scary it was going to be for them. For now, I told them to sleep.

9:00 p.m.

I took a shower and lingered. I turned the warm water to as hot as I could bear. The water formed a force field around my psyche and I folded my arms against the world. Those moments in the shower would be the last private moments I would have for a very long time.

I spoke with Di and Dave briefly. I thanked them for their love and for helping us. They shrugged it off and simply let me know that they were there for whatever we needed. They never wavered from that stance. God bless her, Di tried to get me to eat something. I declined and decided that it was time to return to the hospital. Larry called and told me that Cathy had been moved out of the MICU and into a hospice room, #8465.

I was going back to 8–South.

10:00 p.m.

Driving Coolidge Avenue this time seemed surreal. There was no rush. No panic. No doctors to see, no therapy to promptly attend. Christina had given me the timeline of it all, and although Cathy could pass away at any time, I was confident in the timing. She was no longer in pain and we had already said good-bye. All that was left was for her body to shut down.

I arrived at the hospital and found my way back to 8–South and Cathy's new room. I took a seat on the bed next to her. I held her hand and noticed that she was already breathing a "double breath" and making an almost snoring sound as she inhaled. I hadn't shared what Christina had told me about this and I seemed to be the only one in the room who knew.

11:00 p.m.

Cathy's breathing was gradually getting worse. Larry and Jill took turns at Cathy's side opposite me. When one sat on the bed, the other would sit in a chair or go out into the hall. Larry told me that Cathy's cousins, the Kreiners, and her Aunt Terry had arrived and were in the lounge area. I was glad they were close. Cathy loved these people and it was right that they be near her now.

Around 11:30 the door to the room opened and someone walked in. I didn't look up, I just knew. My brother Rick had arrived. He walked into the room with his usual gait. I felt him come up behind me, but this was not the time for hugs and hellos. He merely put his hand on my shoulder and squeezed. Without speaking he had announced that he was here and he was at my service.

This was how we would do it. This group from different cities, backgrounds, faiths, and experiences. Larry, Jill, Dad, Rick, me, and, of course, Cathy all formed a tableau that would remain in place for the next hour as we watched this incredible woman pass from this existence to the next. Nothing was spoken. No one moved except to shift in a chair or clear throats. All of the rush and fury and chaos of this morning, and the agony and pain of this afternoon, was now replaced with an odd calm.

MIDNIGHT

We watched Cathy intently. Her breathing was almost painful to watch. It reached a point where you would wish it to simply stop, out of mercy. For almost a half hour I thought each labored breath was going to be her last. The nurse came into the room briefly and checked Cathy's pulse. She noted her breathing, and as she left, she put a sympathetic hand on my shoulder.

"It won't be long now, honey," she told me. I prayed she was right.

At approximately 12:34 a.m., Cathy took in a large breath, this time without struggle, and let a long, deep breath out. I watched as her body seemed to relax significantly as most of the air left her. My father and I looked at each other. Neither of us had ever seen a soul leave a body.

He said, "Do you think that was . . . ?"

"Yes," I replied. That was it. I asked someone to get the nurse. Rick got up and called for her. In actuality, Cathy's heart lasted another handful of beats. By the time the nurse arrived, however, my dearest love, in body and soul, was gone.

The nurse came in and checked the vital signs. "I'm so sorry, honey," she said. "I have to call a doctor to pronounce. I'll be right back."

No one moved. Not a sound was heard. Cathy was gone. I could not believe this was happening.

Then a tall man in a white coat entered the room . . .

CHAPTER 22

the dream

gina

It felt like I was trying to get in shape after a long lazy winter. I had been taking in a steady dose of junk food in the form of discouraging thoughts and longings for the past and I was finding it difficult to move. I tried giving God the silent treatment, but that only made me feel foolish. I resented myself. I couldn't remember Matt before he was sick and it tortured me. Not even old photographs brought him into focus.

I did seem to have perfect clarity when it came to seeing my failings as a wife. I knew the better person was taken and didn't mind wrestling with God about it. Some days I envied Matt for being whisked off to perfection in heaven with not a care in the world, literally. I was left to comfort our children through pain that reaches deep into the soul, changing the character of a child and anyone listening to the sounds of their suffering.

The end of a long day seemed to bring the pain of Matt's absence to the surface, so I tried to preemptively lighten the mood in our home. While the kids ate a bedtime snack at the kitchen island, I performed my "mystery trapdoor" trick. I pretended to walk down an escalator by moving forward and gradually bending my knees lower and lower. From their vantage point on the other side of the island, I was walking down into a mystery trapdoor only grown-ups can see. As I came back up, Drew and Sam belly-laughed. Music to my ears. This was followed by a long, sudsy bath with lots of squirt toys, and finally an uplifting storybook, which meant no *Bambi* or *Lion*

King. Despite all this, there were many nights I could not stop the barrage of painful questions.

"Mom, did Dad die because I wasn't a good boy?" Drew asked. My heart ached. Where does a child come up with such thoughts?

"First Dad died. Then you'll die. Then Drew will die. And who will take care of me?" Five-year-old Sam had been giving thought to this scenario.

My answers were short on detail but filled with love and reassurances. For now, the boys seemed satisfied, but I sensed that this was going to get harder as time went on.

The evening of February 27 I was up throughout the night, restless and staring at the clock once an hour. When I finally drifted into a restful sleep in the early morning hours of February 28, I had a long-awaited dream of Matt. He was perfect, beautiful and fair-skinned, almost aglow. I was in awe of the sight of him, yet somewhat fearful. He opened his arms to me and I hugged him. Then I began to turn away like an embarrassed child. I felt unworthy to be so close as to see his radiant perfection. In the dream I was humbled, and although I turned, I deeply desired to see more of him. He enveloped me from behind, around my shoulders, and I felt safe in his embrace. He kissed the side of my neck and suddenly I awoke. I tried desperately to fall back asleep to him.

The dream lingered with me all day. It felt so good to see him alive, like a ray of light seeping through the impenetrable pall of grief hanging over me. In the dream Matt was so real and pure. Throughout the day I crossed my arms and imagined feeling him around me again. I couldn't stop the replay in my mind.

CHAPTER 23

telling the kids

michael

When a person dies in a hospital, there is paperwork. Surprisingly, there is not a lot. One form attests that you are the next of kin and another gives permission to release the body to the funeral home. That's about it. I asked the nurse outside of Cathy's room what was next.

"I need you to sign these papers," she said with a matter-of-fact tone that told me she had done this a thousand times. "Then an attendant will come and prepare her body to be moved down to the morgue. You can go home now. I'm so sorry for your loss."

"I want to stay with her." I was still being Cathy's husband, refusing to resign the job I loved so much.

"No," she insisted. Kindness was finding its way into her voice. "Go home and be with your family." I could tell that she was trying to help me. Still, I was adamant.

"I want to know where she is." I needed to be with her. I needed to know where she was going to be.

The nurse seemed to understand. "I'll call you when they are ready and you can go with her downstairs." Rick was with me. He had not left my side since arriving. Now he put his hand on my shoulder and squeezed slightly.

"C'mon, Michael," he said. "Let's go sit in the cafeteria. She'll call us when it's time."

I sat in the lifeless hospital cafeteria with my big brother staring at an untouched glass of Coke and wondering about what was to come over the next weeks and months of my life. Not much was said. Just two men, who'd spent their whole lives taking care of things, fixing things, and making sure that everyone was okay, now sitting in the reality that they actually were not in control at all. A stunned quiet came over us. Inside, though, was pure terror.

After about thirty minutes the nurse called. They were ready. By the time we arrived, they were wheeling Cathy's body out of the room on a gurney. She was completely covered by a red vinyl zipper bag. I rested my hand on the side of the gurney for just a moment and then began to walk down the long hallway. There were four of us: an orderly pushing the gurney, a nurse with all of the paperwork, my brother, and myself. Rick and I walked slowly a few paces behind the others. We walked past dozens of patients sleeping in dozens of rooms. They all had come here to get better, I thought. Now this grotesque procession, walking slowly through the corridors at 2:30 a.m., proclaimed the limitations of this hospital and of modern medicine itself. I hoped everyone was asleep.

The doors of an oversized elevator slid open and we entered. The ride down was silent but for the creak and strain of the elevator itself. No one spoke. The doors opened at a sublevel basement of the hospital. The cement floor had no markings on it and at the far end there was a ramp for cars to enter and exit this level. This wasn't lost on me. This would be where, tomorrow, a hearse would come and a stranger would drive Cathy's body back to Rochester.

My wife's body. My wife's dead body. God help me.

We approached a steel door with a plain sign that said "Morgue." The attendants stopped me. "You aren't allowed in here. It's against the law, actually."

I didn't believe them. It sounded like one of those responses you get from salesclerks about not being allowed in the back rooms "for insurance reasons." In a different time, perhaps only a few hours ago, I would have fought them over this. Now, however, my circumstances were sinking in. My day was nearly over. There was nothing left for this husband to do. In fact, I no longer was a husband.

"Thank you," I told them, and Rick and I walked out.

He offered to drive me home, but I didn't want to leave my car and, truth be told, I just wanted to be alone for the few moments that driving would provide.

"Follow me," I told him and we drove through the empty streets.

I began to realize that my primary duty over the next day or so would be telling people. My brothers and sister knew. My dad had been in the room. I decided to call my best friend, Dan, in California. My cell phone battery was dead, so I put my car into park right in the middle of the road at the next stoplight and walked back to Rick's car. He lent me his and I placed the call. Bob had alerted Dan to the fact that Cathy was not going to make it through the night. So my call wasn't a complete shock.

Through the years, Dan and I called each other with the big news that life's road provided: "I'm getting married. . . . It's a boy. . . . We bought a house!" This time all I could tell my friend was, "Danny . . . she's gone."

I wasn't crying. I was numb. Tired. Empty. I hung up after a brief conversation that involved love and prayers and ended with, "We'll fly right out."

As I drove farther through the cold and lifeless streets of Michigan, a thought washed over me. "How will I tell the kids?"

I would have to tell my children that their mother was never coming home. I thought about how cruel this was and wondered why God had given me such a task. How in God's name does someone tell children such a thing? Can there be a more painful thing to say to a child than that? What words would I use? Where should I do it? How would I prepare them? I was awake all night talking to myself, and to Cathy, and to God. Asking them, and myself, questions. I was never quite satisfied with the answers.

I went upstairs and looked in on them. Jack and Dan were in the same room. These two boys with such beautiful spirits went to bed as normal boys with a mom and dad. They were going to wake up completely different. They were going to be "those boys whose mom died."

Across the hall was sweet Charlotte. Nine years old and just beginning to become a young woman. She would have to face this life without a mom, without a woman to guide her and push her and hold her and shop with her . . .

"*Really*, Lord. Tell me! How will I do this?"

The next morning, the kids woke up and found that not only was my dad (their Grandpa Hoke) back in town and sleeping in our house, but so was Uncle Rick. I told the kids that they would be taking the day off of school today. I let them have breakfast as normal. I had decided that I would tell the older kids first. Charlotte and Jack were old enough to grasp what this all meant. Danny would have to wait until later when we could all surround him and help him through with lots of love and understanding.

When they were done with breakfast, I told Charlotte and Jack that I needed help upstairs. We went up to my bedroom and I locked the door. Everyone else in the house knew what was about to transpire except for the kids. My heart was slowly ripping apart.

We sat on our bed and I put my arms around them. I had a box of tissue on the bed next to us. After sitting quietly with them for a moment, I began.

"You guys know how bad the sickness is that Mom has, right?" They nodded. "Well, yesterday she got even more sick and Mom was in terrible pain that kept getting worse and worse." Charlotte began to sense that something was terribly wrong. She turned her back to me and lay on the bed close.

"Well, the doctors tried to fix this, but it just got worse all day long. They told me there was nothing more they could do for Mom. She was in such terrible pain and the doctors told us that they couldn't fix it." Jack began to cry just a little. Charlotte tensed up but was silent.

"Guys ... I'm so sorry. Mom died last night."

There are sounds that no man should ever hear. Sounds so evil and racked with torment that they will haunt him forever. Such is the sound of a child hearing that their mother has died. It is a guttural cry; a wail that cuts so deeply that the English language offers no words that can express the magnitude of darkness.

It is pure, black pain.

We sat together for more than two hours. Holding each other. Wailing. Crying. Shaking. Jack had many questions.

"Why did Mom have to die?"

"I don't know," I said. "We won't know until we go to heaven and ask God. But it is his plan and we do have faith."

"Was Mom suffering?"

"No," I lied. "But it is good now that her head doesn't hurt anymore." I tried my best to answer them all. He cried and cried. I cried with him. Charlotte was mostly quiet. She cried, but softly. She never spoke. She listened for more than two hours. Then she said the only thing she said the whole time.

"Dad," she said.

"Yes, my sweet."

"Will you promise me one thing?" she asked me softly.

"Anything in the world." I meant it.

"Promise that you will never marry another woman."

There it was. To a nine-year-old girl who had just found out that her mom was in heaven, this was the thing that had to be settled first. Lucky for me it was an easy one.

"Yes, my love. I promise."

With that out of the way, she and Jack had a few more questions.

"What's going to happen to us?" Jack wanted to know. I tried to be realistic but at the same time hopeful.

"Some things are going to be a little different. I am going to have to learn how to do the laundry and cook a little bit. But most things are going to be the same."

"Will we still live here?"

"Yes," I said emphatically. I was firm about this. They would not be moving out of their house. They would not be moving across the country to live with an aunt or uncle. I would have to figure out all of the details. But for now, I wanted them to have as "normal" a life as possible.

After a while it was clear that they understood what I had told them. They were scared, but they were strong as well. I decided to prepare them for the next few days. "This house is going to fill up with a lot of people," I told them. "You're going to see a lot of adults doing a lot of crying, because everyone loved Mom so much and they are sad that she is gone now. But this is important for you to know: If you feel like crying, it is okay to cry. But if you feel like laughing, it's really okay to laugh, too. You don't have to feel the same as everyone else. You can feel the way *you* feel, and that's okay."

I could sense they were calmed by this. Their postures relaxed a little and they seemed quietly glad at this permission to just be true to themselves.

I decided to take it further. "For instance, if I feel like chasing you and spanking your butts, I might just do that!" I got up and they let out a shriek. They took off out the bedroom door and down the stairs. They ran past my father, who was listening on the stairs, and they yelled as they tore around the corner and past the other adults who were now in the house. Danny joined in, and I followed after them, never quite catching them but coming close.

The four of us all ended up in the kitchen and caught our breaths. We had a good laugh and I played up how old and out of shape I was and that they were brats for not allowing me to catch them. It was a relief, if only for a moment. The rest of the adults in the house were clearly confused by this outburst. Had I actually told the kids? Did they understand? Why is everyone laughing?

Soon everyone exchanged knowing nods, indicating that they understood what they were witnessing. The children were experiencing the very first step in their grief. If grief is the toughest and most relentlessly unpredictable golf course in the world, then we had just teed off on hole #1, and we were already using what would become our rescue club: laughter.

Things were calming down now in the kitchen. The adults were uneasy and not exactly sure what to say. Everyone wanted to act normal, but when nothing in the world is normal anymore, how do you know how to act?

I still had one more heartbreaking task: telling Danny. Little four-year-old Daniel was at an age where he had not yet broken away from his mother. Danny and Cathy were buddies. He made her laugh and she made him feel safe. It was the truest form of love, that between a mom and her little boy. Now, with the help of Charlotte and Jack, I would have to tell him that his mom would never be able to hold him again. He heard my words and cried, knowing it was bad, but I wasn't sure he really understood. I suspected there would be a day when it would hit him. For now, I thanked God for helping me through the worst morning of my life.

CHAPTER 24

not again

gina

There is a special bond between sisters. Best friends too. We have a need to connect every few hours or days lest we feel adrift from one another. For Colleen and I, going more than just a few hours without talking to one another or, at the very least, texting would cause withdrawal symptoms.

On February 28, the Schomakers were finally due home from Florida and I couldn't wait to catch up with Colleen. She was still in the car with her family on the way home from the airport when she called to fill me in on the last few days of their vacation. There was always some hilarious parenting drama to share, but these days the dramas were more serious. I told her about Sam grieving his dad over a popped balloon and she told me about a debacle involving Tommy's heart medications. Not your typical mommy talk.

After swapping stories about everything else we had missed, we moved into the second phase of our call, anticipating the week ahead. She had a cardiology appointment with Tommy at the University of Michigan, and I had to deal with COBRA plans, insurance companies, and the Social Security Administration. We made it around to talking about laundry, grocery shopping, kids' field trips, and play dates. Play dates were code for the next time she and I would be getting together. The third and final phase of our call was the wind-down, where we covered everything we missed in phases one and two. Many times this took longer than the first two phases combined. After thirty minutes on the phone, Colleen was almost home and we were about to say good-bye.

"Have you heard any updates about Cathy Spehn?" Colleen asked.

"No. I've been kept out of the loop. People think they are protecting me by not giving me information. I was hoping you had heard something."

"I'll check when I get home and let you know."

"If you think of it, please copy me on the emails. I want to know what's going on."

Within a few minutes the phone rang again. I knew before I looked that it was Colleen. We had covered everything else ad nauseam. This could only be one thing.

"Gina?" She said my name like she was trying to hold herself up on it. "I don't even know how to say this."

"Don't tell me."

"It's Cathy. I cannot believe it."

"She's gone?"

"Yes."

"Oh God! Not again!" I knelt down behind the counter where the kids could not see or hear me. "This is not happening to those kids! She was fine last week. What happened?"

"All I know is that she was getting progressively worse throughout the week. They were talking about chemo and bringing her home, but she took a sudden turn. I guess it was a brain hemorrhage."

Colleen tried to explain, but the details didn't matter. Cathy Spehn was dead. Her babies didn't have a mom. Matt was dead. Our sons didn't have a dad. And I was filled with anger.

I regained my composure long enough to calmly send Drew and Sam to the basement to play. Before they hit the bottom stair, I threw a stack of papers with bills and sympathy cards off the kitchen counter, along with a napkin caddy and a box of Junior Mints. Thank God there were no breakables within reach. My rage was momentary, but heavy-laden with cursing and gnashing and hair pulling. I smacked my own head three or four times. I was out of my skin like never before in my life. I ended up in a heap on the kitchen floor with the phone in my hand. I dialed Pastor Karl Galik. I needed to hold someone accountable.

He answered the phone after one ring. "Gina Kell," he said in low voice, dragging out the *l* in my last name. "I was anticipating your call."

"Oh, I'll bet!" I snapped back. "Another young parent dies at St. John, and I go right back to square one!"

"That's understandable."

"Please tell me that you weren't one of the people trying to protect me from the news about Cathy."

"Well, I didn't run to the phone to call you. You're pretty raw right now. It makes sense that people would want to shelter you from more grief."

"Yeah, well maybe they're right, 'cause I'm goin' outta my mind right now!" I was yelling into the phone; then I started to cry. "I can't take it. I can't take knowing this is happening to another family. First Matt, then Tom Larkin. As if it weren't enough for those five kids to lose their fathers, now Cathy Spehn's kids don't have a mom! Why so many young people? Old people are supposed to die!" I was inconsolable.

"I know it's hard to reconcile all this." Karl instinctively knew not to attempt trite explanations. He was feeling everything I felt. He recalled the night of Matt's biopsy when we received the news of a terminal diagnosis. "I gave you and Matt a Bible verse that night that might be helpful now."

"Habakkuk. I remember. It was obscure so I wrote it down somewhere."

He recited the verse from memory. "Though the fig tree does not bud and there are no grapes on the vines, though the olive crop fails and the fields produce no food ..." Tears were streaming down my face again as I remembered the verse. I said the last two lines with him. "Though there are no sheep in the pen and no cattle in the stalls, yet I will rejoice in the Lord, I will be joyful in God my Savior."

"It's just coming from all sides, and sometimes I can't be joyful." I kept sniffling into the phone.

"I get it. You don't have to try to make sense of any of this right now. I know that there is unspeakable pain in this community. I'm with you. Even though I don't have the answers, yet I *will* rejoice in the Lord ..."

Karl got right down into the pit with me, grabbed my hand, and turned on a light to guide me out. He had something I didn't: clarity of mind. He took my misdirected anger and set it on the right path. He didn't try to banish it or make me feel guilty for having it. He allowed me to be angry, but he guided my anger to a safe place. Our conversation was brief. My fit ended tearfully. We set up an appointment to meet for lunch. I was grateful that the kids were playing quietly. I went into the den, and with my hands shaking, I pounded out an email to an out-of-state friend who wouldn't be tempted to do anything other than listen.

Date: 2/28 6:24:30 P.M. Eastern Standard Time
From: gvkhome
Subject: perseverance

I have to vent and ask for prayer. An acquaintance of mine from St. John, Cathy Spehn (she went to school with Matt) died after a three week stint with a brain tumor ... she went from having headaches to an inoperable brain tumor to swelling on the brain to radiation to death.

I AM SO fgjrawcno[vmtahwinctjdkbawovt;hkba ANGRY right now I could nfdsa;hfeiowa;fmnskagnv;tnujaw;gj SCREA{M!!!!!!!!!!!!!!!!!!!!!!!!!!!!

Pray for the Spehn family ... three kids 9, 7, 4 ... I can't seem to do it right now. I'm meeting Pastor Galik tomorrow ... I honestly feel like I'm going nuts with anger and frustration.

One other thing I'll share ... I was up throughout the night, sleepless, restless, not my typical M.O. When I finally got back to sleep around 4am I had a dream and I saw Matt. It's been lingering with me all day.

We rejoice in the hope of the glory of God. Not only so, but we also rejoice in our sufferings because we know that suffering produces perseverance, perseverance, character; and character, hope." Romans 5:2–4

I'll go with that.

Peace ... g

The day had started so beautifully. I wanted to wrap myself in the haunting beauty of my dream, but the news of yet another family suffering sent me back into the darkness, like a cloak being pulled over my head.

I originally wanted to be copied on emails about the status of Cathy Spehn's health. Instead, I was now receiving emails about funeral arrangements and making meals, copied to all the same people who helped my family through the days after Matt died. It was humbling to get a glimpse of what was going on behind the scenes. I was acutely aware that I would never be able to repay everything they did for us, but I was certain that because of them, we survived well.

I also received another series of emails, sent to me by Colleen. She forwarded the last email exchange she had with Cathy Spehn less than a month earlier.

From: Cathy Spehn
To: Colleen Schomaker
Sent: Thursday, January 26 2:41pm
Hi Colleen and Mike

I hope that you guys are doing well.

Colleen, I saw in your care pages that you have copies of Matt's service. I would love to get one from you if I could. It was such a wonderful service —I would like for my husband to see it. There are many messages in it— from the strength of love and friendships to the strength of relationships with God. Looking in from the outside on can see that Matt led an amazing life in those relationships—as well as do all of you. I think of you all often, and mostly of Gina and the boys. Take care.

Cathy Spehn

In another email, Cathy told Colleen that she wanted to invite the boys and me to her house for pizza and "letting the kids run wild in my basement." I was supposed to be friends with her.

I struggled to reconcile yet another loss and all that would never be, and at times it was more than I could bear. Yet I realized the privilege and responsibility that came with my experiences. I had a perspective and means of helping the Spehn family that no one else in our immediate community could offer. I wasn't sure how that would manifest, but I knew I had to reach out.

I reread the emails between Colleen and Cathy several times. Emotionally exhausted, I crawled into Matt's side of the bed hoping to drift asleep to another dream of him.

CHAPTER 25

she wasn't there

michael

Making arrangements for Cathy's visitation and funeral service was pretty standard. Rick, Lynn, and Larry accompanied me to the funeral home. It was a low-key meeting that addressed all of the necessary issues. Once it was all taken care of, I walked out with the others, but when we got to the cars, I pretended I forgot something inside.

"I'll be right back," I told Rick. "Wait here for a minute."

I walked briskly back into the foyer area and caught the funeral director just before he went back into his office.

"Tell me," I said, "when will the room be ready? When will Cathy's body and the casket and flowers, etc., be ready and fully prepared?"

"By Thursday afternoon. Why?"

"I'd like to come by and see it. I want to make sure everything is okay for my kids. I just want to put my eyes on everything before I bring them here so I can prepare them for what they're going to see."

He was very accommodating. "No problem. Come by around 2:00 p.m. Thursday, and you can spend all the time you wish."

Pastor Galik from St. John was to preside over Cathy's funeral, and he asked if he could come to the house to meet everyone. He wanted to know the people to whom he was ministering. Relationships mattered to him. I liked that.

I was running an errand and was late getting back to the house. When

I arrived, I saw something remarkable. Little Danny was sitting in Pastor Galik's lap on the kitchen floor and they were deep in conversation.

Just moments before I entered the room, Danny had approached the pastor as he waited for me to arrive.

"I know you," Danny said. "You're Pastor Galik from school."

"Yes, that's right!"

"Did you know that my mom is in heaven?" Dan said with the raw truth of a four-year-old.

"Yeah, Danny, I did know that."

With that, Pastor Galik removed his suit coat and sat himself down on the kitchen floor. Danny melted into his lap. This trust was not something that came easily to Danny under normal circumstances. I admired his instincts here though. He was in good hands.

"I really don't want her to be in heaven," Danny told the pastor.

"I don't either," the pastor said.

When I thought about that simple reply to a four-year-old by a pastor, I was impressed. The two of them went on to have about a five-minute conversation about Jesus and Mom, and heaven, and caterpillars and butterflies. It was right out of Chicago. A Dick Spehn everything-else-can-wait approach to things. It didn't matter that he was wearing his best suit. It didn't matter that there were fourteen other adults in the room staring. It didn't matter that this was going to be heartbreaking to talk about. A child was hurting and somebody needed to get on the floor and give him some face time. I had never seen a pastor or priest or rabbi or any other man of the cloth do this before. I smiled as I watched the scene unfold. My respect for Karl Galik took root at that moment. He and Danny sat together for quite a while. Then, as four-year-olds will do, Danny ran off to play.

The adults needed to talk about the order of the service at Cathy's funeral. We sat at the kitchen table: myself, Pastor, Lynn, Larry, and Jill. Just in the next room but well within earshot was the delegation from Skeptic Valley: my brother Bob, Dad, and my Uncle Mel.

We dispensed quickly with the basics. Pastor had suggestions ready, and I availed myself of almost all of them. At some point, just before it was clear we were close to wrapping up, I asked a question.

"Where would be a good spot in the service for me to say a few words?"

There was the kind of silence in the room reserved for the fool who has just proposed something ludicrous. Karl was clearly surprised, but he was gentle in his reply.

"I would advise against that," he said with all of the pastoral care he could muster.

"Why?" I shot back.

He wasn't as prepared for this conversation as he had been for all of the others.

"To be perfectly candid, I am concerned about you making it through. I would hate to have to rescue you midway. Plus, I'll be honest ... in twenty-five years of ministry I have never seen a spouse do that."

The others in the room concurred with the pastor. Except for my sister. Lynn knew. She knew I could get through it. She also knew that I was someone who simply had to speak to the crowd that would surely be there. She nodded affirmation to me and helped me get through that moment of debate.

Finally I declared, "I want to do it."

"Okay," said Pastor. "What shall I tell them to call this in the program?"

"Words of thanksgiving," I said.

I walked Pastor Galik back to his car as he left. In the driveway I shared with him the story of Cathy telling me that I should call Gina Kell. He thought on it for a time. Unbeknownst to me, he had become a close friend of and theological shepherd to the Kell family. Matt Kell was like a brother to him in the last years of his life.

"You should call her," he said.

"No. I just told all of that to you to let you know what kind of woman Cathy was. She was thinking of others in her last moments ..."

"You should call her," he repeated. Then he got into his car and left.

Later that day Lynn accompanied me to a print shop in town that would print the memorial card I designed for the visitation. It had several photographs of Cathy and the kids that I'd taken and that were very special to me, along with some text that I wrote.

I knew the print shop owner, but I could tell he didn't recognize me yet. I had used him to print the memorial cards I designed for my mother's service just fourteen months prior. I handed him the disk that had the artwork on it.

"I need this by Friday afternoon," I said. "Is that doable?"

"Lemme check this artwork," he said, walking into the back room.

My sister and I waited at the counter out front. He shouted to us from the other side of the wall. "Is this for a funeral or something?"

Lynn and I exchanged a glance. *Oh boy*, we thought.

"Yes," I told him. "A visitation. So I really have to have them for sure by Friday."

He came around the corner to join us back at the counter. It was starting to come back to him now.

"Did I do one of these for you about a year ago?" he asked, scratching his cheek.

"Yeah. You printed some for my mother's memorial services."

He thought about this for just a moment. Without a hint of emotion or compassion, he said, "Hmm. Who died this time?"

My sister's eyes went wide. He just looked at me as if he had asked me where I had parked my car. There really was nothing left to do but to answer the man.

"My wife passed away two days ago," I said. Lynn gripped the counter with both hands and silently prayed for this moment to end. But he wasn't finished. He thought on this for a moment and then, as he turned and headed for the back room, he summed it all up in one concise word.

"Bummer," he said. Then, as he walked into the back, "Yeah, I can have this to you by Friday."

Bummer. He actually said "bummer." Lynn was frozen, not knowing how this would end. Was I going to get in this guy's face? Was I going to break down and start crying? She literally didn't move. I sensed her fear, but I couldn't resist the awkward perfection of this moment. I looked at her, then toward the back room, then back at her.

"You know," I said, "I think he took that pretty well, don't you?"

Lynn burst out laughing. I, too, could not contain myself. "Bummer!" we both said at the same time through hysterics. It was the understatement of the century, yet it was just right. Pulling out of the parking lot, Lynn and I could not stop laughing.

Back at the house, friends, neighbors, and relatives all seemed to come and go. I spent a lot of time talking with people on the phone in my den or dealing with the kids. There was a constant clamor by people wanting to "do something." There was an almost nonstop line of questions regarding the most mundane things. "Where is the can opener?" "What time does the mail come?" "Where should we take the kids for lunch?"

I was alone in these waters. It would be up to me to do everything. And "everything" meant so many things that I didn't even know about. I would have to learn about all of these things, and soon. For now, though, I had somewhere to be.

"I'll be back," was all I said.

The funeral home director met me at the door and walked me into the room where Cathy's casket was. There were hundreds of flower arrangements and they were scattered everywhere.

"Take your time," he said and closed the door behind him, leaving me alone.

I took it all in. The flowers. The casket. The semi-darkened room. The reality of it was brutal. I slowly moved closer to the casket. My hands rested on the edge as I looked directly in. I was shocked by what I saw.... Cathy wasn't there.

She wasn't there! I had waited all week to be able to spend a few moments alone with my wife. There was only one problem: she was already gone. Yes, her body was there, but she — Cathy — was gone. To the casual observer, this may have seemed completely obvious. Yet to me it was an epiphany. Of course my dead wife was gone. I knew in my head that she was gone, but standing there, at her casket, I had an extraordinary moment of clarity. Cathy was in heaven.

She told me she was going. In those God-awful moments back on 8-South just days ago, she said, "I'm going to heaven." Here was proof. She was gone. I stood before her casket and she wasn't there. If there was anyone on earth who deserved to go to heaven, it was Cathy Spehn. I had no tears. I actually smiled and shook my head in disbelief. Or perhaps it was in *belief.* I can't describe the overwhelming sense of peace I felt.

"Good for you, Cath. You made it!" I whispered.

Finding a chair on the side of the room about fifteen feet from the casket, I took a seat and noticed the quiet. I was very much alone. I was worried about what was to come, but for now, I was at peace. It was the most manifest moment of faith I have ever experienced.

I was filled with the spirit of Cathy. I was filled with the spirit of my late mother, my Uncle Jack, and Gram too. I was filled with the Spirit, for the very first time in my cynical life. There wasn't a theologian alive who could have taught me what I learned that day. It had nothing to do with religion and everything to do with faith. My God was real and he was alive in my life. I had looked for him my entire life. I looked for him in prayer and penance, in cathedrals and crashing surf, in baptisms and the Bible itself. Who would've thought that now, in my most grief-stricken moment, I would finally find him, right where he said he would always be. At my side.

CHAPTER 26

the only one i know

gina

For the third time in three months, I was attending the funeral of a young parent from St. John. Matt's was the first in this season of misery, and I felt like I was becoming the resident widow on call. Within a month we said good-bye to Tom Larkin, whose son was in Drew's class. Having two fatherless boys in first grade left twenty other kids wondering if their daddy was next. Heaviness hung in the air at St. John. The repeated loss of young parents was affecting all ages within our church community. The loss of Cathy Spehn was another devastating blow.

Her visitation was held on a cold and dreary Friday evening. I planned to meet Colleen at the funeral home around six o'clock. We arrived early, knowing all too well what kind of crowd to expect.

"Are you okay?" Colleen asked as we walked through the front doors of Pixley Funeral Home.

"I don't know. Just stay close." My stomach felt tight, and I could feel the heat of my perspiration intensify. The customary funeral home scent of lilies filled the air, making me want to hold my breath. We walked past the sign-in podium and immediately recognized several of Matt's high school friends who had consoled me in the exact same room just two months earlier. As the head shaking and words of disbelief were getting started, a man came alongside me.

"Are you Gina Kell?" I turned to meet his eyes and nodded. He hugged me tightly.

"Thank you for coming," he said. For a moment I thought he was one of the high school friends, but quickly realized that it was Cathy's husband, Michael.

"I'm so sorry for your loss." I regurgitated the same words that so many had expressed to me. Receiving those words meant the world, but speaking them felt trite and inadequate.

"Can I speak with you for just a minute?" he asked. The crowd of friends and family was growing, and they were all looking for some face time with Michael. This didn't seem to matter. He was focused on me.

"Sure," I replied, glancing at Colleen for reassurance. Her eyes followed us as we walked a few feet away from the crowd to a more private sitting area. Michael pulled together two upholstered chairs, and we sat closely facing each other to talk over the din of conversation that filled the room. He was composed, yet I recognized the pain in his eyes and in his posture.

"How are you holding up?" I asked, sounding like an idiot. "I'm sorry. That's a stupid question. You'd think I'd know what to say."

"I was about to ask you the same thing. I feel terrible doing this, but I need to know something." Michael was sitting forward in his chair.

"What is it? Anything," I replied in a matter-of-fact tone.

His words came haltingly, but not out of nervousness. It felt more like regard.

"Well, you're ahead of me in this process. Tell me about your kids. How are they doing?" He leaned in to listen for my answer and quickly added, "Lie to me if you have to."

"I don't have to lie. They're grieving, but they really are okay. We talk about Matt all the time, and we laugh and cry together, but they go on living the way kids do. Our faith, and being surrounded by people who love us, makes it doable."

We talked about the kids for a while. Our conversation was intense. At times Michael was overcome with emotion and filled with uncertainty and confusion. In many ways I saw myself more like him three years ago when the newness of Matt's diagnosis was washing over me. Michael had no time to process Cathy's illness, let alone her sudden, unexpected absence from their lives. I so much wanted to comfort him but I didn't know how.

I became increasingly aware of the growing crowd around us. Hundreds had come to express condolences to the husband of the deceased, and he was spending an inordinate amount of time away from his post. Michael was keenly aware too, but unfazed.

"I can't tell you how much it means to me that you're here," he said in a clear voice. "When I was getting ready to come here tonight, I wondered if you would show up. I hoped that you would. The day before Cath died, she talked about you. She told me I should call you."

"Really?" I was shocked. I tried to comprehend how and why Cathy would speak of me on the last day of her life.

"Cath was like that. She thought of others. She had hours to live and she was thinking of your boys and who would teach them to play basketball. I'm a basketball coach at Lutheran Northwest. She told me to help your boys learn the game. There were just things that she knew. She thought we could help each other."

"That's unreal," was all I could muster. I was humbled and grateful that he shared this with me. "I only met Cathy a couple times, but she was like a ray of sunshine. I'll never forget her smile and her genuine kindness."

As I described the first time I met her, Michael handed me a memorial booklet that he created. The cover photo was a large closeup of Cathy, and three smaller photos with her children. Inside, there was an even more stunning photo of Cathy sitting on a boat, with one arm stretched back over the rails. With a radiant full smile, she was tilting her head back, her face being kissed by the sun. It was the perfect visual summary of my impression of her. She was a beauty.

My purpose for being at the funeral home became clear. I was there to listen, to console, and to simply be present in our shared experience. I received far more than I gave that night. Through our mutual grief we found empathy in one another. It was like a parachute opening during a freefall. I stared at the memorial booklet, and we sat silently in the stuffy, crowded room for what seemed like more than a minute until Michael broke the silence.

"Lots of people here tonight," he said, looking around the room.

I nodded.

"Friends and family from forty years of life." Michael turned toward me and looked me straight in the eyes. "You and I just met, but you're the only one I know here tonight."

I half-smiled at the stranger sitting across from me and understood him completely. "I know," I replied. I was relaxed in my chair but quickly sat up straight, realizing that our time together was coming to an end. He had responsibilities and I needed to reconnect with Colleen.

As we said our good-byes, Michael introduced me to his Uncle Mel, who was holding a plate of food.

"This is Gina Kell, who I was telling you about."

Mel shook my hand, offered his condolences, and immediately handed Michael the plate. Michael winced at the sight of it and turned to greet an old friend. From a distance, I watched Mel offer him the food several times, insisting that he eat. Michael finally grabbed a cookie, took a bite, and threw it back on the plate, making a face like he had just eaten sand.

It's as if everyone becomes an Italian grandmother around the bereaved. "Eat! Eat! Mangia!" It's been my experience that the grief-stricken don't want to eat, especially in the middle of a crowded funeral home. In the throes of grief it's hard enough to swallow your own saliva, let alone choke down a turkey sandwich. But feeding the bereaved becomes a mission for helpless onlookers who don't know what else to do.

My protective instincts kicked in and I couldn't help myself. When Michael was at a safe distance, I gently approached Mel.

"I know you want Michael to eat, but I don't think he will," I said softly.

"He needs his strength," Mel replied.

"I understand your concern, but right now he's getting it from another source. You just need to be here when he finally says, 'I'm hungry.'" Mel knew that I was speaking from experience and agreed to let it go. He proceeded to fill me in on the cast of characters around the room. We went on to discuss responses to grief, the differences between men and women, and the best way to help Michael through the next year. I felt like I was talking with a dear old friend. Mel was incredibly insightful and thoughtful.

Colleen found me. "So much for just 'staying close,'" she said.

It was time to walk into the room where Cathy's body lay in precisely the same place Matt had been two months earlier. Déjà vu. Cathy's father, Larry, was standing in my spot alongside the casket greeting a line of people. He appeared a broken man, thin in stature and weary from the nightmare he was living.

While waiting in line, we approached the open casket. I observed Cathy's hands. They were delicate. I tried to avoid looking at her face, perhaps because I knew that I wouldn't be looking at Cathy. I noticed the beautiful cross necklace she was wearing. I bowed my head to pray for Michael and the children.

When we finally reached Larry, we shared tears and sorrowful hugs.

He was a proper and gentle man who considered others before himself. He thanked us for coming and said, "I know this must be difficult for you."

I tried to hold it together, but I began to cry again. We reminisced briefly and shook our heads at the senselessness of it all, reminding each other that ultimately the Lord is in control. We sought the silver lining that Matt and Cathy were together in heaven, mostly because it felt like the only right thing to say.

It took another twenty minutes before we made our way through the throng of visitors toward the door. Colleen and I walked out into the bitter March night and headed to our cars. We planned to meet Mike for dinner at a nearby restaurant.

"You want to just ride with me?" she asked.

"Yeah, I think so." I needed to process everything that had happened. "I might want a second glass of wine tonight."

"That was crazy. What just happened in there with Michael Spehn?"

"You saw that, huh?"

"Everyone saw that. You two were in deep conversation for twenty minutes. I thought the funeral director was going to lose his mind! He wanted Michael to greet guests, but he knew better than to interrupt you two."

"I don't know what just happened. I felt like I've known him all my life."

She didn't press. For possibly the first time since I've known Colleen, we drove to the restaurant in complete silence.

CHAPTER 27

five pews

michael

We held a memorial service for Cathy on Saturday at St. John. I took care to call it a memorial service and not a funeral. This was a quirk that I had with some phrases. For instance, I never say that I am anxious for something to happen. I use "eager" instead. My uncle noticed that I never said the word "died." I always told people that Cathy had "passed." Tomato, to-mah-to, I suppose. I didn't know why, but it felt better to me to say, "My wife passed away," and that we were having a memorial service to celebrate her life.

We took our seats at the front of the sanctuary. There were flowers and songs and the Northwest High School choir sang beautifully in honor of my beloved. Pastor Galik conducted a perfect ceremony. It was heartfelt and prayerful. There was even a children's message that, although a bit corny, worked for the kids.

Then Pastor introduced me and I walked carefully up the four marble steps to the altar, turned, and looked out. The church was overflowing with people and they spilled out into the lobby. There were people everywhere; familiar faces and many I'd never met. All had come together for one reason: they loved this lovable woman.

I hadn't written anything down, but I'd thought about what I might say. I thought that if I prepared a "speech," it just wouldn't be as genuine. I wanted to speak from my heart and I just assumed that the words would come to me when I needed them. As I began, I noticed that, although there were hundreds of people, young and old, not a sound was heard. Not a rustle of paper, not a dropping of a pencil. Not a single clearing of a throat. There was absolute silence. It was deafening. My words reverberated back to me as I spoke.

"Pastor Galik very gently suggested to me that I might not want to do this, this morning. He was afraid that I might not get through it.

"But these are the things that Cathy relied on me to do throughout our life together. She would give me one of these [I motioned as if she were elbowing me in the ribs] and say, 'You should say something. You should say a few words. You should go make a toast.' Although I never really needed much encouraging in my life.

"So I guess that if I cry a little bit today, that'll just have to be okay. We've been doing a little bit of crying at our house. We've been doing quite a bit of singing, too. And dancing and concert-giving, and making fun of things.

"But it's a sad day. It's a sad time. We are saying good-bye to one of the great people of all time. We are saying good-bye to our friend, our neighbor, our daughter, our mom ... and to our one great love.

"It is also an amazing day of thanksgiving. It is. I am so thankful for so many things that I had to stand up here and tell you all. I am thankful that I am alive. I am thankful that I am among you, the living. For I have seen up close—too close—how fragile our existence is, and I am determined to take every day, every breath, as a gift to me. I am determined not to waste them.

"I am so thankful for my time with Cathy. You all were blessed because you knew her. But I won the lotto; I got to live with her. Every day and every night, and every boring car ride was spent in the presence of an angel on earth. And every morning I'd wake and see her and I'd think, 'My God, she's still with me!'

"Someone asked me, when we were preparing to have children. We were talking about it and thinking about it and thinking how are we going to do this, and should we do this ... and this person asked me outright, to my face, 'Why do you want to have kids?' And I thought *I* was cynical. But I had an answer right away. I didn't hesitate. I told this person, 'I have met the most extraordinary person on earth. I have met the most compassionate, the most loving woman. And I have the power to make more people just like her.'

"And then we did. And I am so thankful for you guys. I am so thankful for the brightest, smiley-est, happiest, most loving children that God ever blessed this planet with. They are messy and they are noisy and they spank my butt when I'm not looking. But they are their mother. I am so proud of them. And every day with them will be my blessing, forever.

"And I am so thankful for all of you. During the last three weeks of our lives, you all have showered us with love. Look around the room. There are people from everywhere, every walk of life. People with nothing much in common, except that they were touched by this beautiful spirit of a lady.

"You have showered us with your love and with your prayers and with your offers of help ... and God knows, with your baked goods. Our home is bursting with food and we are going to keep the dentists of Rochester busy for a long time.

"This time of amazing grief, this time of pain that cannot be spoken ... I'm telling you, has been matched step for step and ounce for ounce with love from you all. And with the same amazement that I would wake every morning and thank my God that my wife was still at my side, I tell you all I am amazed that you have flooded our lives with pure unconditional love.

"We do not know what tomorrow brings for us. We are a little bit scared. But I know absolutely that we will be lifted up by that ocean of love that has come from you all. I know absolutely it will lift us up and carry us. I know that as sure as I have come to know anything. And on behalf of my family, from our hearts, thank you."

The service ended and everyone filed out of the sanctuary. The aisle leading to the back of the church was jammed with people wanting one more hug, one more opportunity to tell me they would pray for us. I was appreciative, but there was someone at the very back, standing in the aisle, whom I needed to get to. Dad.

He stood alone in the crowd. No one talked to him; no one queued up to hug him. He was now just a quiet giant of a man, having been so completely humbled by this experience, standing at the back of a church, waiting for his son. I approached and gave him a tight-lipped smile. Like when I was young, he put his large hand on the back of my neck and pulled me close. I kissed his cheek, and as his eyes welled, he whispered into my ear.

"Michael James, you did good. You did good."

His massive hand cradled my head and he looked me square in the eyes. "I love you, my boy. She would be proud of you."

That meant everything to me. I did what Cathy wanted me to do. I did what he would have done. I did what God called me to do.

A luncheon was held after the service in the basement of the church. Several hundred people lined up to a buffet generously prepared by the good Lutheran women of St. John. I didn't eat; instead I spent much of the time hugging and being hugged. The ocean was beginning to lift me up. After a short time, Gina Kell approached me. I thanked her for coming. She too hugged me and told me that my remarks had touched her. I was glad about that.

Later, as most were still eating, I found my way back upstairs and into the sanctuary. It was mostly quiet now as I made my way up the long aisle. The huge centerpiece flowers were still on the table at the center of the altar up front. Underneath the flowers, discreetly placed and unknown to most in attendance that day, was the urn containing Cathy's ashes. I reached out a hand to touch it.

"You were wrong, my love," I said quietly. "You filled up a lot more than five pews today."

I left the sanctuary and stepped out to the parking lot to clear my head. It was cold and my coat was somewhere else, but I didn't mind. At least it was quiet. I squinted in the midday sun and put my hands in my pockets to shield them from the chill. Leaning against the brick wall of the church, I thought about things.

I couldn't believe this had happened. I hated this. This new life—our new normal. I wondered why he had given this to me. I knew that whatever *this* was, the really hard part was likely still to come.

I rested my head against the rough surface of the bricks for just a moment. I knew I had to get back inside. The kids would need me.

PART 3

the new day

CHAPTER 28

calling gina kell

michael

I'd been lying on the kitchen floor for a while. After driving the kids to school, I faced another day alone in the house and as soon as I closed the door behind me, I literally collapsed to the floor. At some point I tried to gather myself. I needed to get to work but couldn't quite seem to make it to my feet. Cathy surrounded me. She was everywhere I looked. Her chair at the dinner table, her coat in the closet, her hair in the brush, her ring, her soap, her pack of gum, her pillow, her magazines, her calendar, and a thousand other meaningless things that were connected to her.

It ravaged my soul; this pain that grabbed me by the throat and shook me like a rag doll. One minute she was here and the next ... "Where did you go!?" I screamed to the emptiness. Agony. And it was getting worse each minute. Just when I thought it had passed, it would wash over me again, relentlessly. I wailed and gagged on the hurt, and then it seemed to fold over onto itself, increasing in magnitude. I couldn't stop it. Like never before in my life, I needed to weep. It became so intense at times that I began to make unrecognizable sounds. Pain-filled, guttural sounds. The sounds of my own private hell. "Where did you go!!!?" I shrieked at the emptiness. Of course, there was no response. Only silence and the cold, hard floor.

The phone rang, and I was startled long enough to stop crying for a moment. The mundane sounds of everyday life had a way of jarring me back to sanity like some grief defibrillator. Caller ID told me it was Pastor

Karl Galik. I wanted to let the machine pick it up, but thought twice. I liked him. It wasn't easy for a pastor to impress a guy from Skeptic Valley, but this Galik fellow had been more than kind to all of us as he presided over Cathy's funeral. I gathered myself before picking up the phone, but knew that I couldn't clear all of the tears from my voice. I kept it brief but stayed on long enough for him to invite me to lunch.

Settling into a booth at the local Panera Bread, we sized each other up. I knew why we were there. The pastor had brought his emotional white gloves to see if my psyche needed a little therapeutic dusting. I was there to see if this man of the cloth was for real. After some pleasantries and a few bites of our sandwiches, he got down to it.

"I wanted to check in with you and see how things were going," he said.

Here we go, I thought. "Things are okay," I offered, and nothing more.

"Look, I understand if you don't want to talk to me. We don't know each other very well, and I'm prying a little here. But I do have some experience in this area, and I want to offer myself in fellowship to you if you could use it."

"I appreciate that," I said, still at arm's length.

He sensed that I needed more credential from him. He offered just the right one.

"You're from Chicago, right?"

"Yeah, the West Side," I told him.

"I'm from the South Side," he said. "Although I still bleed Cubbie blue."

I was warming a bit. A Chicagoan, and a Cubs fan. Hmm.

"I will ask you one thing. Obviously you can choose to talk to me or not. I really am interested in hearing about your family. If you don't want to talk, I understand. But if you do, I only ask one thing. Don't try to sell me any crap."

I stopped chewing in midbite. He knew that he had made an impression and went in for the kill.

"Tell me about Cathy. What was she like?"

That got me. People don't ask that simple question of widowed spouses. They should. Instead they talk about how sad it is that she's gone. They speak about her illness and her funeral, how shocking it all was. They ask about the kids and the future. Nobody asks me to talk about the love of my life. "Tell me about her," he said. That was it. We became friends at that moment.

We spoke for a long time that day, and again a week later. We began to have regular lunches together. His counsel to me was invaluable. We spoke a lot about grief. People grieve differently, he told me, and he wanted to know about mine.

"The pain is unbearable some days," I confided. I told him about the quiet of the house and the times when I couldn't stand up. I told him about the sounds that I made yelling at the emptiness. I told him about the tears that seemed to never stop.

"I saw a video once," I said, "of the waves coming ashore during the tsunami in the Indian Ocean.... Out of nowhere, on a clear sunny day, as people all around did normal things, this massive wall of water rushed over the beaches and into the streets and neighborhoods, destroying everything in its path and leaving behind only death and despair."

He nodded as I spoke.

"That's what it's like for me," I said.

I knew that all of this sounded like an exaggeration. It wasn't. So I explained further.

"There was a woman who sang in the choir at St. John and she sounded like ... well, like a turkey. She didn't sing so much as she warbled. This used to make Cathy and me laugh hysterically during church. And they kept giving this woman solos!"

Karl knew exactly of whom I was speaking. He laughed heartily.

"When she began to sing," I told him, "all I had to do was look at Cath and she giggled uncontrollably. It was our running joke."

I continued, telling him about the first time I heard the turkey woman sing after Cathy died.

"I could feel the tsunami wave coming straight at me. I told the kids I had to go to the bathroom. Instead I went outside and cried for twenty minutes."

We were quiet for a moment, then I added, "There's just no stopping it."

Being able to talk with Karl helped me tremendously. He counseled me with the lightest touch, not trying to browbeat me with Scripture verses or telling me how to live my life. He offered little prescriptive advice, opting to listen more than speak. On a few occasions, however, his carefully chosen words stopped me in my tracks.

"You know, Michael," he started. "You're not just grieving for the loss of Cathy. You lost someone else that day. You lost yourself. The man and husband you were when she was alive. I suspect you liked that guy."

"Yeah," I said. I was beginning to tear up now.

"Well," he said, "he's gone too now."

This hit me like a thunderclap. Cathy was my context. I missed being "us." We did things as a couple, we were known as a couple, and we had friends as a couple. But when the couple ceased to exist, so did I. I spent years becoming that guy. But he died with Cathy. I was going to have to get to know me, without her. Although I hated that notion, saying it out loud brought a measure of peace.

Pastor Galik asked me if I had called Gina Kell yet. Cathy's eyes flashed in my mind as I recalled her telling me that Gina and I would help each other. She was so determined, so sure.

"No," I said. "That woman's got enough to deal with."

Karl wouldn't let it go. "Cathy and I have something in common. We both knew Matt and Gina, and I wouldn't tell you to call her if I didn't think it would be helpful to you both."

He could see he was getting nowhere, so he tried to swing for the fences.

"Cathy didn't have many words left the day she told you to call Gina Kell. I don't think she would have wasted them."

I agreed to think about it. In the end my dilemma was solved for me when, after our first Sunday back at church since Cathy passed, I received an email from Gina Kell.

From: Gina
To: Michael Spehn
Subject: hello...
Hello Michael ...

I heard you were at church today.... I know how hard it can be to attend church ... not because you don't want to worship or draw near to God, but because people can very unintentionally overwhelm despite good intentions to comfort.

I would like to get together with you soon to talk. I have a few things to give you for the kids ... resources and such. You can email me or call ... my phone numbers are home 248-XXX-XXXX and cell 248-XXX-XXXX. I am reachable any time. ANY time.

Goodnight. Peace ... gina kell

I stared at that email for a very long time. First Cath, then Karl, and now the woman herself. I wrote back later that night.

"Thanks for the note. I was in church with the kids. It helps, I guess. Sometimes it feels like I'm the one who now has a terminal disease. Take care. Michael Spehn." Then I added, "PS, Careful about that 'call me any-time' stuff. My 'anytimes' these days are going well into the wee hours. Would love to talk sometime but you need to give me proper hours to call."

She shot back a few minutes later, "Anytime means anytime. If you think you're the only one up at three a.m., you're fooling yourself. gina."

I had been instructed, encouraged, and invited to call Gina Kell, but I still couldn't bring myself to pick up the phone. In the midst of my long days filled with medical bills, school schedules, and out-of-town visitors, making the call would cross my mind, but it just wasn't a matter of urgency.

I spent days looking through Cathy's things, her calendar and notebooks and even her purse. I spent an entire evening reading through her old emails on our computer. It was comforting to hear her voice through her sent email. I found an email trail from January between Cathy and Colleen Schomaker, where Cathy proposed inviting Gina and her boys to our house for pizza and fun.

"Pizza and letting the kids run wild in my basement might be a good get together," she wrote. That was Cathy. She wanted to bring people together and ease the pain of those who suffered. She wanted to fill her house with the sounds of children playing.

After reading through the emails, I realized that what she had said to me in the hospital was not completely out of the blue. I knew that calling Gina Kell was as much for Cathy as for me. I would honor her desires and fulfill her promise of love, life, and laughter. It might bring smiling children together in her house. And it could help me too. Simply doing what she asked me to do might make me feel closer to her. It wasn't what I wanted to do, and it wasn't "perfect" to me. But it was right. I picked up the phone.

Gina and I exchanged some small talk and then I asked her and the boys to join us for dinner. She immediately offered to cook, but I had a different plan. I told her of an experience that happened about a week after Cathy passed away.

I had received a phone call from my neighbor Ed, asking if I would be home around four o'clock.

"Sure, what's up?" I asked.

"Just open your garage door and leave it open the rest of the afternoon," he told me.

This was strange, but I followed Ed's instructions. Around 4:30 I heard a commotion in my driveway. Ed and two other neighbors were wheeling a large deep freezer toward my garage.

"This is yours," he told me, in take-charge mode. He and the others put the freezer against a wall in the garage and plugged it in. "There."

"Thank you," I said, thoroughly confused. "What's it for?"

"I know how you feel about those little red coolers, so everybody pitched in and got this for you. Now you can just keep meals frozen in here until you need them."

"That's great ... thank you. But I really don't have that much food to fill it up with."

"Yeah, I know," he said. "I've seen you cook. Don't worry. We've taken care of it. Just keep your garage door open."

Over the next two hours, one by one, more than twenty neighbors, some of whom I had never met, filled the freezer with home-cooked meals. Some came to the door with hugs and memories of Cathy. Others simply came and went without a word. The experience was an astonishing and overwhelming display of love and kindness. This was exactly what I needed. I could take care of my kids without having to worry about the next meal.

The thing that made it so ideal was that Ed knew exactly what I needed, and he knew exactly what I didn't want. Most importantly, he simply did it. He didn't ask, he didn't wring hands, he didn't call me with petty details. He simply took care of it. It was a perfect act of friendship I'll never forget.

Gina and I agreed to cook something from the freezer for our dinner together.

"Anything but a casserole!" she said with a quick laugh.

She insisted on bringing a salad, and we talked just long enough to set a date and time. I agreed to email her directions to my house. I hung up the phone and just stared at it a while.

I had called Gina Kell.

The kids were upstairs asleep. The house was quiet again. It was the time of day when my private tidal wave of sadness would soon begin its nightly swell. High tide in grief land was swiftly approaching.

I hunkered down.

CHAPTER 29

dinner with strangers

gina

After two months of receiving meals from friends, neighbors, and members of the church, I politely requested that people stop cooking for me. When politeness didn't work, I sent in Colleen, my consigliere, to get the job done. I could always count on her to represent me, even with delicate matters like telling people when enough is enough. I didn't want to seem ungrateful, but I was a widow, not an invalid. People weren't considering that I had been abruptly let go from my job as a caretaker. I needed to become productive and relevant again. Not being allowed to handle my own mundane tasks, especially the ones I happened to enjoy, was worse than being unemployed; I was starting to feel helpless and irrelevant.

Michael Spehn could relate. When he called to invite us to dinner, he told me about the brand-new freezer friends and neighbors had generously purchased and installed in his garage, stocked with enough meals for a month.

"What do your kids like? We have four casseroles, three lasagnas, and several unidentifiable chicken dishes. I'm like my own personal food bank," he kidded. We agreed that he would defrost a mystery chicken dish, and I would bring a salad.

Michael sent an email confirming our dinner plans, including directions to his house. The route took us directly past Stoney Creek Cemetery where Matt, along with a part of me, was buried. I sighed deeply as we drove by, and glanced in the rearview mirror, wondering if the boys remembered. They were quiet as I stared at the gates and spoke to Matt in my head. *I miss you. I love you. Going to see Cathy's family. Tell her I said hi. I can't believe you're gone. Where did you go?*

Michael and his three kids were waiting in the driveway to greet us. Drew and Sam immediately ran off to play with Charlotte, Jack, and Danny, and Michael helped me unload the car.

"What is all this?" he said, smiling. "You said you were bringing a salad."

"I did," I replied, handing him the fourth grocery bag from the trunk. I had packed up one mixed-greens salad, one fruit salad, three types of dressing, including all the ingredients for my homemade vinaigrette, a bag of dinner rolls, and a few gifts for the kids.

As we entered the mudroom, I noticed a dog bowl and a collar. "There must be a dog around here somewhere," I said, anticipating a crotch sniff.

"Not so much." Michael instantly tensed up. He stretched his neck around the corner to make sure the kids were out of sight and then mouthed the words, "The dog died," with a blank stare on his face. "I haven't told the kids."

"Oh my Lord God in heaven, have mercy," I blurted. My eyes widened, and then I did the unthinkable. I started to laugh. As if in a stunned stupor, he threw his hands up, shook his head, and started to laugh with me.

"I am totally inappropriate. I mean, this is not funny. I'm so sorry, but what else can you do?" I was fumbling for my words.

"I know. I know. It's ridiculous." The tone became more serious. "I can't bring myself to tell the kids. It's been six days, but I just can't do it."

He proceeded to tell me that Maggie, the dog, died of an abdominal tumor.

"While I was at the vet's office having her put to sleep, I walked into the lobby to try to make sense of what was happening. Sitting on the table was a front-page *Oakland Press* article featuring my family with a big photo of us with Maggie," he said.

"I remember seeing it."

"Everyone in the office started realizing it was me, and pretty soon people were in tears and trying to console me. All I kept thinking was 'How am I going to tell the kids?'"

He had been using every excuse he could think of, but Charlotte was missing her dog and becoming unsatisfied with Michael's stall tactics. Even at her young age, she knew something was up.

Their wife and mother had died of a brain tumor a few weeks ago and now the family dog. Two family members gone from their home just like that. Michael was beside himself, but in a very controlled way. He kept running his hand through his hair. I felt helpless, and for the first time I understood how everyone in my life must be feeling around me.

We stood at the kitchen island and talked about the dog and the kids and our lives. Sometimes it felt as though we were talking about other people. But this wasn't a headline in the newspaper. It was us. We both leaned on the island with our elbows, our body language screaming exhaustion and a need to be held up. Leaning in toward Michael, with the light coming from the windows behind me, his eyes seemed to change like a mood ring, becoming a more vibrant blue. In a quiet tone, he recounted Cathy's last days.

In the lulls of our conversation we could hear the kids playing in the basement. It was a refreshing sound. Once in a while, nine-year-old Charlotte appeared in the kitchen. It was obvious she wanted to be around her dad and the adult conversation. Michael gently asked her to "move along" a few times so that we could talk. While I understood asking the kids to leave the room, my heart didn't want to send Charlotte away. I wanted to hold that little girl and tell her that she would be okay without her mom. I couldn't help but wonder how my life would have been different without my mom, the person who knows me better than I know myself. I ached for Charlotte.

On her last trip into the kitchen, the four boys followed closely behind, begging Michael to play "Ball of Peril," a game exclusive to the Spehns. The energy and excitement in the room shifted, and now five kids were screaming and running around in a loop from room to room in anticipation of what came next. Drew and Sam had no idea what was going on, but they jumped right into the madness. Michael grabbed a beach ball that was tucked behind the couch, got on his knees, and started slapping it against the wall in the living room. He shouted hilarious danger warnings in an awful French accent, then he would flop to the ground as the kids screamed and ran past him trying to avoid being hit by the perilous flying beach ball!

"If the ball hits you, you must sit in the 'chair of doooom'!" Michael shouted.

No one made it to the notorious chair of doom because they all ended up climbing on Michael. Kids were sitting on his head, smacking his butt, tickling his feet, and "burfting" his belly with their mouths. He was a dad who got down on the floor, rolled around, and laughed louder than anyone, but he never ceased being the dad. It was obvious that Michael was an attentive father who had the respect of his children. He played with the kids, but he wasn't one of them. When he announced, "Game over," it was.

We transitioned into dinner with a buzz. The kids were giggly and punchy and I quickly regretted a candlelight dinner I had shared with Drew and Sam just a week earlier. The boys wanted to have a formal dinner, which I thought meant not sitting at the kitchen counter, but they wanted to sit at the table and have candlelight. I set the table with fancy dishes, complete place settings of flatware, and kiddie stemware, also known as brand-new Buzz Lightyear cups. I could tell by the looks on their faces that the boys thought it was pretty special. The candles mesmerized them.

I made linguini tossed with broccoli. We did a comparison to determine if slurping noodles was better than twirling the fork. I don't know if the broccoli had anything to do with what happened next, but our special evening turned into a full-blown farting and belching contest. We laughed hysterically, but what really put the boys over the edge was when I joined them. It's a little-known secret that the petite Valenti women can belch like a three-hundred-pound beer guzzler at a saloon. Both of the boys fell out of their chairs laughing. In all the fun, I had forgotten one important detail. It became painfully evident at the Spehns' dinner table that I failed to teach my children that this is not something we should do often, or in the presence of others. I had created monsters.

At our dinner with strangers, as if on cue, Sam let one rip at the table. The five kids erupted in laughter. Michael let out a surprised, "Well!" and I was horrified and amused at the same time. As I tried to scold Sam to engage his manners, my shoulders were shaking because I tried to repress my laughter. I couldn't help it. Gas is funny. It is the lowest common denominator for humor, I realize, but it was a wooden chair! The sound reverberated throughout the kitchen. The comic relief just kept coming as Charlotte accidentally squirted ranch dressing all over her shirt and pants. When she left to change clothes, Danny spilled his milk and it poured through the seams of the table onto the floor. In less than two hours, all pretense and politeness had gone out the window. We were just raw and real. First impressions were completely overshadowed by the practical realities of humanity.

After things quieted down a bit, I threw out a question to the kids, wanting to gauge how much they knew about each other.

"Does anyone know why we're having dinner together tonight?"

Jack answered enthusiastically, "Because we're new friends!"

"Exactly right," I said. That was the right answer for the moment. I should have known better than to attempt to tackle the elephant in the room when everyone was just getting to know each other. But at the same time, I wanted it known that we were all in the same boat. Michael and I had the benefit of that knowledge, and I wanted the kids to have it too. I had told Drew and Sam how the Spehns had experienced a loss like ours, but it wasn't on their radar in that moment. I left it alone, although I was disappointed. They needed to know that they were not alone. I wanted them to know that we understood.

In the short time we had been together, Michael and I shared tears, laughter, and embarrassment. We grieved together, played together, and dined together. And then it came time to do the dishes. Together. Or so I assumed. I started clearing the table and rinsing the dishes. It's my Pavlovian response to my last bite of food.

"No, please don't," Michael politely insisted, trying to close the dishwasher.

"What's the problem?" I said casually, looking him in the eye as I put my knee on the dishwasher door to hold it open. My display of defiance seemed to amuse him.

"You're not doing the dishes," he said, shutting off the water.

"Oh, but I am! See!" I continued loading the dishwasher and smiling.

"No one does the dishes in my house, especially not guests."

"Clearly, someone does do the dishes, and after what we just went through at the dinner table, we no longer qualify as guests. I wouldn't leave Colleen's house without doing the dishes, so why would I leave yours?"

This comparison to my best friend gave him pause and seemed to put him at ease. When I confessed that I, too, had requested that people stop "helping me," he knew that letting me do the dishes wasn't charity or an admission of weakness. And it certainly wasn't robbing him of something he loved to do. It felt like I had been playfully arguing with someone I'd known for a hundred years. It wasn't awkward or tense. It was everyday comfortable. I hadn't had an exchange like that in months. It energized me and made me feel alive. Michael relented and let me finish loading the dishwasher while he prepared dessert.

"Are those brownies?" I asked, knowing the answer.

"My grandmother's recipe. I made them from scratch," he said proudly.

"Wow. Impressive!" Michael looked pleased with himself. "Oh, no frosting on mine, please," I said as he held a glob of chocolate on a knife.

"Really? But this is Grandma Mayzie's famous buttercream frosting."

"I like an unadulterated brownie. I'm a purist," I said, certain that I didn't want frosting.

"Oh, c'mon, you've got to just try a bite!"

I had to admit, the frosting looked pretty good. It obviously wasn't Pillsbury out of a plastic can. I took a baby step, agreeing to half with, half without.

The kids were back in the basement and it was just the two of us with our brownies. We talked about what our new sudden reality had done to our perceptions of the world. And also how we were being perceived by the world. In the midst of suffering, loss, and grief, it is impossible to explain how you feel from moment to moment, yet the overriding question people ask is, "How are you doing today?" When you are numb, there are no words to convey what you feel. It was comforting to know that I didn't need any with Michael Spehn. After a long silence I commented, "That was the best frosting I've ever had on a cake or a brownie. You converted me."

As if he hadn't heard me, Michael looked up and asked, "How is it that you are here, sitting on my couch tonight?"

I stopped eating my brownie. We were two grieving people who needed to be known, not fixed. For the first time in my life, I was in a place of great need, and sitting across from me was my mirror image in Michael Spehn. I didn't know how I got there. I wanted to reach out and help him, but he was merely my reflection, suspended between the past and the future. I hadn't a need or a want but to be left alone to heal, and that was exactly how my mirror image felt. As I sat and stared into the mirror, it became clear.

"By the grace of God," I whispered. There was no other explanation.

Before heading home, we presented the Spehn kids with journal notebooks, like the ones Drew and Sam had been given by the Schomakers. We wrote, "For memories and thoughts of my mom" on the covers. This gesture opened the door for us to share our loss with them. They seemed surprised and comforted to know that they were not alone. Charlotte remained quiet but seemed more at ease. She hugged me before we walked out the door.

I quietly cried as we drove past the cemetery on the way home.

CHAPTER 30

you can't do this alone

michael

Life was different in almost every way. One of the more significant ways was the fact that my dad was back in our lives. The kids loved having their Hoke back. He called several times a week. He sent gifts and cards. (The thought of Dick Spehn actually shopping in a Hallmark store made me smile.) We spoke often. I called him after the kids went to sleep and vented about life's inconsequential things that were getting to me. He also came to visit several times that first year.

From: hoke
Subject: Re: misc
To: mspehn

It is difficult. Reminds us of how fast tragedy can strike, how very mortal we are. Some have said, in talking with me, that they question why God "let it happen." The very question is an answer in itself. The "load" is very heavy and needs to be shared in some way. One reason why I am very proud of your brothers and sister for their willingness to take some of the "load" on their shoulders.

A word ... If you feel that my presence will help the kids in any way, just holler. When all this happened I said I would be there for them and you and I meant it. As long as I can still move, I can be wherever is necessary, whenever it is necessary. Your Call!!

Dad

It was nothing short of a miracle that Dad and I were back in each other's lives. There was a twinge of guilt that came with that though. Why did it have to take a death in the family to bring us closer again? Would we ever have reconciled without that death? That thought haunted me.

My sister, Lynn, said it was like Dad's heart grew back again.

"Like the Grinch," she said. "In the Christmas movie."

In so many ways she was right. Dad seemed to be a new man. He was infinitely more patient than I had ever seen him be. He was softer in his approach to life. He seemed to not only notice the little things in life but also appreciate them. He had become sentimental and comfortable expressing those sentiments.

From: hoke
Subject: Re: misc
To: mspehn

I remembered the "moments" that I had with Cathy ... the very memorable moments ... all that has come and gone since. I am sure that she would be proud of the job you have done. It has been incredible really.

Certainly one to make a father proud.

She was right, "Michael is strong."

Dad

When Cathy passed away, several people stepped forward with suggestions on what I should do. On several occasions there was talk of everyone's new role. Cathy's mom, Jill, wanted to take over a lot of the basic "mom chores" of our family. I resisted. I grew frustrated with the blurry lines defining everyone's "new roles."

I was adamant that each of us remain in our same role. We were missing Cathy but I was still going to be Dad. I had some new chores to do but I didn't have a "new role." Neither did anyone else in our lives. Cathy's death seemed to throw everyone into a tailspin. Grandparents, aunts and uncles, even neighbors all seemed confused about what they should "do" when it came to the kids.

I think it had something to do with the fact that I'm a man. If Cathy, the mom, had been left behind, everyone would be confident in her ability to handle the home. Dinners, laundry, school volunteerism, etc., would be in good hands. The aunts and uncles of the world would likely show up and take the kids to ball games and out for ice cream. Because I was a man, I think the collective opinion was "He can't do this alone ..." and the "this" was primarily related to the home. Apparently I didn't inspire confidence when it came to making meals, changing sheets, staying current with the kids' homework, and the like. Everyone seemed to show up randomly ready to help out, which should sound great, except when you're a man—especially a stubborn one like myself—you don't want people from all sides telling you what to do. To me, everyone wasn't helping me; they were letting me know I was doing it all wrong.

In the midst of it all I'm sure I handled some things wrong. I know I could've been more gracious with those willing to help. It just was unsettling to come home and realize that your mother-in-law had been there ... and she folded your underwear!

Something more was buried deep down in there that took me awhile to understand. My job as husband and father was to provide for and protect my family. For nearly thirteen years, that is what I did. Then one night, a thief named cancer came into my home and stole Cathy from us. And I didn't stop it. I failed at protecting our family from this evil. Now everyone seemed to be saying that I wasn't capable of doing these other jobs either. I responded like most men in that situation: I circled the wagons and tried not to let anyone in.

One suggestion that persisted was that I move to Chicago to be closer to family. I could keep my job and travel as normal. My sister, Lynn, and sister-in-law, Patti, would be nearby to help with the kids. Patti had raised three fantastic boys and Lynn was a wonderful and capable aunt, so while the idea had some merit, I was steadfast in my desire to keep things as "normal" as possible for the kids.

For months I was bombarded with ideas and suggestions and offers of help from all sides. My instincts, honed by a lifetime of watching the two finest fathers of all time (my father and my brother Rick) do it, told me to guard the kids closely and keep their interests above all others. I may not have known the answer to the question, "What are you going to do now?" but I was starting to see clearly what I was *not* going to do.

My responses to ideas like these became consistent and firm.

From: hoke
Subject: Re: misc
To: mspehn
There are lots of opportunities to make changes in your schedule that are worth considering from time to time. For instance a move to Chicago.

There are real advantages to such a move. You would have Lynn and Patti available for situations that you related to in your e-mail. Lynn has it pretty well defined, i.e. you need "stop-gap" people available that would allow you to work well, rest well, and have a life of your own. I do believe that it may warrant further talk when we are together at Thanksgiving. Everyone has the same priorities, i.e. what is best for those kids, your general good health, and a good life for all of you. Once again, it is YOUR CALL ... there are lots of opinions around as to what is best for all.

Dad

From: mspehn
Subject: Re: misc
To: hoke
   No.

From: hoke
Subject: Re: misc
To: mspehn
   Never let it be said that you are a wordy fella. Good enough.

Dad

It was time to take a step forward. I had worked as a franchise consultant since moving to Michigan. The travel required with that job was not going to be possible anymore. I needed to create a different life for us, starting with my career.

For years, while I worked my day job in the franchising world, I slowly nurtured a passion for photography. Beginning around 1994, I developed an interest in Adobe Photoshop, the photo enhancement software. Soon I was attending Photoshop conventions and studying for tests to become certified —I was completely immersed in it. However, because I had a day job, this passion would have to remain a glorified hobby for the time being.

I decided to talk over my decision with Gina Kell. Together we processed through the challenges and risks of starting a new business, but in the end, she enthusiastically agreed that I should pursue my dream. She offered to help in any way she could, and within a few weeks, Spehn Photography & Design was born.

Getting a small business off the ground in southeast Michigan during a recession was hard. Trying to come up with three meals a day, keep up with the laundry, and handle the paperwork that comes home from school for three children under ten years old was impossible. Each day around 5:00 p.m., it hit me that I needed to prepare something for dinner. Which means that I should have *shopped* for something for dinner prior to this moment!

Our dining room became the dumping ground for all things school. With three kids bringing home projects, homework papers, permission slips, volunteer sign-up sheets—more every day!—I could not keep up. I developed a "system." If it didn't have to be dealt with immediately, I would put it into the dining room. Soon the stacks resembled our own paper Stonehenge; a monument to procrastination. It was really quite beautiful when the light hit it just right.

One evening, I was preparing another gourmet dinner (of chicken tenders and french fries) and I noticed the three kids huddled together in the living room. They were working on something and clearly didn't want me to see it. Yet.

After dinner, they presented me with their work. A handwritten contract they prepared for me to sign. It read, "I, Daddy Spehn, promise to never, ever, forever, marry again. But, only if you ask your darling three children, Charlotte, Jack and Dan, and they agree. If you, Dad Spehn, marry without our approval, you will have to face us crying, mad, shouting and more."

I considered having my lawyer, Dan Pelekoudas, review this contract, but in the end, I signed it with a laugh. The kids were all smiles. Charlotte especially seemed at ease.

Several months after Cathy passed, I was walking through the hallway at church. I noticed Mike Schomaker with two of his three kids at the drinking fountain. He was struggling to organize them all and, though he was smiling, I could tell he was losing his patience. I realized that his wife, Colleen, was with all of the other mommies at a women's retreat in central Michigan. He was alone—with the kids!

I couldn't resist giving him a little jab. "I see a man whose wife is out of town," I said with a smirk.

Mike was good-natured about it and (half) joked back. "I only have to make it another three hours. She's back after lunch, so just one more meal!"

We had a laugh about it. As I walked past Mike and the puddle of water at his feet, I couldn't help think, "Welcome to my world."

From: mspehn
Subject: Re: misc

To: hoke

Dad

Things are pretty crazy here. School is in full swing. The kids seem happy where they are. They get a lot of attention and care. Charlotte is loaded with homework each night. I have to help her with math especially.

Lots of missing Cath going on now. The kids have moved into a phase of "Dad, can we talk about mom?" Then we do for a half hour or so. Lots of crying still—lots of "why." Danny is moving into a tough phase. He is verbalizing more and missing Cathy so much right now. It is hardest for him at night when he is extra tired. I try to be that comfort to him—that soft, head-petting parent, and not the harsh father who always yells. We both know it's not the same though. He needs his mom.

It is going to be very tough to stay on schedule. There is very little margin for error right now. The pace here is staggering. With all of the above, laundry, groceries, cooking, cleaning the house, staying on top of the outdoors stuff, making sure the kids have winter things and not summer things, dealing with the extra school functions practices, assemblies, teacher conferences, half-days/day offs, etc.

When "hiccups" occur it gets extra hard. I hope the kids are ok. I try to stay positive for them but I know that I am not 100%. I realized the other day that, since Cathy passed away, I have not had so much as a cold. I have been so lucky.

For now—got to go.

                                                  M

I began to get a couple of clients for the new business and I settled into some routines at home. The kids were simply unbelievable in their patience with their new circumstances, and with me. They loved each other and trusted me and remained faithful to God. They talked about Cathy often. "That's Mom's favorite song," "Mom loves mushroom chicken," etc. I always encouraged that and never corrected their tense. It kept her close and present. I was in awe of how strong they were.

Those telling me, "You can't do this alone," didn't really get it. It was true that I was the only one wrinkling the laundry or burning the dinner, but I wasn't alone.

From: hoke
Subject: Re: misc
To: mspehn

We advance into each new day with some fear and dread. As we age, we experience more of the joy and the grief that all living holds for us. Too bad that the grief most often leaves a deeper mark, often filled with anger, whys, and terrible loneliness. Just as when our children are born and in our joy we wonder, with some fear, what the future holds, it is when we come face to face with death, the ending, that our wonder is deeper, our fear more personal and very mortal.

The new year will come, as will a second new year and another after that. Your children will bring to you new joys, new laughter, moments of unbelievable sweetness. Within that framework, I, as your father, hope you take time to realize a very real life of your own, a life that your children will be proud to share. The life with Cathy is behind you, like a beautiful sunset, and you and the kids move on to your happiness that awaits. You do not forget those beautiful colors. They make up the sweet part of your life, the memories. They are there for your "Decembers" when you will need the sight and smell of your "rose."

You and the kids have a vault full of roses. They are there forever even as they dim. Use them as needed. I promise you that the enormous love and caring that you share with your children will see you through any pain, any grief, any loneliness. Your family is rich and alive with love, and *that* is Cathy's legacy.

Do not fail her.

Love

                                    Dad

I'd never heard my dad speak this way. This was not the same man I grew up with. I believe that it wasn't a death that ultimately transformed him. It was love that softened his hard heart and put those beautiful words into his mouth.

He wrote, "Your family is rich and alive with love ..." He was right. But that wasn't just Cathy's legacy. It was his as well.

CHAPTER 31

working mom

gina

Six years after I resigned from my position as an account executive at the local CBS television affiliate, I reentered the workplace as a receptionist in the school office at St. John. The security of making a living while being near my kids was the comfort I needed for my new status as a single working mom. I wore a headset for answering phones and had a sliding glass window in front of my desk.

I sat adjacent to beloved receptionist Sheri Aman, the eyes and ears of St. John. She knew everyone's name and story. Most of my on-the-job training was spent observing her interactions with students, faculty, and guests. She tended to kindergarteners with tummy aches and eighth graders with attitudes, all with the same grace and humor.

I had developed decent "people skills" working in sales, but when it came to remembering hundreds of students, all dressed in identical school uniforms, I couldn't seem to get the gears in motion. I once confused Haley with Riley and called the wrong mom to pick up her sick daughter! Thankfully I worked in a forgiving environment.

The biggest adjustment to my new position was figuring out the tricked-out office machines that could fold paper any which way short of origami. When I started taking notes to help me remember how to use the Xerox machine, Sheri gave me a sideways look.

"Did you really work at a television station?"

"I sold air!" I said in my defense. "There were no mechanical skills required!"

When I discovered that the postage machine not only stamped the letters but also sealed them, I asked the obvious question, "Why am I even needed?"

"You're pretty much here just to undo paper jams," Sheri teased.

My job had little to do with temperamental equipment and everything to do with serving our community. Sorting mail and answering phones were secondary to bringing smiles and solutions to every person who approached our window.

The first several months I worked in the office, I had what felt like a personal drive-thru therapy window. Many acquaintances, and a few strangers who had known Matt, stopped to offer consolation or ask about the kids. Sheri was patient, graciously covering the phones during more than a few unusually long and even emotional conversations.

My favorite visitors were those who shared stories about Matt and the impact he had on their lives. Those exchanges were like gifts to me, yet there never seemed to be enough. It was surprising how many people avoided or hesitated to speak Matt's name. To a grieving person, there is no sweeter sound than the name of the one they grieve.

After school hours, I was working alone in the office when Larry Lutz appeared at my window. I hadn't seen him since Cathy's funeral. We exchanged pleasantries and Larry mentioned that he and Jill were planning to move up to Mullett Lake permanently.

"Don't worry," I said, "I'll make sure Charlotte, Jack, and Danny stay out of trouble while they're in school."

Larry and I shared comforting stories about our memories of Matt and Cathy. I told him about the first time I met her in the St. John atrium, just outside the office door where I now sat. Larry shared a story about coaching Matt's winning eighth-grade softball team. Our conversation quickly turned to grief, our common ground, and we began validating one another.

"You know what I find so difficult?" he asked. "No one seems to want to talk about Cathy."

"I know what you mean. They think they are protecting you from heartache."

"It's disappointing," he said sadly.

"It's tough, Larry. People just don't understand."

"No, they really don't," he agreed, and quickly changed the subject. "I hear you've been helping Charlotte with her new contact lenses."

"I'm glad to do it. It's a big transition from glasses."

I didn't mention how much I loved that Charlotte came to my window whenever she needed help. Since the first time we met, I hoped for any connection with her. Those opportunities increased when Michael and I began volunteering together on a project to update the atrium at St. John.

For many years I used my advertising background to serve the church and school, but we always lacked two critical ingredients: a budget and a graphic designer. When I was approached by the leadership team at St. John about a substantial project to "give life" to the atrium, I jumped at the chance. They had a budget. All I needed was a graphic designer. I immediately thought of Michael for the project, not only because he had the design background, but also because I knew that, like me, he had a strong desire to give something back to the community that had given so much to his family. In one phone call he understood the vision and shared my desire to use this project as an outlet for gratitude to our St. John family.

We brainstormed over sandwiches at Panera Bread and met with church leaders to present our ideas for softening the brick-and-mortar feel of the atrium. We focused on what church is all about: people. Michael coined the phrase "the Living Mural," and this became the name of the project. Phase one was planned as a mosaic using images of all sizes, representing the history and service of St. John's people. We planned phase two as an abstract work of art filled with symbolism designed to reveal something new each time it was viewed.

The Living Mural became a new focal point for Michael and me and provided a perfect excuse to get together with our kids. We'd spend thirty minutes or less talking about the project and hours getting to know each other's kids, processing our losses and revealing our histories. Sometimes the weight of our conversations was too much, but Michael's sense of humor provided a perfect balance. Once in a while the sound of my own laughter caught me off guard. I wasn't sure that it was okay to laugh so loud, but I knew it felt good.

One beautiful afternoon on our way home from the Spehns' house, I turned into Stoney Creek Cemetery. Matt's headstone had been in place for several weeks and I decided it was the right time to show Drew and Sam their father's grave site.

We approached Matt's grave and Sam went right to the headstone and sat down in front of it. Drew began wandering and taking note of our surroundings.

"There are a lot of dead people in here," Drew said plainly.

We calculated the math on several headstones and noticed many young people, including children.

"That kid was eight!" he said, surprised. "Look, Mom. That was a baby! What happened to him?"

"I don't know," I replied.

I wanted to have all the answers for my kids, but standing in a cemetery a few yards from their father's grave, I began to feel helpless.

"Sometimes, we just don't get to know."

Sam sat cross-legged and traced every letter on the headstone with his finger. He asked me to tell him the story of the caterpillar and the butterfly. Midway through, Drew came back from wandering.

"I want to go home."

"Come sit with us, Drew," I said, pulling him close.

The boys sat on my lap together and we talked about Matt, the beauty of the day, and the peacefulness of cemeteries. They had endless questions but I had almost no answers. I tried to think of what Matt would say and reminded the boys that when we don't know, we just have to trust God. The boys sat still in my arms for a long time and I rocked them.

"Ya know what I think when I look around here? We're not alone. There must be a lot of people who feel the same way we do."

"Like the Spehns?" Drew said.

"Exactly."

My words made me think about my conversation with Larry Lutz several weeks earlier. I may have been wrong. People do understand. We are surrounded by so many, silent and heartbroken, who long to hear the names of the ones they grieve.

Sam lay down on the grass and quietly cried. I stroked his head while Drew remained restless.

"Can we go *now*?"

"No!" Sam said.

He didn't want to leave, but I scooped him up in my arms and promised to bring him another day.

"Can we have ice cream?" he asked.

"You bet."

CHAPTER 32

turquoise lake

gina

It was my first trip to Colorado since Matt died. My parents invited the boys and me to join them at their condo in Beaver Creek. Drew and Sam were out of school for the summer, and I was ready to escape Rochester for a while. This was going to be *my* vacation, my opportunity to take a deep breath and get reacquainted with my sons without the distractions of home. I hadn't anticipated that my parents had other ideas.

In their desire to help me, they offered to take the boys to see the sights, or sign them up for day camp so I could have some alone time. The truth was, more than anything, I just wanted to be with my kids. I had been passing them off to friends and family for three years. With Matt headlining the Cancer World Tour, I was functioning as his stage manager, and we had doctors to see and treatment protocols to follow. As much as we tried to maintain balance during that time, the kids often came second. There, I said it. The kids came second. This was my struggle and my heartbreaking reality, and a huge source of my volley with God. As hard as I tried to strategize our lives and make a happy home, cancer trumped everything. I needed to make up for lost time.

At the urging of my parents, I attempted to unwind with some early morning hikes, but I wasn't getting the usual refreshment from my time in the mountains. Instead, I was pushing myself along until my lungs burned.

My typical easygoing style became a rush to the finish, and the joy of hiking escaped me.

My desire to be more agreeable was not always reflected in my attitude. In fact, I was perpetually annoyed. I have come to learn that being annoyed at others rarely has anything to do with them. It almost always has everything to do with me. I was frustrated by the general lack of understanding for my wants and desires, which, by the way, I never clearly expressed, nor could I, given that I didn't really know what they were. I simply expected everyone to recognize and navigate my moods.

My dad always had a plan for having a good time, and for the first thirty-five years of my life, I was fairly agreeable to his plans. If he sensed hesitation or resistance, he jumped into salesman mode. It began the same way every time: "This will change your life!" he said as he popped the side of his fist with an open hand.

Throughout our week in Colorado, however, I was interested only in my own plans. Yes, my parents invited me, but this was my trip, with my boys, to my favorite place. Therefore, in my mind, the plans were all mine too. Perhaps I should have conveyed this, but instead, every time my father made a suggestion, I snapped back with a reply to the negative. In my grief and adjustment to being a single parent, I needed to make my own way. Regrettably, I chose a family vacation in Colorado to make this stand, and I did it in a way that seemed ungrateful and dismissive of all that my parents had done for us.

At the end of our first week, my sister, Tara, and her husband, Bob, arrived, the kids were having a blast, and I hadn't even begun to unwind. If anything, the coils were wound even tighter. I found myself obsessing about a hike to a place I had found on the trail map called Turquoise Lake. The name alone intrigued me, so I inquired about it at the Beaver Creek Hiking Center. They strongly suggested I not hike it alone. It was four miles past my usual destination of Beaver Lake, which was a stunning, steel blue mountain lake at 8,000 feet, the kind of place that could find its way into a John Denver song. I had made the three-mile trek to Beaver Lake several times over the years, but I was intrigued by the thought of a new destination; something farther, more challenging, and possibly more beautiful. I needed to see Turquoise Lake with my own eyes.

To get to this mountain Shangri-la, I would have to venture outside of the Beaver Creek ski boundary, to 11,000 feet, along a trail maintained by the U.S. Forest Service. Apparently, that meant that the quality of the trails and terrain would be uncertain. None of that mattered to me. I needed to find a hiking partner.

My mom had been to Colorado with me enough times to know that hiking was my passion. Even when I attended Horsemanship Week at Lost Valley Ranch, I'd skip full days of riding with my mom just so I could take all-day guided hikes. While she appreciates my interest in hiking and enjoys some herself, my mom had absolutely no interest in going to Turquoise Lake. For her, the thought of becoming the Blue Plate Special for some grizzlies at 10,000 feet was enough to scare her off.

"A single mom should not be taking risky hikes," she scolded me. "It's irresponsible. What about bears?"

"What about bears!" I shot back. "I would never hike it alone, Ma. C'mon. You raised me better than that!"

"If you can find someone to go with you, it would be okay, but I don't like it."

I hoped that Tara and Bob might be up for it, but they weren't interested either. I started asking random people along the trails and at the Hiking Center. I couldn't find an interested party for a fourteen-mile hike. I resigned myself to the fact that I would not be making the trek.

On the last day of our vacation, Tara and Bob offered to take Drew and Sam out for a couple of hours so I could take one last hike. I filled my backpack with the usual stuff, but before I got to the door, I stopped, went back into the kitchen, and grabbed four additional bottles of water and a protein bar. My pack was heavy but I didn't care. In the back of my mind I had hope for a new adventure. This would be my last hike for some time and I wanted to be prepared for anything.

I savored my time along the trail, taking it slow and documenting every butterfly and bridge. The path was quiet and serene. And familiar. When I arrived at Beaver Lake, I walked around and attempted to capture its beauty on camera. Impossible. I found a spot on a log and sat resting in the quiet. Just then I noticed a man and woman, probably in their early twenties, having lunch. Both had blond hair, blue eyes, and matching blue resort staff shirts. I wandered over to them.

"Have either of you ever been to Turquoise Lake?"

"Funny you should ask. We are heading there today," the man answered.

"Seriously?" My face lit up and I started to laugh. "I have been wanting to go there all week and I couldn't find anyone to go with me."

I decided to press my luck. "Would you mind if I tagged along? I won't hold you up, I'll just follow behind."

"Sure, no problem."

I knew it! I felt it in my bones before I left. I was giddy with excitement albeit somewhat concerned, but I was unable to check in with my family. I resigned myself to the fact that it would be an "ask forgiveness later" situation. I would be gone at least three hours longer than I had planned, and my parents, in particular my mom, would likely be furious. If the bears didn't eat me, I'd certainly be killed when I got home.

I tried to call, but apparently the "middle of nowhere" is not a big market for the folks at Verizon. I began to rationalize and offer myself some comfort at the same time. Surely everyone would realize that I found a way to Turquoise Lake. It was all I had talked about all week. I could not pass up this opportunity. I had to take it. I was so excited.

The next two hours I weaved my way through the forest. The path was narrow and steep in some places and the terrain was far more rugged than the lower half of the Beaver Lake trail. I had fun crossing over bridges made of tree trunks and climbing through heavy brush and along boulder fields to find where the trail picked up. I documented as much as I could, including videotaping my new friends for proof. At thirty-six I still needed a good reason to break curfew. There is no cure for first-born syndrome.

"Audrey! John! Wave to the camera so I can show my parents that I was responsible!"

We all had a good laugh, but it was only funny because it was true. They knew I was freaked out. John and Audrey, whom I later discovered were brother and sister, stopped a few times to catch their breath along the way. I had been hiking for nearly four hours. Though I tried to keep a brave face, I was grateful for the rest. The hike was more difficult than I imagined. Our pace was steady and challenging, the air, thinner and thinner. I tried to eat a protein bar but it was difficult to walk, chew, and breathe at the same time. We approached a large meadow adorned with patches of snow and wildflowers, like a visual overture to Turquoise Lake.

We climbed up the south side of the ridge. I could see the snowcapped mountains that surrounded the Turquoise Lake basin. Audrey and John were ahead of me, as they had been the entire trip. We made our way over the low ridge and a wave of sadness came over me. Although the journey had been incredibly demanding, I didn't want it to be over. I slipped a few times and had cuts and bruises on my arms and legs, but I could have gone farther. I wanted to go farther.

My legs were tired and heavy. There was silence, but for the sound of my last few steps. I had made it to Turquoise Lake. My throat tightened, making it difficult to catch my breath. I had been waiting for this moment. The mystery was over. All that was left was stillness and beauty. Tears began to flow freely.

It had taken over three years to get to this place. I knelt down and touched the surface of the water with my fingers, watching the ripples unfold into the lake.

"Good-bye, Matt," I whispered. I had fulfilled my promise.

This wasn't about a hike. It was the convergence of my past and my future. It was reflective of my time in the wilderness and the new path that I would forge with God. He and I were having it out on that mountain. I carried my grief and my fear, and my failings as a wife and a mother. But more important than what I brought to that place is what I would carry back.

The lake was not turquoise; it was midnight blue leaning to black. At 11,000 feet I was not having a mountaintop experience; rather, I was standing at the foot of a basin. Not what I imagined. I wandered through the forest, trying to follow the path before me through the fallen trees and unpredictable terrain, all the while guided by not one but two guardian angels. It was all so unexpected. It was invigorating.

"Gina, look! Top of the ridge!" John loudly whispered, pointing toward the northeast side.

A mountain lion was sauntering along the ridge. I took a deep breath, but I was not afraid. I considered it a privilege to be in the home of this elusive and majestic creature. Before I could snap a photo, he swiftly slipped down the back side of the ridge.

I thanked John and Audrey for safely guiding me and we parted ways. I headed back alone and as much as I could, I ran. I was focused for the seven-mile jaunt down the mountain. Downhill is significantly easier, although not without its dangers. Momentum got the best of me and I tripped a few times, but I didn't stop. I had to get back. Excitement laced with fear kept me running.

I hit send on my cell phone forty times trying to get a signal. The moment I did, my sister answered the phone. It was worse than I thought. My hope of sharing the meaning and depth of this experience was erased in one call. I had disappointed and angered my family.

When I got in the door, my mom would not look at me or speak to me. With tears in his eyes Drew asked, "Why were you gone so long, Mom? No one knew where you were."

Tara and Bob were shaking their heads, wanting to understand me, but I had worried them and robbed them of a day of their vacation. They expressed more disappointment than anger. My dad was great. He supported my mom's position but also pulled me aside privately.

"How was it?" he asked with a glint in his eye. "I'll bet it was stunning."

"It was, Dad. It was the hardest hike I've ever made, but it was worth all of it. Even this." There was a long pause. I continued, "Thank you for asking. I'm sorry that I worried everyone. I knew it as I was heading up the mountain. I had to make a decision in the moment and I went for it."

"I would have done the same thing," he said. "Your mother is going to need a few days to get over this one. But she'll get over it." These are the moments when I am my father's daughter.

Dinner was very quiet. My dad was the neutralizer. After the kids were tucked into bed, I made small talk with Tara and Bob. My mom declared that she was not ready to speak to me. I was a selfish brat who thought of no one but herself. It stung. I had many apologies to make to my family, but not once did I try to offer an explanation. My apologies felt hollow in light of their disappointment and anger. The irony was that I had finally unwound, for the first time in two weeks. Or was it three years?

I left the condo to call Michael from the courtyard, where massive flowerpots lined the walks. The sky was pink and periwinkle at dusk and the cool air smelled clean. I couldn't wait to tell him about my hike, and unload a bit of my guilt about hurting my family. I told him about every breathtaking step. Michael listened to me prattle on for a long while. When I finally took a breath and gave him a chance to speak, his words were brief and insightful.

"I can hear it in your voice, G. You sound great. I'm sorry about the stuff with your family. You know, you *were* selfish today. But I'm proud of you. For the first time in over three years you put yourself first. I know how hard that is for you."

I cried quietly on my end of the phone. He had touched a nerve. Today began my journey back. My identity died with Matt. I couldn't remember myself before him, and I could hardly remember our life before cancer. I knew one thing for certain. I was a mom. Beyond that, I was lost.

I was literally guided to a place that reflected the fulfillment of my promise to Matt, and it became a symbol of renewal for me. I found myself beside quiet waters at Turquoise Lake, being restored. I said good-bye to Matt, yet he remains alive and vital in my life. I carried back the lessons he taught me throughout our marriage. They run deep and I struggle to share them, but as much as I can, I will wear them in my thoughts, words, and actions like a robe of honor and remembrance.

Michael and I talked for a long time as we always did, comforting each other, laughing, reassuring. The night sky became the color of Turquoise Lake, and the stars emerged brilliant. Nothing was as I had imagined or planned, but I realized that I was beginning to feel something I hadn't for a long time. Hope.

CHAPTER 33

because she knows

michael

"Whoa!"

I yelled, rubbing my eyes as I walked out of my office.

"What?" Gina looked around. She was in jeans and a hooded sweatshirt with the arms pushed up to the elbows. Her hair was pulled back and messy in a cute kind of way. She had music playing, a pan of garlic sautéing, and she looked incredibly happy.

"My eyes are burning!" I rubbed them vigorously.

"Well then, it looks like I've done my job. My grandma would be proud!"

"My God, it's like some sort of Italian weapon of mass destruction went off in here," I said, playing it up.

"Oh, come on ... it's just a little garlic." Gina was starting to laugh at me. "It's good for the soul!"

"Well, there won't be any vampires here tonight, that's for sure." I looked around at what used to be a perfectly good WASP-y kitchen that now looked more like a Fellini movie. Gina grew self-conscious as I began touring the mess.

"I'm cooking," she said, stating the obvious with such quiet contentment that I put away the next four or five punch lines I had locked and loaded. She was at ease in my kitchen, instinctively knowing where to find things that I didn't know even existed. She started up a small machine that made a horrible grinding noise. I came up behind her and peered over her shoulder. I went back to my sarcasm.

"Are you mixing grout for the tile?"

"It's a food processor, you goof. I'm chopping onions for the sauce. Take cover!"

Her hair had fallen over her eyes, and she tried to tuck it behind her ears with her forearm because her hands were covered with onion and garlic. I moved in close and gently brushed the strands away from her eyes. "I hope you understand, this smell is never going to come out of these walls."

She just smiled. "That's the whole point."

We both moved around each other in the small space of the kitchen. We laughed and flirted and I made fun of her Italian heritage. She gave me a little bump with her hip.

"Move along. I want to cook and you're distracting me."

"Move along?"

"Yes, move along."

"*I'm* the one who says 'move along.' People don't tell me to move along ..."

"I know. How does it feel?" She was smiling but never stopped her work.

"Not very good, I will tell you ..."

"Okay then, seriously, skedaddle! The sauce needs my undivided attention."

"I need to take cover from your next pan full of onions anyway," I said as she raised a ladle in my direction.

I retreated back to my home office, pausing just inside the door to take it all in. There was a woman in the kitchen—Cathy's kitchen—and she was cooking for my family. This was strange to consider. For the first time in the months since Cathy passed away, I felt okay. More than that, I felt normal. Being around Gina made me feel more like a man again. I liked making her laugh. I liked that she was cooking for me. I liked the intimacy that was building between us.

The sounds and smells that continued to fill my home that day were glorious. It is often said that animals mark their territory by urinating on a particular area of the forest. This makes it "theirs." Likewise, Italian women mark their territory with sauce, garlic, fresh basil, and mozzarella.

Dinner, of course, was out of this world. The girl can cook, that's for sure. We finished dinner and the Kells went home. As I put my kids to bed,

I checked the time and knew that Gina would be calling soon. This was becoming predictable. Sometime after the kids were down, one of us would dial the phone and initiate our now nightly ritual. I tried to get most of my chores done prior to the call. I knew that often the conversation would go long past midnight. A couple of times we had the sun come up on us while we were in midsentence. There's an awful sinking feeling when you realize that you have three kids to wake up and get to school, and you've just pulled an all-nighter.

Our phone calls had progressed from basic introductions of each other to in-depth background stories, and lately we'd been venturing into the minefield of religion. Gina had a strong Christian faith, and she spoke eloquently about it. I had a strong faith in God but an equally strong cynicism of the men who proclaim (or was it pretend?) to serve him.

I knew there were millions of people just like me, who had a strong faith in God but also still had questions. They want to know why only some of the Old Testament is no longer a problem (see working on a Sabbath, or planting two kinds of seeds together, or cutting the hair on the sides of your head, or withholding part of a man's wage for more than one day ...) but other parts are quite a problem indeed (see ... well, anything having to do with sex ...).

These "lost believers" are driven from the very Word they need the most. They are not allowed to question or discuss. They are kept at arm's length because they are not "one of us." Ironically, it is precisely these people whom Christ talks about reaching in the Great Commission: to reach (and save) the lost.

When Gina finally called, it was late and she was talking as if we were already mid-conversation. "I love Regis Philbin."

"Who?"

"Regis. I adore him. He's on *Letterman* tonight. I mean, come on! How can you not love Reeg?"

I decided to play a little. "Because he's a hundred and fifty years old."

"Oh, stop it. He's adorable!"

"Little-known fact about Regis Philbin ..."

"What?"

"He was actually Abraham Lincoln's first vice president ..."

"Whatever. He's hilarious! Unlike someone else I know."

"I'm sorry, I didn't realize you had a personal relationship going here ..."

"You know, you have a little Regis in your personality."

"Really? How do you get that?"

"Your little tirades and your sarcasm. Plus, he's funny and cute and ..."

"Easy there. The man has had something like nineteen bypass surgeries."

"Hey, I like him and he reminds me of you. You should take it as a compliment."

"When the light hits you just right, do you know who reminds me of you?"

"Who?"

"Ernest Borgnine."

Gina laughed hard. I loved that about her. She knew a joke when she heard it. Some women would've been upset, or maybe not even understood the reference.

"Granted, *McHale's Navy* was taken off the air in 1966, but come on! His work on *Love Boat* alone makes him one of America's most beloved actors. And ... he's easy on the eyes!"

"Ewww," she said, still laughing. "You're insane!"

"Hey, did you see that email about the Schomakers' friend?" I asked, changing the subject.

A little girl was having heart surgery and an email was sent around asking for prayers. A few days later another email came saying that the surgery was a success and that God had answered all of our prayers.

"Yeah, I saw it."

"What do you think?" I tested her to see if she'd bite.

Gina's voice told me she knew where this was headed. "Well ... what do you think?"

"I have trouble every time I hear that someone's 'prayers were answered.' I mean, we all prayed really hard for Cathy to get better. I would bet that you had hundreds or even thousands of people praying really hard for Matt to recover too. So what do these people think, that we didn't pray enough or in the right way?"

"It isn't like that ..."

"I mean, the way it sounds on these emails is like they are holding a prayer telethon — 'If we can just get enough prayers up to God, we can change his mind and get him to save our little girl.'"

"It's called 'intercessory prayer' ..."

"You mean these people think that they can actually change God's mind? That they can 'intercede' in his plan for all of us? Then that means that our prayers and yours for Matt were just not quite enough for the big guy upstairs. He would've 'interceded' but the prayer production was not quite up to par . . . I really have a problem with that."

"Michael, you're simplifying it way too much. Prayer isn't like that."

"But that is how it comes across. It makes prayer sound like a huge mystical wishing well that, if we do it right, makes our wishes come true!"

"Then why pray at all?" she challenged.

"Well, for many people that's exactly what they say. Why bother praying? If he is all-knowing and all-powerful, then will he be changing his Grand Plan for the universe based on my little prayer?"

Gina pursued me. "I've seen you pray. Why did you bother?"

"Because I use prayer to simply talk with God. I use prayer to stay in relationship with him, to regard him. I learned a long time ago, you don't want to disregard The Boss. I don't use prayer like some kind of Christmas wish list."

"Good, because that's not why we should pray. Prayer is a means to an end, but the end is not simply getting what we want. It's always bigger than that. God wants to hear from us and he wants a relationship with us. He knows us completely and wants us to be in continual pursuit of him, relying on him for hope and our understanding, even when we don't like it or it doesn't make sense."

"That sounds a lot like my father," I said sarcastically.

"It's actually a lot like that. The relationship is the key. You should call your father not because you want something from him but because he is your father. Period. It's not about a transaction. It's about the relationship. People confuse answered prayer with getting what they want, rather than getting what God wants. I think it's great to give God the credit when a prayer is answered according to how it was asked. 'The heart surgery was a success' was not just an answer to prayer; it was the answer that we all wanted. Great. I don't know whether he changed his mind through intercessory prayer or if our prayers happened to line up with his plan. Either way, give God the glory. But if that child had died on the table, we would continue in our pursuit of God's will for that as well."

Gina was on a roll and she needed to get one more thing in. "And by the way, trying to assign human logic to divine matters is perilous. God is just way too big to be factored into our simplistic views. Part of the very reason for leading a prayerful life is to get more comfortable with that idea. Am I making any sense at all?"

I took a deep breath, trying to take it all in. "Yeah, I get it." I thanked her for trying to help me understand. Every time we talked I seemed to get a little closer to God. We agreed that I should call Pastor Galik. He seemed to be the one "man of the cloth" who could meet me where I was and talk to me in ways that I understood. I needed these conversations and sought them out whenever I could. For now, I could tell Gina had reached exhaustion with this particular subject.

"You should go nigh-nigh," she said, slipping into a sleepy-toned voice.

I still had the day's last few drops of sarcasm on my tongue. "Nigh-nigh?"

"You know, sleepy time."

"Aren't you missing some letters there on the end?"

"I got it from my kids when they were little and it stuck."

I volleyed back, "Okay, well, I have to go tinkle now, so I'll say good night. I mean, nigh-nigh."

Our conversations over the next days and weeks grew more intense as we dealt with some weighty issues. Some topics took us so far afield that it took hours to find our way back to "nigh-nigh." We always did though. Many nights I shouldered the phone under my chin while doing my best to fold the kids' clean clothes, a chore I despised. I tried to do it during our nightly phone calls in hopes that I would somehow be distracted long enough to forget that I was actually folding laundry. I think I hated it because I was terrible at it. (Perhaps it was the other way around.)

Several nights a week I stood at the side of my bed with a mountain of clothes piled high. While Gina and I laughed, argued, and rambled about heaven and hell and all things in between, I struggled with trying to make a simple polo shirt lie flat. There are some people (warning, sexist alert!), mostly women (and really "artsy" guys who work at the Gap), who can fold a shirt or pair of pants as if they were masters of the ancient art of origami. They can pile those clothes six or seven high and they stack perfectly one on top of another. Three weeks later, you can pull a shirt from the middle of this pile and it drapes on your body impeccably, not a visible crease or wrinkle. When I did it, I was more like a one-armed man trying to make a balloon animal.

To save my patience and my sanity, I developed a new laundry system. They say necessity is the mother of invention. That may be true, but necessity's lazy cousin, "frustration," was in town and he said the clothes didn't need folding. I began draping all the clothes across the side of my bed. I was only using one side to sleep, which left a perfectly good side for my new "system."

On the rare nights when Gina and I couldn't talk, and I was left all alone with my piles of clothes, I sometimes let Charlotte stay up late. She liked hanging out with me after her brothers went to bed, and I liked that it gave us a chance to talk.

One night I was lying on the floor of our family room, exhausted from the day. She sprawled on the couch, and we talked about the nothings of our lives. Her friends, my work projects, something funny on Nickelodeon that night ... I loved those simple times with her.

"Hey, Dad, I was thinking," she started. "I bet I know why you and Mrs. Kell are such good friends."

This surprised me even though Charlotte had a knack for being very quiet about a subject for a very long time and then, out of nowhere, addressing it head-on. She and I had not spent much time at all talking about the "whys" of my relationship with Gina, so I was eager to get a glimpse inside her thoughts.

"Really?" I said. "Okay, why do you think?" I expected Charlotte to list the simple things that can be seen through the eyes of a ten-year-old girl. Instead, she took a moment, smiled, and found the clarity that most adults lack.

"Because she knows."

I was in awe of her answer. I was in awe of *her*. "Yeah." I smiled. "She really does know."

CHAPTER 34

take the walk

michael

Being the widower in town makes people treat you differently. Sometimes it works out, sometimes it doesn't. There were countless examples of this. Once I called my children's school and got the receptionist. I asked to speak to the principal and was told that she was unavailable. When I told her my name, the receptionist said, "Oh ... um, hold on, please." Within seconds the principal was on the line. Okay. Except it felt like pity.

Heather from across the street told me that a woman who heard about our family wanted to bring us dinner. I balked. After all, I didn't really know her at all, and besides, I had my freezer full of food.

"Just let her," Heather said. "She wants to do something nice."

So a time and day was set up for this stranger to bring us dinner. I raced home from Jack's Little League game so as not to miss her. When I got home I saw a takeout package from the local pizza parlor with a pan of lasagna inside. I called Heather, raging.

"*I* can pick up the phone and order takeout! I left Jack's game early so as not to be rude and miss the meal she cooked for us. And by the way, if you're going to order something from the pizza place on the corner ... order a *pizza*!"

Then there was the twenty-dollar–bill episode.

I was at home in my office trying to get some work done but finding myself really unmotivated. The midday sun showing through my office window was starting to make me drowsy. Looking to stretch my legs and shake the cobwebs a little, I walked out to get the mail. Half jogging in bare feet and shorts, I was hoping not to run into any neighbors today.

The actual mail hadn't arrived, but something caught my eye. A plain white envelope with "Mr. Spehn" written on it in pen was inside the mailbox without postage. This wasn't completely unusual. Neighbors and friends from time to time would drop notes into our box; invitations to kids' birthday parties, or moms' Bunco night, or the latest kid on the block who just turned thirteen and wanted to start babysitting.

I could not see what was inside and decided to go back in the house before opening it. Good thing, too. When I opened it, the only thing in the envelope was a twenty-dollar bill. That's it. No note. No explanation. Just twenty bucks, cash.

My head swirled. I was livid. This was the backbreaking straw. I flew into a rage inside my house. No one was home, of course, but I let fly some beauties. I paced across my family room carpet, back and forth, waving the twenty and venting my wrath. There was only one thing to do. I had to call Gina.

"What's wrong?" she said, noticing my tone right away.

"A twenty-dollar bill!" I said through gritted teeth.

"What?"

I told her the story. Gina listened, but I could tell that there was confusion in her voice. "Well ... that's okay, right? It's just a twenty-dollar bill. I mean ..."

"I'm a man! You don't do that to a man. That's just insulting!" I was almost screaming now. Not at Gina, just in general.

"I mean, if it's a kid who is trying to do a good deed, great," I said. "Let's help a kid learn about helping others. That's a good thing. I understand that. Or if it's a local mom or dad who has seen our story and they didn't know what else to do ... they wanted to treat my kids to ice cream or whatever ... okay, fine. But tell me! Write a note. Knock on the door ... No. They just leave it in the box."

"Yeah, I get it. That's a little weird," Gina interrupted. "But this isn't just about a twenty-dollar bill, is it?"

"It's everything!" I exclaimed. "It's people at the kids' school, it's my job, it's the woman ordering us lasagna from a pizza place.... Life is throwing me nothing but curveballs." I took a breath and tried to calm myself as I explained further.

"I don't need to hit a home run. I could use just a basic single to right. But I can't get any decent pitches. There's nothing normal coming my way ... no easy fastballs down the middle of the plate. Life's throwin' me nothing but junk in the dirt!" I was ranting, but I let her in for just a second.

"Then take the walk." Gina's voice was clear and firm. And startling.

"What?" It didn't register.

"Take the walk. Stop swinging wildly at the junk.... Just take the walk. Get to first base and see what happens next."

I was stunned. I had a habit of using metaphors and analogies to get my point across to others. The baseball analogy was one that simply popped into my head at that moment. Gina then did something that had never happened before. She took my analogy and used it back on me to offer a solution. No one did that. Certainly no one ever did it with such elegant precision.

I sat in stunned silence for perhaps a full minute. The amazing thing about Gina was, she did too. She had sensed that something deeper was bothering me on this day. She took my analogy and turned it right around on me with perfect accuracy. And now, when I needed to absorb the truth and magnitude of her statement, she simply let the silence linger for a while. Amazing.

She was 100 percent right, of course. I needed to stop fighting what the world was throwing at me. I needed to take the walk. I needed to get to first base and see what was next.

I really was staggered for a bit by this. I told Gina I needed to hang up. We said nothing more except that we'd talk later.

I sat in my chair thinking for a long time. As I thought, I realized Gina was right. I needed to adjust my perspective. Life had been throwing me garbage. Curveballs. Pitches in the dirt. Instead of flailing away trying to make contact, instead of arguing with the umpire or trying to force something unnatural—something perhaps from my former life—I quite simply needed to relax a bit and let some pitches go by. I started looking at the annoyances in my life and tried to see them differently.

Ball one. My mother-in-law, Jill's, efforts to help—with the kitchen, laundry, kids' pickup times, and so on. I would let her do more for us. Yes, she did some things differently than we were used to, but the truth was, I could be clearer as to exactly how I wanted those things done. Perhaps we could find a middle ground.

Ball two. My sister, Lynn, wanted to come and stay with us for several weeks. She was willing to take a leave of absence from work and essentially move in with us for a month. This would mean a change to our routines, a certain amount of lost privacy. But the kids loved their aunt and it would be nice to have the help. Plus, if Lynn were here to watch the kids, maybe Gina and I could spend time together without the distractions and obligations of parenting.

Ball three. The mommies at St. John. Those tireless, relentlessly helpful, and overly organized women I tried to avoid as I dropped my kids off at school. They wanted to help. They weren't trying to run my life or change my life. They were simply trying to help. I would begin to let them. I would let them take my daughter for a sleepover. She wanted to go so badly anyway. I would let them take Danny for the whole day every Wednesday. He loved having playdates and it would give me time to clean, shop for groceries, get some work done, and every once in a while, have a meltdown.

Ball four. I would get my family to church on Sunday. I was ready to admit that, despite my natural tendency to resist group worship, I did feel refreshed when I came home from church at St. John. Pastor Galik was a gifted speaker and his weekly message was always meaningful to me. I was actually learning to recognize Bible verses and it felt good. I decided to wade into those waters a bit deeper.

Gina was the one who had given all of this to me. She was the one who was able to come alongside me and speak to me in the language I understood. She gave me not only the construct of "take the walk," but also the peace of mind to actually do it. Then, miraculously, when I got to first base, she was there with me. She began to take her own advice and let some of life's curveballs go by.

I wouldn't have made it to that place without Gina Kell. I trusted her completely. I was open to her and so very grateful for her. And like it or not, I was falling for her.

Charlotte had said, "Because she knows ..." And that was true. Gina did know. She knew about loss and pain, grief and challenge. Yet it seemed we were about to move past all of that. We were beginning to take the walk, together.

CHAPTER 35

date night

gina

Human suffering and loss bring out the best and worst in people. They also bring out the awkward and absurd. Words can be difficult to choose when dealing with the bereaved. It's why there are professions and billions of greeting cards dedicated to helping us do it. It is hard enough to string together a coherent sentence when trying to comfort a grieving widow, but things get really dicey when people try to give advice.

Michael and I spent a considerable amount of time trying to help each other make sense of the things people would say and do. We laughed about Michael's "bummer" guy from the print shop and the kindhearted women who treated him like one of the mommies, inviting him to playgroups or coffee when the kids were in school.

"I've got one for you," I said, trying to one-up Michael. "I was given some really interesting advice about men and dating."

"Really? Do tell!"

"The deaconess at St. John—"

Michael couldn't resist interrupting. "The deaconess at St. John!?"

"Yes. She told me that widows are magnets for men who want sex because they view us as vulnerable and needy."

"The deaconess got it right!"

"Oh geez!" I replied, exasperated.

"It's not just widows. It's women in general. It has nothing to do with being vulnerable or needy. It's a little thing called natural selection. We want it, you guys have it ... makes the world go 'round."

"Oh, well, imagine my relief!"

"Glad to help!" Michael said, smiling through the phone.

"I guess that would explain the time I got asked out by a total stranger at Target."

"Really? Who was he? I'll kill him!"

"Wow. Jealous?" I said, teasing.

"Heck yeah! I go to Target all the time, and no one ever asks me out!"

I laughed out loud.

Then he added, "If I saw you at Target, I'd ask you out too."

"Aw. That's sweet."

"Don't be too flattered. The smell of popcorn and hot dogs in the air clouds my judgment. But ya know, for an Irish boy from Chicago, I do know where to find some pretty good Italian food."

"Oh, really? You're going to show me good Italian in my hometown?"

"Yeah, I know a place."

"Like, what? Olive Garden?"

"Just because you're Italian doesn't mean you're the only one who knows where to find good food!"

I sensed where our conversation was leading and I was glad we were on the phone, because I could not erase the smile from my face. The thought of a "date" in its truest form was abhorrent to me, but the idea of having an evening out to sit across from Michael was an opportunity to laugh and feel present in my own skin.

Through him, I felt myself pulling away from destructive thinking. For months I had been asking the question, "Where did Matt go?" but the emerging question was, "Where did I go?" and more importantly, "When will I be back?" To be a healthy mom in service to Drew and Sam, I needed to be a complete person, but I had lost my identity and become depleted by my longing for what was and what could have been. Living in the rearview mirror was turning me into a walking cliché of regret and "coulda, woulda, shouldas." Feelings, thoughts, ideas, and energy had been replaced by numbness, anger, and indifference. I had been trying to live in the moment by sitting in one place, waiting for something to happen. Before despair could take root, something needed to move, and it had to be me. Every conversation with Michael was a means to that end. And now, a date. Something stirred in me. I couldn't define it. I didn't know how to do this.

Society has strong views on when a widow should or should not start dating. Ambiguous and subjective as they are, protocols exist. Dating too soon can be perceived as callous. The underlying assumption is that you didn't have the right kind of love for your spouse. It's the "body isn't even cold yet" factor. Too late means you're clinging to the past and need to move on. You need companionship, but not until the world is comfortable with it. Throw kids into the mix and the opinions really start to fly.

I didn't want our evening out to be scrutinized. Michael and I came to know each other well over the phone and through working together on the Living Mural. Our friendship began to extend beyond our mutual grief. No one really knew but us, and even we weren't sure what was happening. I only told my parents and Colleen about my plans with Michael. I needed to leave the rest of the world out of it. I had enough internal strife.

I was thirty-six years old and I was going on a date for the first time in over fifteen years. I had butterflies in my stomach and nothing to wear in my closet. My clothes hung like shapeless, weathered willow tree branches. This did little to help my confidence. As I flipped through the hangers, my mind screamed, "Wrong color. Out of style. Trying too hard."

The last time I had a real date, men were boys, there were no cell phones, and my parents didn't have to babysit my kids. One thing that hadn't changed was my need to find the right outfit. My endless supply of zipper hoodies and cargo pants was six years strong, and any outfit worthy of a first date was buried beneath piles of clothes worthy of nothing more than a playdate.

I went to the mall in search of an outfit that said stylish but not trendy, youthful but not slutty, simple but not boring. I found a cropped jean from the Gap, a cap-sleeved navy blue tee from J.Crew, and a short summer tan blazer from Anthropologie, with the sleeves rolled up, exposing the flowery fabric inside. I had cute sandals in the closet to complete my look.

It was a beautiful August evening. Michael was due to arrive so I checked my hair and lipgloss one last time. I watched through my office window as he pulled up in a Chrysler minivan, another difference from the last time I dated. My parents would never let me date a guy with a van.

Michael was wearing classic khakis and a light blue pinstriped oxford. Playing it cool, I waited for the doorbell to ring before I moved. The boys ran to the door ahead of me, excited to see Mr. Spehn.

"Where are you guys going?" Drew asked.

"We're going to an Italian restaurant," Michael told him. "But something smells good here."

"Nona made pasta and clams."

"Nona?" Michael asked, glancing at me.

"My parents are babysitting," I said, realizing how weird it was to have both my parents and my children greet my date. I suddenly felt like I was standing in the corner, observing my life. My husband was gone. A new man was in my house and we were having a "Meet the Parents" (and the kids) moment. It wasn't like dating as a teenager. We were two experienced, broken adults who needed a reprieve from the demands of life. We also saw the value in getting to know each other without five kids, a phone line, and a wall of grief between us.

After introductions and pleasantries, Michael and I said good night to my folks, I kissed the kids, and we were out the door. Sitting next to him in the car felt familiar. For so many years, Matt occupied the driver's seat to my left. There was a confusing mix of emotions swirling inside me. I missed Matt, but I felt good with Michael. I was a grieving widow and mother of two, a strong and independent woman out for the evening with a man, and a nervous girl on her first date.

We sat in the corner of a large half-circle booth that could have easily seated six adults side by side. Michael immediately won over our waitress with playful teasing and jokes. He passed the first unofficial litmus test. The way a man treats a waiter or waitress is an excellent measure of his character. I've dated men who lost me on this alone. Treating waitstaff like second-class citizens is unacceptable.

It took a few minutes to get comfortable sitting in an intimate setting, face to face with the voice on the phone. I paid close attention to the expressions and mannerisms that went with the inflections of his words and found it difficult to stop smiling. This was the fourth meal we shared together. The first was a family dinner when we were raw in our grief. The second was a business lunch at Panera Bread to discuss the Living Mural. The third was a family dinner I cooked at the Spehns (Michael is still trying to get rid of the scent of garlic and onions). But dinner at Maggiano's, this was a date; the kind where eating a salad suddenly requires conscious thought, a knife, and extra napkins.

We tucked away grief and business, and for two hours we talked and laughed and became multidimensional to one another. There was very little conversation about the widowed life, yet Matt and Cathy were woven into most every story. We started getting to know each other through them and apart from them. A few times we sat quietly, not feeling a sense of urgency to fill the silence. A second test, passed. I find a certain refuge in anyone comfortable enough to sit in silence without an awkward laugh or fidget. When silence is comfortable, it's a sign of security and ease. Otherwise, I suppose it could be closer to boredom, leading to a nap. I have had dates like that too, but this wasn't one of them. It was comfortable. We talked about our careers, kids, basketball, and all the places we'd traveled. As it had been since the first time we met, our time together was remarkably easy. I felt like I had known Michael for years. We knew heartache and marriage and kids and houses and family and God and sex and love. We'd done it all, and yet there was more to be done. We still had so much to learn about and teach one another.

We drove home with the windows down. I kicked off my sandals and sat cross-legged in my seat.

"Thank you for dinner," I said. "Not bad for an Irish boy."

"I'm glad you liked it."

There was a long pause. "Kinda weird, huh?"

He looked at me and smiled back. "What's so weird is that it doesn't feel weird at all." He reached for my hand and fixed his eyes on the road.

He was right. As we pulled into my driveway, he reached over and gave me a peck on the cheek. He came around to open my door and walked me into the house where my parents were waiting.

CHAPTER 36

happy patio

gina

I grew up in a tiny house on Elmira Street in St. Clair Shores, Michigan, just a few blocks off Lake St. Clair. For two weeks in July each year, every exterior surface was covered in fish flies that resembled a shimmering translucent moss. It was a foul consequence of living in a lake community, but seeing the mansions in nearby Grosse Pointe covered as well, I figured it must not be that bad.

We lived two houses from the end of our block, where my elementary school was located. I grew up thinking all kids walked home for a Campbell's soup lunch. My childhood was simple, even charmed. There was a peach tree in our backyard that grew unexpectedly from a pit that I buried when I was four years old, and a brown and white ice cream truck that drove down our block selling creamy soft serve cones that put Dairy Queen to shame.

In summertime, there were no secrets on Elmira Street. The homes were small, the walls were thin, and air conditioner units were usually isolated to one room, which meant the windows were open and no conversation was private.

I'd sit under the maple tree along the curb in front of my house listening to kids playing, dogs barking, and dads coming home from work to greet their families. Sometimes, if the wind was just right, I could guess what the neighbors were having for dinner. At times I could hear arguments that taught me a few new words, or moms yelling for their teenagers to turn down the blaring music. Many nights I fell asleep to the din of my parents with friends gathered on the front porch, talking and laughing. Content didn't matter. The sounds of summer were soothing.

Sitting on Michael's patio brought me back to those simple days. His house sits on a hill with a tiled patio ten feet off the ground overlooking the backyard. Blooms were bursting on all the flowering trees and every corner of the patio had a trio of pots filled with colorful wave petunias, geraniums, and grass spikes. The sky was clear baby blue, creating a flat, cartoonlike backdrop that gave the foreground a high-definition pop.

This fashionable Rochester neighborhood was worlds away from my humble beginnings in St. Clair Shores, with the exception of the unmistakable echoes of my childhood summers. The rise and fall of kids' voices through the expansive backyards; their laughter and banter brought me back to my maple tree and I couldn't help but smile. Lawn mowers and sprinklers hummed in the distance while dozens of kids discovered themselves through the art and conflict of play. Whenever I heard tension mounting among the kids, I was tempted to intervene, but Michael always stopped me.

"Let the kids work it out," was his mantra. "There's great power in the backyard. It's where kids learn a lot about life. You moms gotta let the backyard do its thing."

Michael's instinct about kids was comforting to me. He was right and I should have known. Before anyone coined the phrase "helicopter parent," I grew up surrounded by people who didn't feel a need to mediate every situation in my life. That was their gift to me. Kids don't need to constantly be told how to live as much as they need a consistently strong example to live by. Michael understood this balance.

I stepped into the kitchen off the patio to help him feed the kids a quick dinner of burgers and fries before we started cooking our own meal from a sea bass recipe he discovered on the Food Network. He was full of surprises. I never expected to hear "Food Network" or "sea bass" come out of his mouth, but there we were, zesting lemons, chopping parsley, and mincing garlic for homemade lemon crumb topping.

We worked side by side in the kitchen, bumping into each other and spinning around the kids as they breathlessly ran in for a cup of water. It was fun and effortless, much like our ongoing experience working on the Living Mural for St. John. Everything Michael and I did together felt easy. We had matching perspectives that we wore like a new skin, void of rough patches, scrapes, and burns. We were still raw and tender in some places, and we carefully protected those, but this new skin brought clarity to our priorities and relationships, making obstacles of all kinds seem fairly insignificant. Little things that once drove me crazy were no longer given such weight.

As we waited for our sea bass to roast in the oven, I tucked my bare toes under my skirt and curled up on the chaise across from Michael. We kept smiling at each other, but didn't have a need to cloud the moment with words. In the quiet perfection of the evening, Michael got up and walked off the patio. I was slightly confused but didn't think much of it. I closed my eyes and could feel my body relax into the chair. When Michael returned he set before me a vase with fresh roses that he had just cut from his yard.

"For you," he said, pleased with himself.

"That's so sweet." I leaned in to smell the flowers. "It seems like everything is right with the world."

"This is a great night," he replied.

"Every time we sit out here, it seems like the weather is perfect, the kids are content, and we don't have a care in the world. And now I get fresh-cut flowers too! I think this is the happy patio!"

Michael started laughing. "I think you're right! Maybe we should live out here!"

We pondered that thought and came up with wild scenarios for how we could pull that off in the winter. We laughed and talked about what Matt and Cathy would have thought of this night, agreeing that they would have loved it too.

Remnants of sea bass sat cold on our plates and the light of day was fading fast. The kids came bouncing onto the patio.

"Mom, can we spend the night?" Drew asked excitedly. Following close behind were Jack, Dan, and Sam, all begging for the same.

"Pleeeeeease! Can we?"

We worked out the details and agreed it would be okay for Drew and Sam to stay the night. The four boys erupted in cheers.

"Mom, are you gonna stay too?" Sam asked.

I glanced at Michael and smiled. "No, buddy, but I'll be back first thing in the morning."

Hugging me, Sam whined, "Why can't you stay?"

"Grown-ups don't have sleepovers, sweetie." I left it at that. "I promise to be back first thing in the morning and we'll have pancakes."

Michael and I got the kids settled in for the night and retreated to the patio for dessert and conversation by citronella candlelight. I wrapped up in a blanket and we spent another two hours on the happy patio casually talking.

When it came time to leave, Michael walked me to my car. I could feel my heart beat just a little faster in anticipation of saying good-bye. We rarely had a good-bye that wasn't on the phone or surrounded by kids, and the thought of a kiss was on my mind. Whether it was nervousness or long-windedness, we talked for another twenty minutes and I was getting cold. Michael saw me shiver and pulled me in for a long hug. He felt strong and it was good to be in his arms. As I began to relax, he leaned back and we looked into each other's eyes.

"Is this okay?" he whispered just before gently pressing his soft lips to mine. The answer was in my kiss.

CHAPTER 37

foundations

michael

Exactly nine months after he died, the first annual Matt Kell Memorial Golf Outing was held. Holding a golf outing that honors a close friend who has died is fairly predictable in the Midwest. Matt was a well-loved man with countless friends and business acquaintances, and there was a natural desire to express their collective grief in a tangible way.

The golf outing was an unqualified success. Corporate sponsors such as WDIV, Victory Honda, Comcast, and others came through with major donations. So many individual golfers wanted to play that there weren't enough spaces for everyone. After the best-ball scramble there was a cock-tail hour, silent auction, and sit-down dinner, followed by a live auction with some very high-end items. Matt's friends Marty, Mike, Red, and the others put it all together, insulating Gina from the burden. For their first attempt at a memorial fundraiser, Matt's friends conducted one of the finest golf outings I've ever attended. It also happened to raise more than $50,000 for charity.

Almost immediately people began to discuss plans for the second annual Matt Kell Memorial. The first order of business, however, was to formally create a nonprofit organization so that the money raised would stay under their control. A meeting was scheduled at Gina's house to iron out the details. Matt's "brothers," as Gina called them, would be serving on the board of directors, along with Gina, of course.

Several days prior to the meeting, Gina ambushed me with an idea. "I want to name the foundation after both Matt and Cathy," she told me.

"No way," I said firmly. I was the newcomer, and while I had lost my wife and everyone was sympathetic to that fact, including Cathy's name on *Matt Kell's* foundation seemed out of place. Gina was adamant, and demanded my reasons for saying no.

"For one thing, the golf outing is named after Matt," I told her.

"Yes, but we want to have more fundraising events throughout the year that all fund the foundation. Some of those will likely be named after Cathy." She obviously was prepared for this conversation. I decided to mention the elephant in the room.

"G. The guys will *never* go for it."

"Yes, they will," she shot back.

A few days later we gathered in the Kells' family room; Matt's closest friends, his widow, and me. Gina presented her idea for a foundation that would serve families like theirs who have small children who have lost a parent to cancer. It would provide financial resources, of course, but also become a central source for counseling services, spiritual guidance, etc. The guys loved the idea. Then she dropped the bomb.

"I want to call it the 'New Day Foundation for Families, in honor of Matt Kell and Cathy Spehn,'" Gina told them. "And I want all of you to sit on the board of directors."

With every word I could see the body language of these four guys visibly change in slow motion. By the time she finished, there was an awkward silence in the room. They weren't going for it.

Gina asked them each to give their opinions. One by one they spoke, and to their credit, they spoke candidly and articulately. Every one of them opposed her request to name the foundation after both Matt *and* Cathy. They were here to create a foundation for their friend — their brother. They weren't interested in attaching the name of anyone else to this thing and they made it clear that this wasn't what they had intended.

Gina was devastated because she couldn't understand their perspective. She held it together as long as she could, but became increasingly frustrated and left the room crying. Her disappointment in these men was crushing. I hadn't known Gina as long as the others, but I knew this was bad — worse than even they could comprehend. After some awkward small talk, everyone left.

I understood this. I was insulted a little, sure, but I got it. At its root was the fact that these guys weren't ready. They were not prepared for the concept of Gina and someone else … *anyone* else, other than their brother Matt. I understood that completely. I was frustrated by it but I was sympathetic to them at the same time.

We spend years building the really important relationships of our lives; the guys you meet in school, the ones you play ball with, the few who make it through all of the years and all of the experiences. These are more than your friends; they are your touchstones that keep you grounded through life's ups and downs. These people, and the collection of memories you share, form the bedrock that gives you the confidence to get married, have children, start new businesses, and so forth.

When Matt Kell died, these men were shaken to their core. They looked around and saw that the foundation of their lives had cracks in it. The grief they felt wasn't simply sadness; it was also fear. Men in general tend to respond to this feeling by shifting into task mode. These guys did that by organizing golf outings and taking Matt's sons to ball games and figuring out ways to help Gina. Which is perfectly well and good, but the core issues remain unresolved. The result is grief delayed. The opposite of those who slip from grief into despair and hopelessness, these folks seem to consciously defer their grief for the sake of the widow and her kids.

I was keenly aware of my status in this group from the start. I was the outsider, so I tried to approach as gently as possible. The problem was that Gina and I were living through an unusual relationship, accelerated by events and proximity. Because we tried to keep our relationship private for a very long time, many people did not know how close we had become. By the time we went public, we were already talking about a future together and everyone else thought we had just started dating.

I did have one thing going for me, however. These guys, Matt's "brothers," were good, honest people. Although it ruffled my feathers a bit at the time, I was impressed with their candor in Gina's family room that night. The next day I received phone calls from almost all of them. They said the right things and I did too. There were no hard feelings and we would all use this experience to take another step toward the future together.

Gina had a good cry, dried her eyes, and went forward with her plan. She admitted to not giving the guys time to ease into the idea. Her heart for this foundation had been growing in step with our relationship. It was tricky, because what was happening between us was unexpected and rather sudden. How could others possibly know the extent of what we were feeling and thinking? Our own sense of self-preservation made it difficult for us to share details with even the closest friends. Gina believed that Matt's brothers would ultimately see what was happening and come to support her, and they did.

We started a nonprofit organization called the New Day Foundation for Families, in honor of Matt Kell and Cathy Spehn. The guys agreed to serve with Gina and me on the board of directors. Together we began building more than a nonprofit foundation to help others. A new foundation of friendship and trust was taking shape as well.

CHAPTER 38

the double rainbow

gina

Whether Matt's cancer journey was going to end on a mountaintop of recovery or in a valley at the water's edge, we realized there was little choice but to unload the massive amounts of minutiae that distracted us throughout our marriage. Cancer, like a machete cutting through the weeds of our relationship, cleared the path to our priorities. This clarity gave me freedom to love more deeply and more purely than ever before; first with Matt, and then again, with a new love, Michael. My deepest personal regret was that it took a terminal illness to bring about this simple change.

I have been in like and in lust. I have been in need and in friendship. Although rare, I have also been in love. I thought I had lived enough to know the difference between these, but the delicate and often confusing boundaries between like, lust, need, friendship, and love can easily blur, especially when moving from one to another. There are a lot of gray areas in those transitions and it is there that people can mistake most anything for love.

I had two children, not to mention a community, watching my every move. I was responsible for the proper healing of three broken hearts. I could not risk mistakes. What began with Michael as mutual grief and understanding had quickly become a comfortable friendship. The relationship between our families grew effortlessly. There were no gray areas. We didn't analyze our tiny gestures, the time we spent together, or our late nights on the phone falling asleep together between conversations. We enjoyed it for what it was, free of expectation or pressure. I savored this simplicity and freedom.

Our relationship was reminiscent of everything I knew about love, yet it remained unspoken. The kids provided a natural buffer, a caution flag, forcing Michael and me to maintain a slow and steady pace. Going slow was easy given proximity, schedules, and a strong desire to protect and insulate them from further heartache. There would be no relationship apart from our children. Falling in love wasn't something we were doing as a couple. This would be a family deal. As the kids became more aware of what was happening, we engaged in gentle conversation about the possibilities, concerns, and hopes for our future. As the questions increased and the conversations ran longer, Michael and I decided to accelerate things by spending time together in a more up-close and personal setting. If this was ever going to work, we needed to test the waters.

We planned a dual family vacation to Florida with the requisite stop at Disney World. Our expectation was that this trip would uncover the realities of togetherness and possibly alter the course of our relationship, for better or worse. Our goal was to put our families under the microscope of coexistence to see how we'd fare. Traveling together is an exceptional measure of character and relationship strength. We were determined to draw out the warts.

Our plan backfired. The trip was perfect. We were like something out of a Disney commercial. Smiling, happy children skipping along the streets of the Magic Kingdom, with wide-eyed and adoring parents trailing behind. There was not one tear, nor a single argument. It was hilarious. Five kids, aged six to eleven, and not one of them complained or moped even once. Everywhere we went, people assumed we were one big family and the kids got a kick out of going along with it. This sense of completeness also went unspoken, but it had everyone smiling on the inside, as if our favorite songs were playing in our heads on a continuous loop.

If this trip was any indication of what life would be like as a family, then we were ready, but our excitement was tempered. It all seemed just a little too easy. I was skeptical. It was Disney World after all. Freakin' happy land. We would need another test.

Despite my Turquoise Lake hiking "incident" from the previous summer, my parents invited me and the boys back to their condo in Beaver Creek. I was ballsy enough to ask them if Michael and his kids could join us. They agreed and offered us the use of their condo for a week before they arrived. This would be the perfect second test.

We quickly discovered this wasn't going to be some cream-puff Disney trip. For two days, the altitude gave the kids dry mouth, headaches, and stomachaches. The cranky factor was exactly what I expected. There was plenty of fun and laughter, but with every challenge of rock walls, hikes, chairlifts a hundred feet in the air, white-water rafting, and trampoline bungee jumps, we were met with the fears, tears, and resistance of five kids. Even putt-putt golf caused stress. Behind every conversation we were processing through much larger issues; overcoming fear, building trust, letting go, taking risks, exceeding perceived limits, and setting boundaries. We even had to get back to the fundamentals of kindness and patience. Now we were getting somewhere. Michael and I were in nonstop parenting and teaching mode. We tag-teamed well, and we knew this because the kids were responsive. This was the test I had been waiting for. We were finally getting a sense of real life as a family. The challenges of Colorado were exactly what I needed in order to say and mean, "Bring it on!" We were meant for this.

For a week we lived together in one condo in the quaint village of Beaver Creek. I had a gorgeous master bedroom suite, the kids shared an oversized bedroom loft, and Michael crashed in the living room.

Since the beginning of our relationship, the children had been our compasses guiding every decision we made. We were hyperaware of their emotions and felt a strong need to protect them from even the idea of Mom or Dad being with someone else. Our vacation was the first time we held hands in front of them. We had never kissed in front of them, and staying in the same room together was simply not an option.

This was the reason Michael slept on a lumpy pullout couch in the living area of the condo. He refused to let me sleep on the couch, even for one night, which was kind, but also drew out my Catholic guilt. For all the comforts and amenities of this luxury condo, the pullout couch was among the worst I had ever seen. Michael did use the master bathroom and kept his clothes in the walk-in closet, but at the end of an exhausting day we said good night to the kids, then to each other, and he tucked into his prison cot as I cozied up in my posh four-poster bed. Not only was his bed like sleeping on rocks, but it was located in the living area where the kids often woke him up for a drink of water during the night or for breakfast before the sun came up. There was little rest for Michael, but it was all worth it when Jack and Drew were lying with him one night and asked, "How come you don't sleep in there?" pointing to the master bedroom.

"Because that is for people who are married," he responded without missing a beat. Simple, straightforward. No gray areas. We had done right by our kids. As a thank-you for enduring the couch for a week, I arranged for Michael to have a ninety-minute massage at the spa.

By week's end everyone was at ease, adjusted to the altitude and reminiscing about our wild Colorado adventures. We had a great group of kids. I was proud of how they laughed together, conquered their fears, argued with one another, and encouraged each other. Our families were brought together by a shared and tragic past, but our new experiences were beginning to create a solid connection between us. "Remember when ..." was no longer consumed by memories of dying parents and times before we knew each other. Now, "Remember when ..." was filling up with a new and shared history.

Michael and his kids were scheduled to go home on their own while Drew, Sam, and I spent another week in Colorado with my parents. Our last morning together was spent horseback riding. The sight of Michael, the ultimate city slicker, on horseback did not compute in my brain. His death grip on the saddle horn was my first clue, but I had to give him credit for being a great sport. He cracked jokes relentlessly. As he sat slumped forward in the saddle, Michael pointed toward one of the rugged, and very handsome, cowboys. "Does that do it for you?" he whispered.

I lowered my shades to get a good look and smiled. "Jealous?"

"Of Billy Bob ...? I don't think so." As if on cue, "Daisy Duke" appeared in the barn door wearing tight jeans, a fitted plaid shirt, and a feminine cowgirl hat. Michael's face lit up. He suddenly looked more relaxed on his perch.

"Everything happening for you in slow motion right now?" I said sarcastically.

"Clearly *that* does it for you! Look at your face!" I cackled.

"Do you see the fog lights and soft focus too?" he joked.

When all seven of our saddles were securely cinched, we headed out on the trail in a nose-to-tail formation, following the lead wrangler. Throughout the ride he twisted around in his saddle to make small talk or play tour guide.

Lupine and larkspur lined the trail, adding splashes of color to the open fields. Puffy white, cotton-candy clouds drifted in the Colorado blue sky. Aspen groves shimmered in the spaces between the spruces and pines, and an occasional mule deer would grace our presence. The kids asked questions relentlessly until the wrangler posed one of his own.

"Can anyone tell me how many aspen trees are in this grove?" he said, pointing to a specific area.

The kids started shouting answers. "Two thousand!"

"One hundred eighty-one!"

"One million!"

They debated about what they would like to win if they chose correctly. Michael sensed there was a catch, but couldn't figure it out. He loves a good mental challenge.

The wrangler held out for a few minutes but finally shouted, "You are looking at one tree!"

After the chatter died down, he went on to explain that trees in an aspen grove are connected underground by the same root system. He told us that new trunks sprout aboveground as older ones die, and after a forest fire, Aspens are the first trees to grow back because their underground root system is protected from the heat of the fire. While the grove might be decimated, the root system remains intact, allowing new shoots to emerge from the devastation.

As the kids grew weary of the trivia, Michael was just getting warmed up. He bounce-trotted his horse up to the front of the line to hear more about the aspens. His interest was piqued and our wrangler quickly learned that the kids had nothing on Michael, who was by far the most inquisitive in our bunch. He has a general "need to know" kind of mind. I was satisfied simply knowing that it was one tree, but Michael needed to know how and why and what it meant to the big picture of the forest and life. I teased him for asking so many questions, but in truth, I loved that he asked. I wanted to be more like him.

We moseyed back to the corral knowing more about aspens than any Google search could have provided. While our sore butts were glad to be out of the saddle, we were sad to see the ride come to an end because it meant the end of our time together in Colorado.

Michael and the kids packed up and, once again, we felt the sting of separation. As the bags piled up by the door, I felt a lump of sadness in my throat.

"It would be nice to actually travel on a plane together sometime," Michael said. "But no matter where we go, can we please make sure that I always have to sleep on a pullout couch? That'd be super!"

"I know. I'm sorry," I said, laughing, but feeling terrible about it.

He held me tightly around my waist. "We'll be waiting for you at home."

"I miss you already and I hate it," I said, fighting back tears.

We hugged and tenderly kissed. He was clean-shaven after enjoying his western scruff all week away from his razor. His lips were soft and warm and I felt like I was melting into him. Neither of us wanted to let go. Holding me close, Michael looked into my eyes and in a low voice whispered, "I love you."

I smiled as the words hung in the air. This was it. We were willing to risk it all again.

"I love you too."

We held each other for another minute. Before we knew it, the Spehns were driving off toward Denver International Airport. I noticed that it had begun to rain.

A lot of our late afternoons in Colorado were planned around the threat of rain. Most days between three and four o'clock, we sensed the telltale signs: a drop in temperature, increased winds, or dark skies either suddenly overhead or in the distance. Sometimes we caught a rare photo opportunity from the chairlift, as a curtain of rain hung in the distance over the Gore Mountain Range. This weather pattern had become predictable. The rain usually didn't amount to much and often didn't even reach us, but dark skies loomed throughout the valley.

Rain gets a bad rap. It is often compared to life's tragedies. The anticipation of rain is a threat. It's gloomy, dreary, and depressing, putting a damper on life itself. It ruins or, at best, alters our plans, our mood, and our hair. Rain forces us to make unwanted sacrifices and compromises. Of course, we want the rain to nourish our crops, make the lawn green, and replenish our lakes and rivers, preferably when it best suits us, perhaps overnight or on the days we need to clean closets. But convenience and predictability are not its trademarks. Rain, like tragedy, keeps its own schedule. I have learned that, despite our collective scorn, both are vital to growth.

The night of the Beaver Creek Rodeo, the sky presented an unusual mix of intermittent sun, dark clouds, and a refreshing light rain that perked up the wildflowers and kept the rodeo dust from swirling. We arrived early for barbeque and beer, and found seats in the crowded grandstands facing due west. The steel gray clouds were layered in a beautiful feathery pattern across the sky. When the sun peeked out from below the cloud line, it was blinding. In between barrel races and bull riding, Drew grabbed my arm in mid-sip of his Coke.

"Mom, look!"

I turned to see what had his attention. What I saw made me gasp a little. Just north of the grandstands, painted against a wall of dark clouds, we saw two of the most brilliant rainbows arcing across the sky. Everything seemed to stop.

These were no barely there, imperceptible rainbows. These were high-def. The colors were vivid and crisp. The second rainbow was nearly as vibrant as the first, with easily distinguishable colors that mirrored the rainbow below. My eyes followed both arcs down to the end where they seemed to touch the valley floor. I swore I could have walked out of the grandstands, through a small field where they parked cars, and touched the literal end of those rainbows.

Everyone snapped photos and seemed to get back to the rodeo after a few oohs and aahs. I was completely distracted. I had to call Michael.

"Hey, it's me. I know you're in flight right now. I'm at the rodeo staring at the most unbelievable sight. And no, it's not a cowboy. It's a *double* rainbow! Have you ever seen such a thing? My gosh, it's gorgeous. I don't want to sound like a cheese ball, but I can't help but think that Matt and Cathy are sending us a message. Everything we are doing is right. I've known it all along and this is our confirmation. I wish you were here. I cannot believe my eyes. There's so much I want to say. I love you. I can't wait to see you. This is amazing! Bye!"

A rodeo clown in the arena entertained the kids, but I could not take my eyes off the sky. I watched the movement of the clouds and stared at the mystical colors as they slowly dissipated. The beauty and significance of rainbows often get lost on leprechauns and pots of gold, unicorns, breakfast cereals and all things childlike and cutesy. But that night in Colorado, the double rainbows symbolized the affirmation, grace, and redemption we were receiving.

The haunting lyric from *Les Misérables*, "The rain that brings you here is heaven-blessed, the skies begin to clear and I'm at rest ..." rings true to me.

Yes, into each life rain will fall, but there is something redeeming in the rain. It hides beauty that can only emerge after the storm has passed. As light enters each drop of rain, it splits the gray and transforms it into the colors of the rainbow. The rain in our life brought Michael and his children to us. God's grace provided the light that refracted our colorless grief into something beautiful. Our season of storms was passing, and the true color of rain was being revealed to us. Our double rainbow was my gift of reassurance.

CHAPTER 39

on both knees

michael

As Gina and I became more serious about becoming a blended family, we paid close attention to the kids. They were our only priority, and if they gave even a hint of resistance to our becoming one family, we would have backed away from the idea.

Gina and I had been careful throughout our friendship, courtship, and now romance to go slowly with the kids. We never forced our relationship on them. We never displayed signs of romantic affection in front of the kids until a year after knowing each other, and even then we took things very slowly. Now we were looking for casual opportunities to mention the subject of becoming a family just to gauge their acceptance. Each time we did, the kids responded exactly as we hoped. There was excitement, but they also had lots of questions and we did our best to make them feel safe to ask.

It was late summer and Drew and Sam were sleeping over at our house. The older boys, Jack, nine, and Drew, eight, were in one room. As Gina and I tucked them into bed, we intentionally lingered a while. I stretched out next to Drew and she sat on the floor next to Jack's sleeping bag.

"Hey, guys, I've been thinking about something."

"You want us to stay up late and watch *Indiana Jones*? Thank you, most excellent father...." Jack never missed the chance to slip in a punch line, even when he was half asleep.

"No, Jack, but nice try." I spoke slowly and eased gently toward the subject. "You guys know ... how we have been talking about ... someday, maybe, in the future ... we might think about becoming a big family?"

"Yeah?" Drew perked up. As perhaps the most anxious one of the kids regarding this big change in our lives, he looked as though he'd been waiting for this conversation.

"I was just wondering. What do you think you guys would want to call us if we ever did that?" I shared a glance with Gina. "So far we have been 'Mr. Spehn' and 'Mrs. Kell' ... or, excuse me, 'Mama Kell.' And even if we were married someday, it might feel weird to call us 'Mom' and 'Dad.' Do you think you would feel weird doing that?"

Drew was quick to offer an answer. "Yeah, that would feel weird, because I already have a dad ... in heaven ... so I don't know."

Jack agreed. "Yeah, and our real mom is in heaven, so ... I mean, we can't really have two moms, right?"

We needed to guide them a bit further. "Well, there are options for what you could call us. 'Mom' and 'Dad,' or 'Daddy Spehn' and 'Mama Kell' ..."

Gina wanted to make a correction. "Except I wouldn't be 'Mama Kell' anymore because my name would be Spehn."

"Okay. So 'Mama Spehn' is an option. Here's the important thing. We really aren't worried about this. If we do someday become a family, it really won't matter what we're called; the only real thing that matters is that we love you and that we would be one big family ... whatever we are called. 'Mom,' 'Dad,' 'Mama Kell,' or ... even 'Phyllis'!" This made them laugh and they needed it at that moment. The boys loved a good punch line. Jack hugged Gina and smiled hard.

"Are you maybe afraid that if you start to call us those names or if you start to love us too much, then that means you don't love them as much anymore?" They both hesitated for a moment and then nodded.

"Well, I want to tell you about something that Jack's mom taught me. When Charlotte was two years old, she was our only child. We loved her more than we thought we could love anyone. Then we decided to have another baby."

Jack interrupted right on cue. "Ta da!"

"Yes, that turned out to be Jack. Well, I was a little confused about this, because how could I love another child as much as I loved Charlotte? Jack's mom told me that when God gives you someone new to love, it's like you grow a whole new heart and it fills up with love for them. It's not that you have to take love away from someone else that you love; it's that you get a new heart filled up with all new love for this new person." They seemed to like what they were hearing.

Cathy was indeed the first to say to me, "You grow a new heart." She had a way of making even a cliché sound practical. The kids liked the idea of growing new hearts and filling them up with love. They understood that if they loved someone new, that didn't mean betraying their late parents. Many adults—some in my own family—were unable or unwilling to grasp this simple concept: Love is not a zero sum game. Loving someone new does not mean that you love someone else less.

Love is not simply a gift from God; it is, in fact, the fundamental nature of God. God *is* love. And like love, he can't be "figured out." He must be experienced. I don't know anyone who has love all figured out. You can read books about it, sing songs about it, write poetry and dream dreams about it. In the end, you can only really *know* love through the experience of love itself.

It's the same with God. I've spent a lifetime trying to figure him out. I've read his book and I've sung his songs. I've recited his Psalms and imagined his heavenly home. In the end, I never really knew him until I experienced him. I experienced him on those trips to Barrington with my dad and diagramming game-winning buzzer-beaters as head coach. I've seen evidence of him waiting for me at the end of the wedding aisle and at the bedside up on 8-South. The experience of God is a sometimes glorious, sometimes painful one. But it is always right. Abundant with rainstorms and rainbows, wedding bells and funeral hymns, it always leads toward love. Our job is to remain open to the love that is revealed.

That can be hard to do when you experience loss. The death of a loved one creates profound grief. However, grief is meant to be an emotion, a transient reaction to the tragic circumstance of loss. It can actually be an extremely healthy experience. Grief honors your relationship with those you have lost and allows survivors to give expression to the unspeakable pain they feel.

For many, however, grief becomes a lifestyle. Instead of simply being strong emotions that someone feels, pain and sorrow actually become their defining characteristics. This disconnects them from the important relationships in their "previous life." Often the most significant relationship cast aside is with God.

When I lost Cathy I felt as though I had lost my context. I called myself the "husband in the forest who fell." If she wasn't around to be with me, did I really matter anymore? I had lost my love, and without it, it seemed I had no life. I instinctively began to avoid friends and even some family. I resisted help and was often annoyed at the "support" of others.

Even in her last pain-filled hours, Cathy had such clarity about these things. She told me to call Gina and that she would help me. Cathy taught me about these things in life and then in death. Gina taught me with her relentless and unflinching faith. Now, unexpectedly, these five children were teaching me. Not simply through the little talks we were having, but also as I watched them, one by one, grow new hearts.

We tucked Jack and Drew into bed. They seemed content for now. As I reached the door, Drew called me back to him. I sat on the bed and leaned in close.

"I think that it will seem strange at first," Drew whispered. "But I think that I'm gonna want to call you 'Dad.'"

"I think that would be great, buddy. Good night." I looked over at the sleeping bag. "Good night, Jack."

"Good night, Dad." Jack waited a beat. For a nine-year-old, he had perfect timing. He called to Gina, "Good night, Phyllis."

It wasn't long before Gina and I called a family meeting. We weren't technically a family yet, but it seemed right to call it that. Before the meeting I did something that was out of my nature. I read the Bible. I looked for a passage to read before we started. I found one that Danny said was his favorite.

Seven o'clock came and everyone was in the family room. With a Bible in one hand, I sat in the middle of it all on a solid wood coffee table. We started.

"Guys, Mama Kell and I want to talk to you about some pretty important things. Before we do, I want to read a Bible verse that I think will help us tonight. It is Jeremiah 29:11.

'For I know the plans I have for you. Plans to prosper you and not to harm you, plans to give you hope and a future.'

"You guys know that, over the past couple years, especially in the last few months, the two of us have come to love each other. And you know that we both love all of you. Well, it's pretty common for people who are like us ... a woman, a man, a bunch of ugly kids ..."

"Hey!" They all laughed.

"It's pretty common for a group like that to be ... a family." They began to look at each other, smiling.

"We want to talk to you guys tonight about the possibility of someday becoming a family for real. We want to talk to you guys about someday Mama Kell and I ... you know, bringing us all together ..." The kids still were not sure what this was about. They held their reactions for further confirmation. I had to just blurt it out.

"Guys, what would you think if the two of us ... got married?"

There it was. All five let out yells and gasps and squeals all at once. They were smiling and talking and hugging each other. They had a million questions. Can we get a dog? No way, not yet. Can we get bunk beds? That is a strong possibility. When would the wedding be? We don't know, but soon. Where will we live? Probably in the Spehns' house. When do we get to start calling you 'Mom' and 'Dad'? As soon as we kiss on our wedding day.

At some point the "meeting" was getting away from us. Gina decided to quiet everyone down and offer a small prayer of thanks for this blessing in our lives. When she finished, I noticed Charlotte and Jack nodding to each other. Suddenly they tore out of the room and headed for my office.

"No!" I shouted as I ran after them. "Do not touch it!" They were headed for the contract they had made me sign two years earlier, promising that I would never marry another.

"But, Dad," Charlotte pleaded. "We have to tear it up. Otherwise you'll have to go to jail."

With the kids' approval, there was really only one thing left to do. I needed to actually ask Gina to marry me. In mid-August the kids went up to Mullett Lake for a few days with Larry and Jill. I had a photography shoot out on the west coast of Michigan and asked Gina to come with me. She arranged for Drew and Sam to spend a day or two with her parents and off we went.

After the shoot I hurried Gina along, hoping she and I could get to a special spot that I knew about some fifteen minutes away on a sandy stretch of private beach near Pentwater Harbor. An unspoiled gem in the Midwest with a quaint shopping district, several extraordinary bed-and-breakfast places, and a pristine beach that stretches for miles with rustic bluffs on one side, Pentwater sits beside the deep azure blue of the greatest Great Lake of them all.

We settled on a spot, and since we had no beach towel or blanket with us, we simply sat on the warm sand. The last few sailboats were making their way back into the small harbor and the gulls were beginning their

evening dance in the sky. Across Lake Michigan, just over the horizon, like
a proud and approving brother, was my hometown of Chicago.

Gina and I were quiet for a time. Then I knelt in the sand on both knees
in front of her. I held both her hands and looked into her eyes. She smiled
at me and I spoke from the heart.

"G. This has been an unbelievable couple of years for us. Neither of us
could have predicted this, or maybe even wanted this. But there's no deny-
ing ... he has plans for us ..." Gina nodded. Her eyes began to water. She
knew.

"I have been confounded by those plans of his. And I have been amazed,
too. I have been heartbroken and I have been lifted up with joy. I have
learned to not expect to know what his plans are going to be and to simply
take this walk one day at a time. And as confused as I get sometimes, one
thing I am certain about ... I want to take this walk with you, for as long as
he will allow. In order to do that, I have to ask you a question ..."

I reached into my pocket and began to pull out the ring box. Gina
smiled huge and put her hand to her mouth. "Gina. Will you marry me?"

"Yes, of course ... you crazy man!"

We hugged and kissed and laughed. It was not unexpected and completely surprising all at once. This most improbable journey was going to
keep getting weird. Now we were going to be planning a wedding!

We calmed ourselves and decided to call the kids. We started with Jack
and Charlotte at the lake. We had them on the speakerphone in our car as
we drove.

"Guys?" I said, wondering exactly what their reaction would be now
that it was going to be real. "Hey, guys ... I just wanted to call you and let
you know ..."

"Yeah ...?" they said in unison.

"She said yes!" I shouted into the phone.

They erupted with cheers and woo-hoos and high fives. The sound on
the phone was the polar opposite of the sound I heard that awful morning
nearly two years earlier on February 28. This? Well, this was pure joy.

What I didn't know, but I found out later, was that up at Mullett Lake,
Charlotte and Jack were out on the dock at that exact moment. They knew
what I was going to be doing that night. They asked me what time I was
going to be doing it. I told them I was going to try to ask her right at sunset.
So they had spent the last hour or so out on the dock at Mullett, just the two

of them. Thinking about it. Talking with each other about it. Once, they confessed, they even pretended to act it out.

They told us that they had been sitting out on the dock wondering if I had asked her yet. They had sat out there for several hours talking with each other, pretending to be us; Jack was me and Charlotte was Gina, while they thought about their life to come. They admitted that they had made up songs and danced goofy dances together. They told us they prayed to God together out on that dock, asking him to bring them a new family.

When we returned to Rochester, we shared the news with Karl Galik. He had become our spiritual counselor, our close personal friend, our brother. He had seen his friend Matt Kell die an awful death. He sat on the floor of Cathy Spehn's kitchen bringing comfort to her children after her passing. He spent countless hours in fellowship and in prayer with both Gina and me as we found our way through unspeakable grief. Now, in the most unexpected experience in his twenty-five-year ministry, he would witness the full circle of God's grace and preside at the wedding of our two families.

We told him over steak and eggs at the Royal Park Hotel, and he was naturally thrilled for us. He asked how the kids were taking the news and we told him about their reactions. He began to tear up. Something occurred to him and it was making him cry.

"I just realized," he said, "the kids will get Christmas back now."

CHAPTER 40

replacement parts

gina

Matt had started a men's accountability group with Karl Galik and two others that met at six a.m. for breakfast every Thursday. A pastor, a doctor, a businessman, and an ad exec each brought their own "cancers" to the table and helped one another find little cures for the moment.

For more than a year, a meek woman named Shirley was their regular waitress at the Star Diner in Rochester. Later, when Matt dramatically changed his diet and began living a holistic lifestyle through Dr. Gonzalez, greasy diner food was no longer an option. Without a second thought I opened my kitchen for the group and became their new "Shirl." It was my complete joy to cook and serve an abundant buffet of fresh, organic breakfast food every Thursday morning. It was also a privilege to be a fly on the wall at this men's group.

After Matt died, the foursome became three, and my role as Shirley ended. It wasn't long before the group was back at the Star Diner with a new waitress and a new guy invited to fill out their foursome. Intellectually, I knew Matt wasn't being replaced, but I had to admit to a twinge of sadness realizing the world was still turning when, for me, it had completely stopped.

It happened again when I went to WDIV-TV to gather Matt's personal belongings and was led past his corner office to the door of a storage closet. In instances where the decision to move on was out of my control, I felt a sense of "How could you?" with an equal portion of understanding that "life goes on."

Upon my engagement to Michael, this same reality became true for many people around me. There were first adaptors who celebrated and accepted our relationship, and contrarians who doubted its validity. Most fell in between with equal parts support and skepticism. Even Colleen made sure to go "on record."

"You'd better be the real deal, Michael Spehn!" she said, half joking, half serious. "That's *my* girl and I'm not goin' anywhere! We're a package deal. You got her, you got me!"

"Oh great, another set of in-laws!" he teased.

Even my best friend, who wanted nothing but my happiness, was cautiously optimistic about my relationship with Michael. Of course, I expected nothing less from her. It was understandable, given that Michael and I became serious in a relatively short time. Colleen modeled true friendship, supporting me, getting to know Michael, and challenging me to read between the lines of my emotions. She asked hard questions, as only a best friend can, and I walked away more certain of my relationship with Michael, despite my increasing awareness of what the world was thinking.

After Matt died I had no intention or desire to have a man in my life. My only desire was to focus on my children. This wasn't some obligatory cliché. Being a widow exposed me to a level of vulnerability that terrified me. My protective instincts were high and my inclination for entering into a new relationship was below zero. I was repelled by any circumstance that increased our risk for further loss. Yet I had spent years learning to live with my heart open to the possibility of unexpected blessings.

In college, Matt invited me to attend church and my reaction was, "We're in college. We don't have to go to church!" Twenty years later Matt described cancer as a "win-win" and I questioned it hard. When Matt said, "After I'm gone, I want you to find a good Christian man and marry him," I plugged my ears and wept. I didn't want to believe that church mattered, or that there could be victory in death, or that I could fall in love with a new man in the midst of grieving another. I could not foresee what God had planned, and if someone had told me that this would be my life, I wouldn't have believed it. I might have even run from it. But I didn't. I went to church and my faith and understanding of God grew. That growth made it possible for me to believe that my husband is living victoriously in heaven. And that made it possible for me to love again.

The perception that I was replacing Matt by marrying Michael was frustrating to me, although I understood it. There are unwritten rules. When a child dies society agrees that the child is irreplaceable to his or her parents. The same is true when a child loses a parent. Yet spouses are considered easily replaceable, at least according to our divorce-laden society. Ironically, my "replaceable" husband was also an irreplaceable son and father, and I was a tad resentful of the implication that marrying Michael meant I was dropping in a replacement part.

Falling in love with Michael was not a measure of my love for Matt, and smiling again didn't mean I was past my grief. I was still in love with Matt. Michael was still in love with Cathy. Having four people in our marriage was our unique blessing. I don't believe this could have happened with any other person at any other point in my life.

No doubt about it, by blending our families we were increasing the number of grandparents, grandchildren, aunts, uncles, cousins, and friends. Questions about family traditions and roles began to creep into our conversations. For all the changes that were about to come, Michael and I remained consistent that every change was a positive. We were expanding our lives, growing new hearts and creating new experiences rather than replacing old ones. Some might call it a second chance, but we saw it as a continuation of the one chance we have to live out our perfectly numbered days.

Our families came together, not as replacements, but as redemption through our willingness to love and be loved. We were being emancipated from grief itself. This didn't mean that grief ceased to exist in our lives. It meant grief could not hold us captive and rob us of our lives. This redemptive season brought forth a profound awareness that although our prayers didn't get answered according to what we wanted, God did answer.

CHAPTER 41

holy water

michael

Larry and Jill have a pontoon boat up at Mullett Lake they call the *Rollie Bea*. Named for both of Larry's parents, the boat has two large pontoons underneath that provide ample buoyancy and stability. The flat floor and multiple seats give these vessels their Up North nickname: party boats. Call them what you will, they were perfect for a landlubber like myself.

Many mornings, before the first light, I quietly slipped out of the cottage with my camera equipment and took the pontoon out while everyone else was still asleep. On rare occasions a diffused fog hovered just over the water, offering a soft filter to the rising sun. This is where I cut my photography teeth, trying to keep up with the ever-changing light. I've always been a big fan of dawn. If only it would come a little later in the day.

The counterpart of my morning excursions alone were the sunset cruises Cathy and I took together. The notion of a sunset cruise may conjure up visions of wine and cheese and long-stemmed glassware. Cath and I preferred simpler fare: a can of Atlanta's finest, Coke, chilled to a perfect thirty-eight degrees and a bag of pretzels. Idling along the shoreline, we'd ogle the summer homes of the wealthier-than-us. Eventually we'd come to a spot a few hundred yards off the sunken pier behind the old train station in the tiny lakeside town of Topinabee. The water was so calm there we never even bothered to throw an anchor.

Sometimes I got Cath laughing with my impressions of the Up North yokels we'd met at the local market that day. Mostly, though, we just sat and smiled at each other. It was so nice to be together in the quiet for those precious few moments.

When Cathy passed away, her ashes remained in our home in an urn with her name on it, on the lower shelf of my bedside table. The kids once asked me if they could look inside. Jack liked that they put her name on the front. We talked about the ashes and how this had been Mom's earthly body, like a vehicle that Mom traveled around in. It wasn't "Mom." It was just what she used while she was here. Now that she was done with it, we could respectfully scatter the remains in a special place that Mom loved.

Cathy and I never talked much about funerals or "our wishes" for what to do if either one of us died. That was a mistake. The closest we ever got to that was when we joked around one night as we were getting ready to go out. Somehow the topic of death and funeral arrangements came up. Exactly how, I still don't remember.

"What do you want me to do with you when you die?" Cathy asked me casually from the bathroom as she was putting on her makeup.

"I'm not sure. Maybe you could have me stuffed in a sitting position and place me at the dinner table."

She returned this serve beautifully. "We could put your hands out in front of you and use them for hot dishes."

"Nah ... that doesn't seem right. I've got it! I think I'd like to be cremated and have my ashes thrown on Elle MacPherson."

"That's disturbing," she said.

"You want to use my dead hands as hot pads for your soup and I'm disturbing?"

Cathy thought seriously about the subject for just a moment. "I guess I'd want to end up at Mullett ..." she said. And that was that. We never spoke of it again.

More than a year after she died, the kids and I were at the cottage. The plain white walls were filled up with photos of Cathy and the kids. Everywhere you looked, a smiling Cath looked back at you. Going to Mullett was different now. The beauty of the place was still there, but a lot of the joy was missing.

This would be our last trip for the summer. School was about to begin and soon the leaves would begin to fall. Before the boats were put away for the season, there was one more ride to take. As the day came to an end, the kids settled in for a movie. Larry, Jill, and I untied the *Rollie Bea* from the dock and headed out for one last sunset cruise.

I drove us slowly out to the spot where Cath and I had drifted together on so many evenings. A layer of clouds created a grayish flat light that made it hard to see the contours of the water. That was okay though. Tonight we wouldn't be taking any pictures. There'd be no cans of Coke, no redneck jokes or knowing smiles. Just three people brought together by an extraordinary woman, now carrying her to her final resting place.

I cut the engine at our spot. For a while there was just quiet. The pontoon rocked a bit right and left with the twilight tide. Eventually we talked about Cathy and her love for Mullett Lake. Then it was time to do what we came to do. I opened the urn and cut open the plastic bag. I asked if anyone wanted to say anything. Both Larry and Jill, tears welling up in their eyes, shook their heads. I knelt closer to the water and spoke softly.

"Like almost everything good in our lives, this place came to us because of you. You insisted that we come. You insisted that we come back. Today we commit your ashes to this place forever. In doing so this ground becomes sacred, these waters become holy. Your soul rejoices in God's kingdom, your earthly remains rest in these gentle, holy waters, and your loving spirit lives within each of us every day. We love you always. God bless you, my love."

The ashes were suspended in the dark translucent water. Some sank to the bottom immediately. After a few minutes we drifted apart from them. I started the motor and very slowly steered for home. Soon we'd lost all sight of the area in which we'd been, with the fading light offering more silhouettes than detail. The ashes, I'm certain, found their rest, mixed among the hungry perch, the fallen mayflies, and the gentle cold springs.

Cathy was now forever joined with her favorite place in this world.

CHAPTER 42

here comes the sun

gina

When I was growing up in the seventies, television reruns were part of my daily after-school ritual. I'd burst through the door, drop my books, and begin to unwind from the pressures of fourth grade by sitting three feet from the television with a bag of Doritos until my fingers were covered with enough powdery nacho cheese film that I had to use my teeth to scrape it off. I tolerated the last twenty minutes of Thurston and Lovey on *Gilligan's Island* until it was time for my favorite show, *The Brady Bunch*.

The still shot of the exterior of the Brady house, which opened every episode, was entirely unappealing to me, but inside was like a dream. Coming from a modest home of about nine hundred square feet, I was in awe of the Bradys' huge living room with the open staircase, and the kitchen with orange countertops, exposed brick, and built-in wall oven. I liked the kitchen so much that when my dad built a desk in my bedroom, he used groovy orange Formica.

The Brady house wasn't the only thing that caught my preteen eye. Unlike most of my girlfriends who thought Greg was dreamy, I had a crush on Peter. He was my first television heartthrob, which lasted only until John Stamos showed up as Blackie on *General Hospital*, followed by a brief infatuation with Kirk Cameron from *Growing Pains*.

Regardless of everything I loved about *The Brady Bunch*, one thing was certain: I never imagined that someday I would be the second coming of

Carol Brady. Being the iconic mom of six kids in the all-American blended family, Carol had many admirable qualities, but emulating her life was not exactly on my "bucket list."

While Mike, Carol, the six kids, and Alice, the lovable housekeeper, looked around at each other from their *Hollywood Squares*–type boxes, the classic theme song explained that a lady and a fellow had "much more than a hunch" that one day they would become the Brady Bunch. Thirty years later, I felt like I was in my own square looking around at my own bunch, sans housekeeper regrettably, and it was clear that I needed much more than a hunch to pull off our wedding in the midst of perhaps the busiest month of my life.

Michael and I became engaged on August 13 and planned our wedding for October 6. There was an element of impetuousness that factored into our wedding date, but we did have some legitimate reasons for the timing. We wanted to be under one roof as a family early in the school year and before the holiday season began. With September overscheduled, late October already bringing Christmas decorations to the malls, and scheduling conflicts with Pastor Galik, we chose the first Saturday in October. Weather permitting we knew an outdoor autumn wedding in Michigan would be beautiful, though possibly chilly. Nothing a few tent heaters couldn't cure.

The day after I happily accepted Michael's proposal on the sunset shore of Lake Michigan, it was game on. During our three-hour car ride home, we called friends to share the good news, picked a wedding date, and convinced my parents to let us have the wedding in their backyard. We drove straight to the Somerset Collection, also known as "the mall" (big eye roll), to get my engagement ring sized. While waiting for the jeweler, we walked to Nordstrom with the notion of looking for a wedding dress. Nordstrom earned my loyalty and my almighty dollar when I discovered their policy to wait until after Thanksgiving to "deck the halls" for Christmas. I practically break out in hives when I see Santa's Castle go up in the mall before I've had a chance to put away the Halloween costumes. Plus, let's be honest, their shoe department is unbelievable!

Michael and I met Brenda, a Nordstrom saleswoman who took an immediate liking to us when we told her that we were newly engaged.

"Congratulations!" she said with a little too much enthusiasm as she glanced at my left hand. "When's the big day?"

"October," I said.

"Of this year?"

"Shotgun . . ." Michael deadpanned. I smacked his arm.

Brenda laughed politely, not quite sure if he was kidding. "Okay . . . well, follow me. We have a beautiful collection of formal white dresses."

Michael kept up the jokes. "I'm not sure white is appropriate for this one. Do you have anything in extremely off-white or maybe a plaid?"

I bit my bottom lip, trying not to laugh and encourage him. My eyes widened. "Stop it!" I whispered.

Without asking my size she grabbed several hangers with white, full-length gowns. We followed her into the fitting room and Michael plopped down on a chair next to the three-way mirror. By the time I came out wearing the first dress, Michael had our saleswoman and two customers in tears as he briefly told them about Cathy, Matt, the five kids, and now the two of us.

"What a story!" Brenda said, hugging me. "We are going to find you the perfect dress!" She looked me over. "And *that's* not it!" She was right. The material hung on me like a satin potato sack.

The second dress I tried was more red carpet sexy than wedding day elegant. Michael quickly noticed the plunging neckline and his eyes lit up. "Perfect! Brenda, wrap it up!" he said with a smile.

"Great dress. Wrong reaction for a wedding!" I said, checking myself in the mirror. I wore the dress more like Kate Hudson than Salma Hayek, but it worked. I wanted any excuse to buy the dress, but I had to give it up. "Maybe I could pull it off if I walk down the aisle like this." I began to stride like a supermodel.

Every woman in the fitting room giggled when Michael began singing, "You're . . . too sexy for our wedding, too sexy to go sledding . . ." as I threw my best runway pose. He stretched his neck to get one last look before I slipped back into the fitting room.

My hair was getting more static with each dress I slipped over my head. I have never been much of a shopper, and although we were having some laughs, I was growing weary of the process. The last dress in the fitting room was a simple satin Calvin Klein that was one size too big. It looked very plain on the hanger but the sweetheart neckline appealed to me. The fabric was pleated across the chest, and the wide shoulder straps crossed in the back. No beads, no lace, no bows, and no plunging neckline.

I walked out of the fitting room with my hands behind my back, pulling the material so the dress would appear to fit. For my final fashion show of the day, Michael sat quietly. He leaned on his elbow and covered his mouth with the side of his fist. I assumed he had grown tired of waiting and being the funny guy. He shifted in his chair and leaned forward. He lowered his head and raised his eyebrows, never taking his eyes off the dress.

"There it is." There was no inflection or attempt at polite convincing. My search was over.

I admired the simple elegance of the dress from every angle. "You think?" I asked with a big smile, completely knowing the answer. Every woman loves to get this response from the man she loves. The only thing better will be to hear that response after twenty years of marriage.

I couldn't believe we were off to such a good start less than twenty-four hours after we were engaged. I thought Brenda was going to pee herself. She ordered the dress in my size and shifted gears.

"Michael, you're next! I'm walking you to men's suits to find John. He's the best!"

A crisp, thin man in his midthirties, John was far less impressed with our story than he was with his sales ranking at Nordstrom and his ability to find the perfect ensemble for every occasion.

"What about this shirt?" Michael said, holding a tightly folded dress shirt against his chest.

With barely a glance, John quipped, "You want to dress like a groom. No button-down collars."

Michael dutifully slipped in and out of several black suit coats. I was having a *Queer Eye for the Straight Guy* moment as John deferred every question about fabric, color, and style to me, and not his reluctant "man-nequin."

We finally found the right suit, a black Joseph Abboud with a barely perceptible thin black stripe that gave the suit a subtle texture. John gathered several dress shirts (no button-down collars) and just about every white tie in the store. We stood by and watched him craft his art, mixing and matching combinations until he narrowed it down to two. He briefly explained his fashion sense, although I had the feeling he thought he was wasting his breath. He allowed us to make the final choice, but we couldn't have gone wrong with either ensemble. I had to admit, Nordstrom's top salesman had chops.

With the reluctance of a ten-year-old going to the dentist, Michael stepped onto a platform in the fitting room to have his suit marked for alterations. He looked incredibly distinguished and handsome, and his eyes looked bluer against the black suit. Watching him in front of the mirror, I smiled as John handled him, trying to check for the proper fit. Michael shot me a look and gave a wry smile as our too-fussy, well-dressed salesman handled his waist. I watched Michael suck in his gut just a little.

"I'm going to be working out a little more before the wedding, you know."

"Is that so?" John replied.

"Nah, I'm just kidding. I mean, look at me! I look good!" Michael teased.

"Well, it's definitely a great *suit*," John volleyed back.

There was a tailor sitting in the corner. He was in his midsixties, with the jowls of a Saint Bernard and a measuring tape draped around his neck. The "seen it all" expression on his face made it clear that he was unimpressed with the banter. Without a word he handed Michael a pair of tassel loafers to slip on before marking the cuff. John stepped in. "I'll mark him up."

"Oh no, no ..." Michael objected. "I want him!" he said, pointing to jowls.

"Oh, please!" John protested. "How do you think I got this job?"

"Let's not get into that!"

John blushed as he let out a yelp. "Oh, you're so bad! I was a tailor for five years. Just relax and enjoy the ride." He began to mark the shoulders.

"Okay, but if you've got a tall blonde around here who could measure the inseam, I would appreciate it."

"Well, there's always Jean Paul in men's shoes. He's tall but I think his blond hair is from a bottle."

The shtick between John and Michael carried on throughout the duration of our time in the men's department. They drew laughs from other salesmen and customers who were in and out of the fitting area. The old tailor in the corner never so much as smiled.

Michael's sense of humor is a carefully timed gift that he uses to elevate people in the most mundane, serious, and even painful circumstances. I've seen him use humor therapeutically, but never in lieu of facing tough issues. It's not a weapon or a mask or a mechanism for avoidance, but rather a shield of protection. His gift of humor and laughter is one of the things I treasure most about him. I have seen him bring laughter to his children even in the midst of their profound loss, and on this random Sunday he was sharing humor with Nordstrom's most persnickety employee. If we had enough time, I'm certain Michael would have had the old, expressionless tailor laughing too.

We left Nordstrom with wedding attire for six out of seven family members, as John, the consummate salesman, insisted on helping us find suits for the boys as well. Though we were off to a good start, I couldn't give my full attention to planning a wedding until the kids were ready to go back to school at St. John. With Michael busy juggling multiple work projects, I decided to get a jump start on my role as Carol Brady. I ran the kids around town, checking off school supply lists and attending open house meetings with teachers. I measured the kids and called Land's End to order school uniforms. The rep was very patient throughout our forty-minute call, making small talk when her computer ran slowly or as I riffled through the catalog to find my "next item."

"How many kids do you have?" the rep asked.

I paused, having to think about the answer. "Five."

"Oh, wow. You've got your hands full!"

"Yeah," I replied, not wanting to explain it all. Her next question caused me to stumble over my words.

"Are they all boys?"

"Yes, um, I mean no, I have one girl," I heard myself say.

I was about to have a daughter. Saying it out loud to a stranger felt like I had just been given an unexpected gift. For something I'd known all along, I was having quite a revelation. It was like the difference between knowing you have the winning ticket for the lottery and actually cashing the big check. We were starting a new mother-daughter relationship. My role in Charlotte's life was more like that of a close family friend or a safe aunt. She associated me with the fun things in her life. We shopped, baked, and wrote notes to each other, and she could see that her was dad was happy. That goes a long way for a child with only one parent. In some respects, I had an advantage over other moms because Charlotte and I started out as friends. Parents have the responsibility to teach and correct their kids as they grow up. We often don't realize the benefit of each other's friendship for many years, and even then, a mom is still a mom. My only hope was that the foundation Charlotte and I built would hold up under the strains of a new mother-daughter relationship, especially through adolescence.

When the first day of school was behind us, it was on to birthdays. Danny, my dad, and I celebrated our mutual September 11 birthday with a Spiderman moon bounce and a store-bought sheet cake for fifteen six-year-olds. Michael's birthday was only seven days before our wedding. Despite the unfortunate timing, I didn't completely overlook it. I picked up a birthday card at the grocery store and made his favorite "Darn Good Chocolate Cake," a recipe I found that Cathy used to make for him.

A handful of memorial dates were scattered in as well, including both of our wedding anniversaries to our late spouses, and Matt's birthday just one day before Michael's. These dates, while significant, did not automatically cause a spike in my grief as many expected. Maybe I had it wrong, but birthdays and anniversaries were some of the happiest days of our lives. Thanks to photographs and videos, my memories were vivid and comforting, bringing more joy than pain. My sorrow was most profound on ordinary days rather than on specific dates of remembrance. There's no rhyme or reason to bereavement and certainly no book of grief etiquette declaring, "Deceased's birthday: mourn accordingly!"

In the midst of our birthdays and remembrances was my twenty-year high school class reunion. Back when I signed up to be on the planning committee, the September calendar wasn't quite so full. For an overscheduled burgeoning Carol Brady, this often highly anticipated, midlife rite of passage had become an insignificant blip on the calendar. Although I was obligated to attend the reunion, the thought of recounting the events of my life for my former classmates was unappealing. I didn't want to show up at the reunion as "the widow" with the story that called for people's puppy dog eyes and condolences. To avoid any "woe is me" exchanges, I worked the reception table, said hello to every classmate who arrived, and quietly snuck out an hour later.

The big event of September was the second annual Matt Kell Memorial Golf Tournament. I had the task of soliciting donations for the auction and writing a speech that I would give during dinner. Thankfully, I was not heavily involved in the planning details. Instead, my focus was the launch of the New Day Foundation for Families, which would be making its debut.

For the golf outing, Michael produced a video that featured the board of directors, made up of my friends and "brothers," talking about their memories of Matt and their hope for the newly formed foundation they were now representing. In addition to producing the video and juggling his clients, Michael was designing our wedding invitations, putting the finishing touches on the Living Mural for the atrium at St. John, and generally trying to stay out of my way. I had become a whirling dervish.

Every day was a veritable buffet of major life events. Any one of these would have been enough, but I piled them high, all together on one plate of delicious insanity. Combining the lives of two families and two houses, planning a wedding, getting five kids ready to start school, planning and attending my twenty-year high school reunion, hosting the second annual Matt Kell Memorial Golf Outing, launching the New Day Foundation for Families, installing the Living Mural at St. John, acknowledging several family birthdays, and keeping the kids happy and organized, all in fewer than six weeks, caused me, I will admit, to be a bit manic. Even in the tidy world of episodic television, I doubt that Mrs. Brady could have pulled all this off. And if she had, I'm certain Alice would have been behind the scenes doing all the heavy lifting.

The weeks leading up to our wedding were some of the most frenetic, joyful days of my life. My rapid-fire pace scared off everyone who would typically be available to assist me. Even Colleen took a step back. She did cohost a beautiful bridal shower for me with several friends, but no one came near the wedding plans. If you weren't running at full speed, you had to get out of my way.

I did have one advantage. I wasn't a rookie. I knew the wedding drill and was determined to have fun with it. I planned my first wedding when I was only twenty-two. Matt and I had a traditional church and country club affair. It was a beautiful, but very old-school, wedding. I wore my mother's hand-detailed dress with a heavy twenty-foot train that detached after the ceremony. My bridesmaids wore crimson velvet dresses, above the knee, and my sister, Tara, the maid of honor, wore a matching pillbox hat. Matt and I danced to "Candy," an old Johnny Mercer standard that charmed and amused us. There was a five-tiered wedding cake, a chicken dance (much to my chagrin), and a long guest list filled with Italians we had never met. A few years after we were married, Matt and I laughed and had a twinge of regret when we realized that we could have taken my dad up on his offer to give us "ten grand and a ladder."

Throughout September my multitasking skills were maxed out. We sought the assistance of an event planner to help us create a comprehensive to-do list that would prevent critical details from slipping through the cracks. Kimberly Allen was also one of Michael's clients, and although we didn't need a full-time wedding coordinator, she agreed to meet at my parents' home to talk with us. She asked a lot of questions, and we filled out a client profile sheet before we began discussing color themes, caterers, and the best rental companies for tents and linens. As she reviewed our information, her expression changed.

"Were you Matt Kell's wife?"

"Yes. For thirteen years."

"We worked together on events for WDIV-TV during the auto show. He was such a great guy. Wow, I guess I've worked with both your husbands on the auto show!"

These moments, when people start piecing together the details, always seem to catch me off guard. I never know if I should explain the whole story, try to fill in a few blanks, or just leave it alone. My instincts tell me that people are not as interested in the details as I might think. But Kimberly was visibly moved and wanted to know more. As Michael told the longer version of our story, she and I were both in tears.

"I don't know what to say first. I'm sorry? Or congratulations?" she said.

Neither, I thought to myself. No pity or applause. I just wanted people to see what I saw. Not a hunch, or a coincidence, or a convenient happy ending. It was just God. With all of his grace, his plans, his freedoms and mysteries, he was present in both the "I'm sorry" and the "Congratulations."

"It's an honor for me to help plan this wedding. I've got about a hundred ideas in my head already," she said.

I liked knowing that our wedding coordinator was more than a valuable resource; she was an unexpected link between the two men I loved.

Kimberly offered, "If you'd like, I'll help you on-site the day of your wedding. I would just love to be part of a day like that."

I was comforted by her memories of Matt, her insights into Michael, and her desire and enthusiasm to help us honor the past while celebrating our new beginning. Kimberly's combination of responses—brokenhearted, joyful, and grateful—remained with me throughout the planning process. She expressed in one moment everything I had felt in stages over many months. It seemed impossible for these emotions to exist simultaneously, yet here we were, missing them, loving each other, and receiving the gift of a new family and a new life. That's redemption. And that's just how God works.

The anticipation of starting a new life gave me such an adrenaline rush that I lost five pounds without trying. My cell phone bill doubled and I was filling up my gas tank three times a week. The ride was wild. I had appointments for both the wedding and the house every day. The caterer, florist, painter, custom closets, photographer, musicians, rental company, church, bunk beds, seamstress, tailor, hairdresser, and marriage license all kept me running in between kids' basketball games, homework, and school projects. I was breathless.

Of all the wedding appointments I scheduled, there was only one that piqued Michael's interest. I had mentioned that I would be going to the florist and the bakery to make selections for the wedding. Instinctively, Michael's face lit up as if his sweet tooth shot a message to his brain: "Must have cake samples ..."

We skipped lunch and went to Christine's Bakery to select the flavor and design of our wedding cake. With a tray full of cake samples in front of us, Michael started asking questions about other items he spotted in the display case. Before long he had the ladies running for additional samples of cookies, cupcakes, and pastries. In the midst of our bakery palooza, Michael discovered what he considered the perfect cookie: a simple bow-tie shortbread with jelly filling and a sprinkle of powdered sugar. His eyes rolled to the back of his head with every bite.

"We gotta have these at the wedding. Unbelievable!" Michael said with a mouthful. It was like a scene from *The Simpsons*. My very own Homer, surrounded by plates full of decadent sweets, moaning with delight.

The face of our dessert table was dramatically altered by Michael's participation in the process. We ordered a modest but elegant wedding cake and added six dozen bow-tie shortbreads, two dozen artistically frosted leaf-shaped cookies, and four dozen glorious cream-filled, poured-frosting cupcakes. Dessert cost more than my wedding dress, shoes, and Spanx combined!

After our bakery appointment, we skipped dinner and later met at the home of Al and Shari Bennett. Their daughter, Lauren, was a high school student with the voice of an angel. Long before we knew her, we had heard her singing a cappella with a youth group band that performed at St. John on rare occasions. We had to do some detective work, but we finally found the source of the voice that had given us goose bumps several months earlier. Acoustic guitar player Eric Hedlund, also from the youth group band, accompanied Lauren. Eric was the son of Katherine Hedlund, a woman who for twelve months had kept a handwritten prayer journal for the boys and me, and presented it to me one year after Matt died. Katherine gave the phrase "I'm praying for you" meaning and power. I have never received a gift like it before or since.

Coming off our bakery high, we were looking forward to enjoying a private screening of Lauren and Eric's acoustic interpretations of the songs we selected for our ceremony. Michael and I sat next to each other on the step leading into the great room of the Bennetts' home.

Eric began to softly play the unmistakable opening chords from George Harrison's "Here Comes the Sun." I kept my head down and eyes closed. The double entendre of the lyrics was as appealing to me as the famous lilting melody that floated on wings of poetic simplicity. Like so many Beatles songs, it had the ability to gracefully elevate the human spirit.

By the time Lauren sang, "Little darling, the smiles returning to their faces. Little darling, it seems like years since it's been here ..." I was a mess. Tears streamed down my face and I clutched Michael's hand. His eyes welled up and we sat in silence as they finished. This little anthem of hope would take us down the aisle on our wedding day, and out of our long, cold, lonely winter. It felt good to be kissed by the sun.

Beyond the details of the wedding was the bigger task of the merging of our families and our homes. I tapped into every available resource, including Michael's friends and neighbors Heather and Tonya, who ran a successful interior design business. These women were dear friends to Cathy and without a second thought they welcomed me into their neighborhood and into their lives. It was fun getting to know them as they helped me redecorate the second story of Michael's home. Whenever I was around, they stopped by to chat or deliver a batch of cookies. All of our kids played together and Tonya was quickly becoming my mentor, as she was also the mother of five children.

Together we selected paint colors for all the bedrooms and bathrooms, ordered two sets of bunk beds, and chose new sheets and comforters for all five kids. Charlotte, Jack, and Danny moved in with Drew, Sam, and me while we tore apart their bedrooms and closets. My goal was to have everyone feel like they were getting a fresh start. The kids seemed excited about all the changes and had input along the way as we switched their rooms, painted everything, and installed closet systems to maximize space.

While details were being worked out for the closets, we hired "Skip the Painter." A clever name, though I have since given him several new ones. The morning he was scheduled to begin, I was running late with the paint swatches so Michael showed Skip around the house. When he stepped outside with his crew, Michael assumed they were gathering supplies or making a run for coffee. After an hour with no sign of Skip or his men, I dialed his cell phone. He informed me that he wasn't going to do the job.

"What do you mean, you're not doing the job? You were just here with your crew."

"I have another job. I am not coming back to your house."

"Ever?"

"No. I have another customer."

"I don't understand! *I'm* your customer! You were just here! I'm looking at your quote."

There was silence on the phone line.

I tried to calm down and reason with him. "Look, Skip, we are getting married in two weeks and I have five kids who need their bedrooms ready. Please don't walk out on us."

Click.

"No way that just happened!" I stared at the phone.

"Did he just hang up on you?" Michael asked. My answer came in the form of a deep breath. I was beside myself. Circling the kitchen island, I squeezed my cell phone so tightly that I might have produced juice. I was raging mad. Michael tried to talk me down.

"Did he say why he quit?"

"No. He just did. Maybe all the closets being torn up freaked him out. I don't get it."

"Was it because I didn't offer him a beer? They say you're supposed to offer these guys a beer, but I mean, it's nine o'clock in the morning, for Pete's sake."

"Seriously?" I wasn't in the mood for jokes.

I walked outside and started pacing the driveway to catch my breath and gather my thoughts. The warmth of the sun felt good on my face, and it helped calm me a bit. I got on the phone with Vince "the painter," who had also given us a quote on our job. He listened to my sob story and informed me that Skip was his brother-in-law.

"Yeah, he's crazy," Vince said. "This isn't the first time he's bailed on a job."

Fabulous! I had found the most unstable, unreliable painter in metro Detroit and I was in the crunch of a lifetime. Vince was in the middle of a job and offered to come in a week, but I needed someone to start yesterday. I walked to the mailbox for a distraction, and I waved to Heather and Tonya as they drove by together. Although they're interior designers, I didn't think to tell them that we had just lost our painter.

The only person I thought to call was my dad, the most connected guy on the planet when it comes to home maintenance. Remarkably, he had an instant solution. James Harris had been painting for my family for more than a decade. After being out of touch for more than two years, my dad informed me that James had returned to the area in the last week and contacted him looking for work. I started dancing in the driveway.

Two days before the wedding, the closet installation was completed and Michael and I were admiring the fresh paint as we put away all the clothing and furniture that had been strewn about during the renovations. I was feeling good about what we had accomplished when I left Michael's house to pick up the kids from school. On my route, I passed a home that sat adjacent to the cemetery where Matt was buried. A lawn sign bearing the name "Skip the Painter" was on the front lawn. I sneered at it and thought, "I'd like to skip the painter.... *Everybody* should skip that painter! You'd think the little sucker might not take a job so in my face!" I had half a mind to pull over and share my thoughts with my ol' pal Skippy.

Instead, I employed the Rule of Forty, taught to me by an old friend from Lost Valley Ranch, Mary Ellen. She said, "Sometimes it takes forty seconds, sometimes forty minutes, but beyond that, you're just wasting your time." It was a seemingly impractical yet totally sensible way to "get over" whatever was bugging me. I was proud to say that my Skip the Painter moment was over in less than forty seconds, because my attention was redirected to the moving truck I almost slammed into while snarling at Skip's lawn sign. Immediately I reached for my cell phone. I wanted a moving company. I had to have a moving company. Bringing a few of my things into Michael's house would really go a long way toward helping us feel like we were waking up in our new home on October 7. The moving company agreed to come to my house the next morning, just twenty-four hours before our wedding. I kept this last-minute addition to our to-do list to myself for fear that someone would try to have me committed. All of this and we still had to install the Living Mural at St. John.

Michael and I carefully mounted over forty images, in various sizes, like a mosaic along the atrium walls. A crowd began to gather and several people volunteered their assistance. I stared up at Michael on a thirty-foot scaffold, holding the last of twelve banners that would complete the Living Mural, and I was struck by the journey we had taken to reach this moment. In a booth at Panera Bread, we had sketched the plans for this day. Unbeknownst to us, God was sketching some plans of his own. We measured and researched and dug through archival photos to design a mural filled with artistic representations of the history of St. John and symbolism of the Christian faith. It took on many forms, but at each stage of the process it was unmistakable. The mural, and our relationship, was taking on a life of its own. The pieces were coming together in unexpected ways to create something beyond what we could have imagined.

After Matt died, I, like the atrium, was lifeless and empty. Many significant events of our lives had passed through the atrium, nestled safely in between the church and the school that had educated two generations of our family. Weddings, funerals, baptisms, graduations, and lifelong friendships had all taken place here. It was also in this place that I first met Cathy Spehn and her little boy, Danny. An incredible experience, in hindsight. Like an ultrasound, I could see him, but he was not yet real to me. I would have to wait two years to have him in my arms.

Michael and I spent a year working on a project that brought color and life to an otherwise empty, lifeless place, and in the process, we did the same for each other and our kids. I never had to become someone new or apologize for my life, past or present. We grew new hearts, new hope, and were on the cusp of a new life.

When the moving van arrived at my house, I knew this was the last of the work to be done before I became the new Mrs. Michael Spehn. While the men loaded the truck, I wandered around my house. I was going to miss it. For more than ten years it had been filled with many of the best and worst memories of my life. Lives began and ended in this home. It would always be a part of me.

I walked outside to the courtyard that was just outside my office window. Under the same tree where I had watched squirrels claw and flail for a few grains of birdseed, I spotted a memorial stone that had been given to me after Matt died. I carefully lifted the stone, expecting to find creepy-crawly things on the underside. Instead, as I lifted it, a tiny rainbow appeared. I dropped it and relifted it three times in disbelief. I quickly realized that the sunlight was beaming through the beveled glass of a light fixture attached to the courtyard's brick entry. Perhaps it was just that, a coincidental refraction of light. But it felt like much more. This tiny rainbow prism was like a message of assurance that our new life was blessed. I was so in awe that I sat down in the mulch, ignoring the spiders and bugs, and continued lifting the stone. It reminded me of our double rainbow in Colorado. Unexplainable gifts. I knew that the light would shift and it wouldn't be long before my rainbow prism would disappear.

Like the atrium the night before, Michael's house was about to be transformed, again. With the upstairs completely rearranged and refreshed, it was time to bring back the female influence to the living area of the Spehn home. Michael moved several pieces of his own furniture to the basement, the garage, and even the curb to make room for my things.

"Why don't you let the movers do that?" I asked several times, not wanting Michael to pull a muscle or slip a disk the day before our wedding.

With beads of sweat on his forehead, he flashed me his Jack Nicholson grin and reminded me that I had brought this on myself. "You can't just bring a house full of furniture into a fully furnished home and not expect me to move a few things!"

I shut up after that. By the time the kids came home from school, the house had taken on a new look. They ran around and checked out all the changes. Drew and Sam were happy to see familiar pieces of their home in the Spehn house. Charlotte, Jack, and Danny liked the changes but had a few questions about what was missing. With so much new, Michael and I felt a strong need to keep the kids close to us. We had no plans for a honeymoon. Waking up together, surrounded by our kids, was perfect. Despite all the changes, seen and unseen, we wanted to assure our kids that they were surrounded by security and love.

On the eve of our becoming the modern-day Bradys, our extended family and friends, many of whom had traveled across the country to be with us, also took notice of the changes they could see all around. New phone numbers, new addresses, new colors on the walls, new brothers and a sister. Everyone seemed to love the house and they marveled at how happy the kids were. While it was gratifying to receive so many compliments for all that we had accomplished in such a short time, none of that really mattered. Like everything else in life, that which is visible to the world is only part of the story. The lessons of our history, and the promises and permissions given for our future, are what impel the unseen current that runs beneath the surface, moving us along through life.

Everything we had done to arrive at this day was motivated by our appreciation for what had been given, and for what had been taken away. We had found the peace that lives in the space between grief and celebration. There was no explaining it, but one thing was certain. Our faith told us that without suffering and loss, we would never come to know such peace. If our children grow up with this understanding, we will have honored God and done our job as parents.

The Brady theme song is true. Blending two families takes much more than a hunch. It requires trust and communication and the ability to express our fears so we can learn to keep them in their proper place. If a dying man and woman can grant permission for their spouses to love again, and if we can teach our children, and ourselves, how to "grow new hearts," then it becomes possible for complete strangers to wake up one day as a new family, with a completely different life, one they didn't even know could exist. The biggest surprise is that it could be as good as, or even better than, the old life. With faith, it most certainly will be.

CHAPTER 43

the new day

michael and gina

We planned an outdoor wedding expecting cool temps and the possibility of rain, but as we've come to learn, our expectations and plans have a way of reminding us that we are not in control. A hint of orange in the trees was the only sign of autumn as temps reached the upper eighties and the sun beat down with the intensity of August in Miami.

Bob and Toni Valenti's home was bustling with activity. Kimberly, our wedding coordinator, feverishly tended to the last-minute details and supervised the musicians, florists, and caterers. As guests arrived, they passed through an elegant white banquet tent with high peaks and seating for 120 guests. Tables were decorated in crisp pale blue linens and topped with small vases filled with bunches of sunflowers.

The natural beauty of the wooded area and small pond behind the house was in perfect harmony with the professionally manicured garden where the wedding was staged. Bright white chairs lined in neat rows contrasted against the grass and cloudless blue sky. The atmosphere was energetic and light. People were smiling and laughing as light keyboard music played in the background. These same people, on both sides of the aisle, had gathered together not all that long ago to mourn. Today they came together again to shake off the shroud of heartbreak and experience some real joy.

Groups of friends awaiting the ceremony gathered around tall cocktail tables that were sprinkled around the yard. Two tall pillars, set adjacent to one another, each holding a large vase bursting with sunflowers, red gerbera, and blue delphinium, framed the area in front of the garden where the ceremony would take place.

Michael was handsome in his tasteful black suit and white tie. He looked out from the tall bay windows in the kitchen nook, taking in the sight of this garden reunion of people who had been led to this place by providence.

Eleven-year-old Charlotte, with her blonde curls and small freckles dotting her nose, was breaking hearts in a powder blue dress that matched her eyes. She graciously handed programs and long-stemmed sunflowers to all of the guests, smiling and moving from one group to another explaining what they were to do with the sunflowers later.

Michael helped Drew with his tie and the other boys gathered in close, all wearing matching dark suits, white shirts, and blue ties. They each had a flower pinned to the lapel of their suit coat. Jack and Drew pretended to be the president and vice president of the United States until they found dark sunglasses and decided they wanted to be a mini version of the Blues Brothers instead.

The children were dressed. The food was ready. The guests had arrived. It was time to become a family of seven. Gina clasped the five-diamond necklace around her neck that Michael had given her as a wedding gift. She glanced in the mirror one last time, a new woman staring back.

The seven of us gathered on the lower patio, out of view of the guests. Sam and Dan held the wedding bands on small pillows and led the group up in a processional. The best men, Jack and Drew, followed close behind. Charlotte, the maid of honor, was next, carrying a small bouquet of flowers. Eric Hedlund, with his acoustic guitar, played the unmistakable opening chords of Harrison's "Here Comes the Sun" as we followed our kids along a stone path to the garden where friends and family were gathered. As we came into view, Danny smiled and waved like a politician at the St. Patrick's Day parade.

While the day was about seven people forming a new family, it was also about four extended families and a community of friends being joined through this union. We planned to visually symbolize this joining of many into one through the use of a unity vase.

As Eric played a soft melody on the guitar, we each placed a long-stemmed white rose in the vase. Then the members of four extended families, the Spehns, Kells, Valentis, and Lutzes, each added a blue iris or a blue delphinium around the white roses.

In the hot sun, with sweat dripping off his face, Pastor Galik joyfully shared a message of deliverance and "all things new" based on Psalm 30.

"You're the greatest example of 'mourning into dancing' that I have ever seen in my ministry," he said. "You're living evidence of the grace of God."

He honored Matt and Cathy and expressed his happiness for the kids, who were the definition of "all things new." The message was brief (likely to prevent anyone from passing out in the heat) and the ceremony closed with every friend and family member placing their long-stemmed sunflower into the unity vase with the white roses, blue iris, and blue delphinium, symbolizing the color and life they'd all brought to this new family.

The celebration continued under the tent with toasts and speeches. Michael, holding the microphone in his left hand and Gina's hand in his right, thanked all the parents and guests for their support and acknowledged the many friends who had traveled across the country to spend the day with us. He then began telling the story of our trip to Colorado.

"In June, Gina and I had the opportunity to bring the kids to Colorado, and if you've ever been there, you know that one of the more stunning features of the landscape is the aspen groves. We had taken a trail ride on horseback ... and if you could for just one minute, try to erase the image of me on a horse, that will help. The trail guide taught us that each aspen grove is actually one tree with many trunks."

The tent was quiet now. Even the kids were listening intently.

"Some aspens are tall, and some are short, and some are broken just a little, and some are ... well, not there anymore. But they are all connected underground by one root system. That's who you are to us. Our family tree may be a bit oddly shaped, but it is beautiful to us. Thank you and God bless you all."

We raised a glass to our friends and family, and Colleen Schomaker stepped to the microphone.

"Take a seat, you two!" she announced lightheartedly. "I've got a few things to say!"

Through tears Colleen spoke at length about the history, depth, and rarity of her friendship with Gina and what it was like having a backstage pass to the events that led to this day.

"I have stood on the sidelines, watching you pull each other out of grief, day by day, in a way that not even a best friend could, and for that I am thankful. I have watched your relationship grow, observed you helping each other with your kids. I have watched you endure hardships and allow joy to be reborn in your hearts. I have also seen you reach out to others in similar painful situations and share your faith and new hope. In this I am reminded that God has a purpose."

Her toast ended with a hope-filled prayer for the journey ahead. Colleen had one last surprise that was a perfect summary of Pastor Galik's message about "turning mourning into dancing."

A soulful rendition of "Awesome God" by Travis Cottrell began playing and twenty-five kids started dancing, with Michael and Gina's kids up front. Colleen had practiced with them to create a routine, but that quickly broke down into kid freestyle. Everyone looked on, laughing and singing, as these five kids, who had lost so much, became the very embodiment of joy. Surrounded by family and friends, and sustained by an unwavering faith, they danced their way into a new day.

epilogue

Weeks in advance of the wedding, the five kids agreed that immediately following the ceremonial first kiss, they would begin calling us "Dad" and "Mom." After a couple weeks of breaking old habits, the names Mom and Dad came freely, sounded normal, and have never needed the prefix "step."

Our first Christmas as a new family was filled with twice the decorations, twice the food, and many old and new traditions. As Karl Galik predicted, Drew and Sam had the celebration of Christmas restored, surrounded by a big new family and many loving remembrances of their father.

In the spring, we brought the kids back to Mullett Lake, this time as a family of seven. Larry Lutz gave his new grandsons a piece of memorabilia that he received twenty-five years earlier: a game ball from his coaching days. It was first given to Larry by the eighth-grade softball team at St. John and carried the signatures of all the players, including a center fielder named Matt Kell.

In early September 2008, Dick Spehn sat on the couch in his Newport Beach home watching his beloved Chicago Cubs lose another game. Near the middle of the sixth inning, he suffered a massive stroke. Four days later he passed away, surrounded by family.

After being on the transplant list for more than a year, Tommy Schomaker graciously received the "gift of life" at the University of Michigan C. S. Mott Children's Hospital through the selfless gift of a donor family. He celebrated his one-year heart birthday on June 3, 2010. Tommy still raids the Spehns' pantry whenever he can.

The New Day Foundation for Families continues to serve the families of young children who have lost a parent to cancer. Since 2007, more than $200,000 has been raised, primarily through events like the Matt Kell Memorial Golf Outing, held each autumn in Michigan.

Michael looks every day at the name handwritten on the discolored slip of paper that sits near his right hand on the top of his desk at home; Christina, the nurse. It reminds this once-cynical man to stop looking for perfect answers in this world and to start accepting the ones that are right.

Becoming a family of seven was a relatively smooth transition. We made the kids the priority and all the grandparents, aunts, uncles, and friends followed suit and quickly realized that their role in the kids' lives was still valued, appreciated, and welcomed.

The kids flowed seamlessly with the living arrangements and have learned to adjust to sharing space. They are siblings in the truest sense, most days loving each other more than annoying each other! There is an ongoing dialogue in our home about kindness, respect, and responsibility. Our family life is rooted in faith and communication. Without these, we have nothing. Perhaps the biggest challenge of blending two families has been the continuous ebb and flow of grief. Children tend to "recycle" their grief as they gain understanding, asking many of the same questions over and over because the answers they received three years ago no longer satisfy their expanding minds. Being surrounded by siblings who understand has been a quiet blessing. Our ongoing grief is a unique part of our family dynamic that will never cease. As long as we continue to use it as a force that propels us to grow our faith and serve one another and our community, we will have honored the lives and legacies of Matt and Cathy.

Michael leads regular family meetings that keep the communication in our home open and honest. We laugh and cry together as a family. We don't always get it right, but we admit our faults and offer forgiveness. The kids are better than okay. They are thriving. Growing up isn't easy under "normal" circumstances, but our kids are surrounded by love, discipline, and communication. If these can be used to continuously reveal God to them a little more every day, then Lord willing, they will be the kind of adults who will make a difference in their generation.

readers group guide

Chapter 1: The Fall

1. Gina and her father share a birthday of September 11. Where were you when the news broke about the terrorist attacks on the United States on 9/11/01? Tragedy has a way of actually bringing people together in ways they never imagined. Other than 9/11, what events have impacted your relationships?

2. Sometimes the simplest notes and letters are the most meaningful—like the one Matt gives to Gina in the aftermath of 9/11. Have you ever received or given a letter like the one Matt wrote to Gina? What made it special?

3. What are some ways you show gratitude to the people most important to you (spouse, children, parents, siblings, friends)? How does showing gratitude impact your relationships?

Chapter 2: Mullett Lake

1. There is a vivid description of morning on Mullett Lake. Where is your favorite place in creation and how would you "paint a mental picture" of it?

2. Michael resisted going to Mullett Lake the first time, but he is pleasantly surprised by how much he likes it and how wrong his images of the experience turn out to be. When have you been delighted by how wrong you were about something or someone?

Chapter 3: Skyline

1. Matt saw two highly regarded specialists that had opposing viewpoints regarding his cancer treatment. Have you ever been in a situation where doctors had different opinions about a health issue? How did it resolve and what was your role in the decision-making process? What are your views about holistic treatments?

2. While lying in a hospital bed after the surgery that confirmed Matt's cancer had metastasized, he offered a prayer not for himself, but for the nun (and her ministry) who came in to visit him. Describe a time when you thought of others in the midst of your own crisis.

Chapter 4: Mushroom Cloud

1. Michael describes growing up Catholic in an area of Chicago he dubs "Skeptic Valley." Many young adults step away from the church when they leave their parents' home. Why do you think this is?

2. "I always question them; I've never once questioned Him." What does this mean to you? Who is "them"? Why do so many question "them"?

3. Richard Spehn began to question his role in his children's lives as they grew up. He was the "old lion" who could still roar but who the other lions didn't respond to anymore. Is this inevitable? As we age, are we destined to become less relevant?

4. As his parents slowly allow their relationship to dissolve, Michael is forced to watch almost in slow motion. Can couples reverse the course of their relationship once it starts to atrophy? As Michael says, "acrimony and scorn had come to live with us ..." Once that happens, can the relationship be saved?

Chapter 5: Win-Win

1. Matt describes having cancer as a "win–win." Why do you think Matt said this to Gina? Have you ever considered that cancer, or any other difficult circumstance in your life, could be a win–win? Do you believe, as Matt did, that having cancer is a win–win situation? Why or why not?

2. What did Matt mean when he asked Gina to walk him to the waters' edge?

3. When you read Matt's journal entry at the end of the chapter, did your perspective shift at all?

Chapter 6: Just Get It Done

1. Cathy tells Michael, "We're moving to California!" Have you ever made a declaration as bold as this and then followed through with it? What was the result? Knowing what you do now, would you do it again?

2. The "rhythm of the kids ..." was sacred to Cathy. Are you in tune with the rhythm of your kids (or nieces, nephews, etc.)? Truthfully, are smiling kids more important than shiny counters?

3. To Richard Spehn, "just get it done" was a personal mantra. He was someone who "just got it done" throughout his life. If you were to assign a slogan or motto to yourself, what would it be?

Chapter 7: Lost Valley

1. Matt's experience with Drew at the Major League Baseball All-Star Game prompts him to generously encourage Gina to take her own "dream trip" to Lost Valley Ranch with their sons. Matt wanted her to experience the same joy he did, but he didn't want to take the trip with them. Do you feel Matt should have taken the trip with Gina and the boys? Why or why not?

2. Gina is in acute pain during her time at Lost Valley but draws closer to God and finds true peace in the midst of it. What draws you closer to God in the midst of your circumstances? What pulls you away? What are the long-term effects of drawing closer to God?

Chapter 8: I'm Home

1. The joy Michael feels when he invites his dad to the World Series quickly deteriorates into another disagreement between the two men. Do you remember a time when pettiness and inappropriate expectations caused a problem in one of your relationships? How did it resolve?

2. Cathy is due to fly home without finding a house in Michigan. On the day of the flight, four-year-old Danny develops a fever that forces them to postpone for a day; just long enough for another house to come on the market. Coincidence? Fate? A God thing? When Michael once again

follows Cathy's "tone," is he just going along or is he slowly beginning to see God at work in his life?

Chapter 9: Freight Trains

1. Matt and Gina wanted to protect their children from the freight train called Cancer that was barreling through their young lives. They couldn't stop cancer, but they guided and protected their sons in other ways. When your children are faced with trials, how will you prepare them to cope with the circumstances? How important is faith in God to seeing our children through tragedy?

2. "Sitting down in front of the camera would mean saying good-bye. Saying good-bye would mean giving up. Giving up meant dying. Dying meant not being there for the boys. Unacceptable." Matt struggled to begin making a video diary, but it is one of the greatest gifts he left for his children. What are the pros and cons of making a video diary? Would you make a video diary for your children if you were facing a terminal disease, or even if you weren't?

Chapter 10: Life Is Good

1. "Cathy could see the righteousness in imperfect things ..." Is there a difference between what is "perfect" and what is "right"? What are some examples? Can something be righteous, yet imperfect to us? How?

2. The title of this chapter is "Life is Good." Is life good for Michael and Cathy? Is it perfect? Is it righteous? Is anything missing? The title of the entire section of the book in these opening chapters is "Life is Good." Do you think the title is intended literally? What is meant by this title? Compare the lives of all four (Michael, Cathy, Matt, and Gina) when considering whether "life is good."

Chapter 11: Connections

1. Mr. Schaffer is a teacher who likes and understands kids. He sets a great example for how to love and respect children. His actions say a lot about how he feels about kids. What do your actions say about what you think about kids?

2. Would your family and friends describe you as a Nike, Thingtime, Snailer, or Mirror? How would you describe yourself?

"Nikes" don't offer to give help, they just do it.

"Thingtimes" offer to help with anything, anytime.

"Snailers" send cards and notes of encouragement.

"Mirror People" look at you and see themselves.

Chapter 12: Bibles and Basketballs

1. Michael finds a new house of worship out on the rocks of Newport Beach, CA. To him, it is a spiritual place where he can talk to God. Is this the same as worship? Can this take the place of Sunday church? If not, why not? What's the difference?

2. Nearly 77% of Americans call themselves Christian, yet only (at most) 40% attend church on a regular basis. This means that more than 110 million people are essentially "out on the rocks" with Michael. What would you tell someone who says, "You have church, I have the rocks... (or any other substitution for church)"?

3. When Michael says to Cathy, "We've been so lucky. We've been so blessed," he is talking about the fact that so many other families have had tragedies and illnesses. Do you ever feel as though you are "lucky" to have avoided these tragedies? Do you feel dread that your luck may run out someday? How does that affect your faith?

Chapter 13: 'Tis the Season

1. Michigan State University basketball coach Tom Izzo and NBA Star Chauncey Billups each came to visit Matt and his family within two weeks of Matt's passing. You are likely not an NCAA coach or professional athlete, but your presence at the bedside of a dying friend can be a tremendous gift. Are you at ease visiting the sick or dying, or are you uncomfortable, tending to stay away? Do the unpleasant, even scary, sights and sounds of visiting a dying person prevent you from being present in the midst of their suffering?

2. Gina balances caring for a dying husband and making Christmas special for her young sons. For Gina, the space between tragedy, joy, and everyday life is the place where her faith provides clarity. What role does faith play in the midst of your circumstances? What source do you rely on to help balance the demands of an ordinary day in the midst of extraordinary trials?

3. After thirteen years of marriage, Matt and Gina share an intimate first when Gina gives Matt a shave. What simple, intimate moments can you find in your life to share with the ones you love?

4. Matt tells Gina, "When I'm gone, I want you to find a good Christian man and marry him." Would you say this to your spouse? If your spouse said this to you, how would you respond to hearing this?

Chapter 14: Coach

1. Coaching high school basketball has become Michael's passion. Cathy doesn't just tolerate it; she supports it fully. She actually involves herself in it to an extent as well. How do you respond to your spouse's (or best friend's or siblings', etc.) passions? Do you simply tolerate them, or do you really support them? How do you actively show your support?

Chapter 15: So This Is Christmas

1. Gina explained that when everything else is stripped away, the only thing left to give is love. "If only we had the ability to live life as though it were so new or so close to the end that all we could do is give and show and become love. It seems that beginnings and endings teach us about this kind of love. It is in between that we tend to forget." Our perspective can easily shift into a much healthier focus when the unimportant things we place above our relationships are forcibly stripped away by cancer or some other tragic circumstance. Why do you think it is so difficult to rid ourselves of unimportant distractions until we are forced to do so? What do you need to be stripped of in order to have a better relationship with God? Your spouse? Your kids? Others?

2. Do you agree with Gina's decision to bring Drew into the room to say good-bye to his father?

3. Describing Matt's final moments of earthly life, Gina writes, "There was an indescribable beauty in this moment." Have you witnessed the passing of a loved one into eternal life? How would you describe that moment?

Chapter 16: Applause of Heaven

1. As you read Pastor Galik's description of taking the journey to heaven, what is your reaction to knowing you, too, will take that journey some day?

Chapter 17: Not a Pinched Nerve

1. Cathy is deeply moved by what she experiences at Matt Kell's funeral. Michael remains cynical and this keeps him at arm's length from St. John, the community, and God's Word. Have there been moments when your cynicism has kept you separate? Did that lead to regret?

2. Cathy tried to connect with Gina Kell in the weeks after Matt died. Is this your reaction when people you know are met with challenge? Do you tend to go toward people in crisis or away from them?

Chapter 18: Gratitude

1. Does knowing the positive impact Matt's video diary had on Gina and her sons affect your desire to create a video diary of your own?

2. If you were to create a video diary, what would be the first thing you would want to talk about?

Chapter 19: Sixteen Days

1. Michael hears the words, "We're praying for you..." as the sound of doom. "No one says that to someone who just won the lotto." Why not? Should they? What is your reaction when you hear those words?

2. "The long meantime" is the time between now and the moment you do what you've been putting off. Do you have a long meantime happening in your life right now? What will it take to end it? Will it take cancer? Death? What is keeping you in your long meantime?

3. What three words would you use to describe the rift between Michael and his father? List three more that describe their reconciliation. Which group of words best describe your relationships?

Chapter 20: Five Balloons

1. Even after receiving a new balloon to replace the one that popped, Sam was inconsolable, wanting only the original balloon. It was easy to identify the connection to his father, who had died only two months earlier. Being aware of the primary source of our emotional breakdowns can make human relationships much easier.

   A. Were you able to recognize Sam's misdirected grief over the popped balloon?

   B. Can you recall a time when you realized that a "popped balloon" in your life was not the primary source of your emotional breakdown?

   C. Can you think back to a time when someone else in your life was directing emotions at you when, in fact, you were not the source of their grief, anger, or frustration?

Chapter 21: February 27

1. Reflect on an experience that created such cataclysmic shift in your life that almost nothing was ever the same afterward. Did that experience move you closer to God or further from Him? Where are you today compared to when you first experienced that shift? Is it possible to make that shift without the tragedy? What are you waiting for?

Chapter 22: The Dream

1. Drew and Sam asked questions and expressed fears, which made it possible for Gina to provide answers, comfort, and guidance in trusting God when there are no answers. How comfortable are you about expressing your fears and how willing are you to trust God when there are no answers?

2. Gina's dream of Matt was like a gift. Have you ever had a vivid dream about someone you love and miss? How did it make you feel?

Chapter 23: Telling the Kids

1. "There was nothing left for this husband to do. In fact, I no longer was a husband." Can you relate to this feeling of emptiness? Your identity has been stripped away and there really is nothing left to do. This doesn't just happen when someone dies. It also happens to those who lose their jobs or get divorced, etc. When have you felt this?

2. Michael gives his children permission to "feel the way you feel." Whether they wanted to laugh or cry, they should feel okay to simply be themselves. Then, to prove his point, he chased them around the house and gave them a big laugh. How did this initial talk and permission impact Michael's kids and their grief? Society frowns on those who laugh "too soon." Michael gave his children permission to do it immediately. Do you agree with him? Could you do that?

Chapter 24: Not Again

1. Who is your best friend? Why is he/she your best friend? Describe three things about your best friend that are different from all other friends.

2. When Gina first heard the news that Cathy Spehn died, she snapped. Why do you think Cathy's death was the catalyst for Gina's meltdown?

3. Pastor Galik did not attempt to make trite explanations in the midst of Gina's fit. What do you think of his response to Gina? Should he have done or said more in that moment? What is your expectation of clergy in moments like this?

Chapter 25: She Wasn't There

1. Pastor Galik comes to Michael's house, sits on the floor, and ministers to four-year old Danny, reaffirming his feelings. "I don't want her to be in heaven either Danny," Pastor Galik says. Is this the right answer for a pastor to give a four-year old?

2. As Michael stands next to Cathy's casket, he is filled with the Spirit. He says, "It had nothing to do with religion and everything to do with faith." What does he mean by this? What is the difference between religion and faith? Are they mutually exclusive? Can either exist without the other? Is it possible to have faith without religion?

Chapter 26: The Only One I Know

1. Michael and Gina meet for the first time at the funeral visitation for Cathy. Do you understand what Michael means when he says, "You and I just met, but you're the only one I know here tonight"? Have you ever had an experience where you feel more understood by a total stranger than you do by people you have known your entire life?

2. Michael tells Gina about his conversation with Cathy the day she died. "Cath talked about you. She told me I should call you." Why do you think Cathy told Michael to call Gina?

Chapter 27: Five Pews

1. Why do you think Michael felt he had to speak at his wife's funeral? He calls this an "amazing time of thanksgiving." How does faith help us reconcile being thankful to be alive here on Earth and still rejoicing that our loved one is in heaven?

2. There is a moment of quiet reflection after the funeral for Michael. He leans "against the brick wall of the church." Why is this line included in the text? Is he still as cynical as always? What does the fact that he leans on the church and never loses contact with the "rough surface" indicate to you?

3. As he stands alone in the cold, he says, "I knew that whatever this was, the really hard part was likely still to come." What does he mean?

Chapter 28: Calling Gina Kell

1. Pastor Galik asks Michael to tell him about Cathy. This simple gesture made a significant impact on Michael. Why is it important to speak the names of those who have died? Do people seem uncomfortable doing that? Why?

2. Michael is told that he is grieving the loss of two people: Cathy and the man he was when she was alive. What transitions have you gone through where you grieved for the loss your "old self"? Did you realize it at the time?

3. Michael's neighbor Ed organizes a gift for Michael's family: a deep freezer stocked with food. This was a classic "Nike" thing to do. Have you ever extended yourself to a friend or neighbor in such a way? How did you feel afterward? How was it received?

Chapter 29: Dinner with Strangers

1. Why do you think Michael and Gina brought their families together for dinner for the first time? Why do you think it was so comfortable and "normal"?

2. If Gina insisted on doing the dishes in your home after having dinner with you for the first time, how would you react? Did you relate more to Michael or Gina in that moment?

3. When Michael asks Gina, "How is it that you are here, sitting on my couch tonight?" what does Gina mean when she answers, "By the grace of God."

Chapter 30: You Can't Do This Alone

1. When family and friends try to help Michael, he only sees people telling

him he's doing it all wrong. How can we better serve the ones we love without trampling boundaries?

2. Perhaps even without knowing it, Michael seems to be articulating his faith in God more and more. When he says that he doesn't necessarily know what he is going to do, but he is certain what he is not going to do, how is this like Scripture?

3. Michael's children present him with a contract to sign, promising that he will never marry another woman. Why does he sign it so willingly? Why not sit the kids down and explain that there actually may be a time when he does meet someone who he may want to marry?

Chapter 31: Working Mom

1. Gina talks with Cathy's father, Larry, and they agree, "People just don't understand" their losses. Later, Gina visits the cemetery with her boys and realizes many people really do understand. Loss is a shared, universal human experience. Do you agree? Do you feel understood in your losses?

2. Sam was comforted by his time at the cemetery, whereas Drew was not comfortable being there. Do you find comfort in visiting the gravesite of a loved one?

Chapter 32: Turquoise Lake

1. Did you understand Gina's need to take the hike to Turquoise Lake? Did you agree with her decision to ask forgiveness later, rather than ask permission first?

2. How would you have responded to Gina after she returned to the condo?

3. Is it ever right to be selfish at the expense of others? Does being selfish always mean somehow shortchanging others? Is it necessary, even Biblical, to be selfish? Consider the second commandment to "Love your neighbor as yourself" when you ponder your answer.

Chapter 33: Because She Knows

1. Michael and Gina have late-night phone calls where they talk about everything, including faith. This is one of the topics (along with politics) that most people want to stay away from. Why can't we talk about our

faith more? Why is religion such a taboo subject? With almost 80% of the country calling themselves Christian, why isn't there more agreement on the subject? Do you think more conversation is the answer?

2. Intercessory prayer is something that many people are confused about. What is your view on intercessory prayer? How do you explain it to those "out on the rocks"? How is prayer a part of your life?

Chapter 34: Take the Walk

1. The twenty-dollar bill hits Michael the wrong way. When in your life were you the recipient of help that felt like pity?

2. When Gina says, "Take the walk," she is once again sneaking a little Scripture into Michael without even him knowing it. Psalm 46 says, "Be still and know that I am God ..." Why is this so difficult to do? Does it ever feel irresponsible to "let go and let God"?

Chapter 35: Date Night

1. Michael and Gina discuss and even laugh about the awkward things people say to the bereaved. What do you think is the best thing to say to a grieving person? Have you ever been in a situation where you or another person said something awkward or inappropriate? Can you laugh about it now or was it hurtful?

2. Gina addresses feeling of regret and destructive thinking. Do you understand what she meant when she wrote, "I had been trying to live in the moment by sitting in one place, waiting for something to happen. Before despair could take root, something needed to move, and it had to be me"? Have you ever been stuck? How did you start moving again?

3. What do you think is an appropriate amount of time to wait before a widow/widower starts dating? Does that time frame have anything to do with the calendar?

Chapter 36: Happy Patio

1. Michael tells Gina about the power of the backyard and that moms need to "let the kids do their thing" without interfering at the first sign of conflict. Do you agree with Michael? What kind of parent are you in these situations?

2. Although the families were spending a lot of time together, do you agree with Michael and Gina's decision to avoid all signs of affection in front of the children? How did you feel about the timing of their first kiss?

Chapter 37: Foundations

1. Who are the people that form the foundation of your life? Do they know it? Have you lost any of them?

2. Gina shows strong leadership by presenting her ideas, asking for support, and proceeding in the face of opposition. What situations have you been in where you proceeded in the face of opposition? Were you successful? How do you discern when to listen to those in opposition and when to follow your heart?

Chapter 38: The Double Rainbow

1. In the opening paragraph of this chapter Gina writes, "My deepest personal regret it that it took a terminal illness to bring about this simple change." When you read this, are you aware of any areas of your life that you could change now, before you have a regret like Gina's?

2. What does it mean to see the color of rain in your life? Describe a time when you have seen the color of rain in the midst of your circumstances.

3. Do you see biblical themes in Michael and Gina's love story? How do they apply these to your own life story?

Chapter 39: On Both Knees

1. "Love is not a zero sum game." True or False? Do you see love as an ever-expanding force in your life? Where in your life have seen evidence that we grow new hearts?

2. "Grief can actually be an extremely healthy experience ..." However, for some, grief becomes a lifestyle. What drives some into this despair? What are the ways you can help friends and family stay connected and out of the "grief lifestyle"?

3. Michael and Gina decide to "take the walk" together and get married. Does this mean that their grief is over? Does moving forward mean the same as "getting over it"?

Chapter 40: Replacement Parts

1. Gina recaps the unexpected blessings that have poured forth in the midst of losing her beloved husband. Can you see how the experiences you have regretted or resented most in your life are things God intends to use for good? He also intends for us to use what we learn to help others. Describe a time your trials or tragedies were used to serve others.

2. Has someone you know remarried following the loss of a spouse? In your opinion was it replacement or redemption? Why?

Chapter 41: Holy Water

1. Michael and Cathy rarely spoke about their desires for funerals and final resting places. Does your family know your wishes?

Chapter 42: Here Comes the Sun

1. Are you in a blended family? If so, what are your biggest challenges and joys? If not, what do you perceive to be the biggest challenges and joys?

2. Do you think grief is more difficult on memorial dates such as anniversaries, birthdays, and other holidays?

3. Gina's friend Katherine kept a hand-written prayer journal for Gina and her boys for twelve months. Have you ever given or received a gift like this?

Chapter 43: The New Day

1. Pastor Galik's message at the wedding was "He turned their mourning into dancing." What does turning "mourning into dancing" mean to you? Does redemption mean "happy endings"? What does redemption mean in your life today?

acknowledgments

Thank you to Dan and Kathy Pelekoudas and Hugh and Betsie Hewitt, who by providence started a chain of events that has carried our story forward. We can't wait to see where it takes us.

To the first readers of our early manuscript, including Mel Spehn, Susan Kell, Toni Valenti, Meghan Kell, Rev. Dr. Karl Galik, Jeff Maerov, Josh Kilmer Purcell, Jack and Ana Maria Chrysler, Meaghan Dowling Chorsky, and Cynthia DiTiberio. Thank you for encouraging us to press on.

To Curtis and the entire staff at Yates and Yates, thank you for being the bridge to new opportunities and experiences. Your quiet strength and counsel have been invaluable and your friendship a true blessing. For you, it was never about platforms or marketability. It was about the story. Thank you for the laughter, patience, and willingness to take a chance on not one but two first-time authors.

We are incredibly grateful to our editor, Sandy Vander Zicht, and the phenomenal team at Zondervan, including Don Gates, Tom Dean, Becky Philpott, Robin Barnett, and Heather Adams, for giving our story wings. Together you have given the legacies of Matt and Cathy the chance to change lives. We deeply appreciate your passion and guidance.

To all of our parents, living and deceased, who did right by their kids: Bob and Toni, Dick and Dolores, Larry and Jill, Susan and Duane; and all those who make up the fun, faithful, and loving twists on our family tree, including Rick and Patti, Tara and Bob, Meghan and Eric, Lynn and Bob. We love you and are forever grateful for your support.

Big hugs and thanks to our circle of friends who love us unconditionally, make us laugh, and always enjoy a great meal! The good news is you won't have to hear about our writing *this* book anymore! Special thanks to Pastor Luke Timm, Chris MacCourtney, and our friends at Salem Broadcasting.

Mike and Colleen, thank you for your unwavering friendship and faith. Your relentless trust in God in the midst of extraordinary trials is a source of hope and inspiration. It's a privilege to walk alongside you through the joys and sorrows of life. Thanks for the endless laughter, honesty, and love.

To everyone who supports the New Day Foundation for Families, thank you for your dedication to "loving your neighbor as yourself." Your generosity is a gift that gives hope to many families of young children who suffer the loss of a parent to cancer.

To our funny, smiley, smart kids who gracefully lived through the events in this book, lovingly grew new hearts, and patiently waited while we wrote about the most tragic and redemptive time in your young lives. Thank you for your gentle nature and faith in God. You make all four of your parents proud. Beautiful Charlotte, thank you for trusting us to share a piece of the secret you hold in your heart. Jack, thank you for your big hugs and big dreams. Drew, thank you for your passion for life and your trust. Sam, thank you for showing love and never giving up. Dan, thank you for the laughter and music you bring to our lives. We love you all so much!

Above all, we give thanks to our Lord and Savior, Jesus Christ, for all that has been lost, given, and received for such a time as this.

NEW DAY
FOUNDATION FOR FAMILIES

www.FoundationForFamilies.com

Michael and Gina began The New Day Foundation for Families, a 501(c)(3) non-profit organization dedicated to bringing hope, healing, and resources to the families of children who suffer the devastating loss of a parent to cancer. Trust the path before you, accept the inevitability of loss and change, and pursue a faith that teaches you to live more pure, simple, and loving lives.

MICHAEL + gina™
FORWARD THROUGH FAITH

www.MichaelandGina.com

Check out Michael and Gina Spehn's radio show, *Your Family Matters*, on WLQV AM 1500 Detroit, every Saturday morning at 9:00 a.m. Streamed live at www.michaelandgina.com.

Share Your Thoughts

With the Author: Your comments will be forwarded to the author when you send them to *zauthor@zondervan.com*.

With Zondervan: Submit your review of this book by writing to *zreview@zondervan.com*.

Free Online Resources at
www.zondervan.com

Zondervan AuthorTracker: Be notified whenever your favorite authors publish new books, go on tour, or post an update about what's happening in their lives at www.zondervan.com/authortracker.

Daily Bible Verses and Devotions: Enrich your life with daily Bible verses or devotions that help you start every morning focused on God. Visit www.zondervan.com/newsletters.

Free Email Publications: Sign up for newsletters on Christian living, academic resources, church ministry, fiction, children's resources, and more. Visit www.zondervan.com/newsletters.

Zondervan Bible Search: Find and compare Bible passages in a variety of translations at www.zondervanbiblesearch.com.

Other Benefits: Register to receive online benefits like coupons and special offers, or to participate in research.

ZONDERVAN®

ZONDERVAN.com/
AUTHORTRACKER
follow your favorite authors